NOTES FROM THE OUTSIDE

Episodes from an Unconventional Life

ALLAN SAFARIK

HAGIOS
PRESS

Copyright © 2006 Allan Safarik

Library and Archives Canada Cataloguing in Publication

Safarik, Allan, 1948-
  Notes from the outside : episodes from an unconventional life / Allan Safarik.

ISBN 0-9739727-4-2

  1. Safarik, Allan, 1948-. I. Title.

PS8587.A245A16 2006   C818'.5403   C2006-904904-1

Edited by Paul Wilson and Donald Ward.
Designed and typeset by Donald Ward.
Cover art: *Ditched*, by Fred Eaglesmith (oil on canvas, 11" x 14", 2006).
Cover design by Yves Noblet.
Set in Adobe Caslon Pro and Felix Titling.
Printed and bound in Canada at Houghton Boston Printers & Lithographers, Saskatoon.

The publishers gratefully acknowledge the assistance of the Saskatchewan Arts Board, The Canada Council for the Arts, and the Cultural Industries Development Fund (Saskatchewan Department of Culture, Youth & Recreation) in the production of this book.

HAGIOS PRESS
Box 33024 Cathedral PO
Regina SK   S4T 7X2

For my father,
Norman Emil Safarik,
and in memory of my mother,
Kathleen Mabel Balmer

CONTENTS

WORKS BY ALLAN SAFARIK

BOOKS

Okira
The Naked Machine Rides On
God Loves Us Like Earthworms Love Wood
Advertisements for Paradise
On the Way to Ethiopia
All Night Highway
How I Know the Sky Is a River:
(selected and new shorter poems 1978–1998)
Bird Writer's Handbook
Blood of Angels
When Light Falls from the Sun

ANTHOLOGY

Vancouver Poetry

CHAPBOOKS

Green Light Stones & Trees
The Heart Is Altered

INTRODUCTION

I AM A GENERALIST, a person who is an expert at nothing but has an opinion in print about everything and anything whenever I feel the impulse to write about it. I have no masters to tell me how many words, what *genre*, or when.

My inability to find a fat sinecure in the middle of some overweight bureaucracy or institution that never fires anybody is probably the singular reason I have had the time to be nearly a full-time dreamer all of my adult life. Herein are essays on four distinct periods of my life on a number of themes and subjects from various regions of Canada with portraits of writers and others. In one way or another all my subjects qualify as "outsiders."

I wrote these pieces while I pursued my literary interests and continued working in trades that are associated with the book arts. A few times I wrote an essay for a magazine that was publishing a special issue on a friend. More often something inside went off triggering a need to document certain people, places, and incidents at different stages of my life for different reasons. You can find these reasons scattered throughout these stories. They are a legacy over a period of time told from a certain perspective from my beginnings until now.

Oddly, they document my coincidental involvement with two major events that occurred in Vancouver, the city of my birth. One essay gives a personal account of Vancouver's worst disaster; another unfolds years of involvement with one of Vancouver's most heinous crimes. I have often found it ironic that my life in the city of my birth was profoundly touched by these two tragedies — the fall of the Second Narrows Bridge in 1958 and the murder of the poet Pat Lowther in 1975.

I stay limber thinking that there will be at least one more generation down the pike in my time that will embrace fundamental change on a wide political front. I am ready to become a revolutionary should the right cause suddenly arise in the affairs of mankind. What other choice do I have — or do you have, for that matter? The environment is already encased in the plastic shroud it will take to its doomsday.

I have produced a steady stream of writing I call "literary journalism," for want of a better term, for a long time on a fairly wide front. Writing is writing. There isn't much difference in the process of producing print in any of the writing *genres*. It always amounts to taking the time to sit down and work at it as if it was a job. Most writers who approach writing that way are inclined to try many different forms while they experiment looking for their own voice. The famous mystery novelist, Raymond Chandler, spent half his life unsuccessfully writing poetry before he finally turned his attention to writing mystery novels.

To be somewhere else for a while is probably a good recipe for writing. A change of scenery and experiences gained along the way bring new ingredients to the feast. A small town in rural Saskatchewan is as good a place as any to find inspiration. In this collection, I have written essays about the place where I grew up, on the Vancouver lower mainland area of British Columbia, as well as about people and places I have travelled to in nearly all the regions of this half-sophisticated, half-rustic country but especially about the northern plains. Along the way over the miles through the years, the more things changed the more some things stayed the same. I still live on the outside looking in, but more often looking out.

BRIDGE TO THE PAST

DOG GONE

THERE IS SOMETHING MAGICAL about the first house you inhabit. Mine had white siding and a green shake roof. It was located on the corner of MacDonald and Yale in North Burnaby, on the lower mainland in British Columbia.

The yard was a brush pile with a scattering of large boulders and clumps of vine maples. We lived on the hillside overlooking Burrard Inlet and the North Shore mountains. In the early fifties the streets were largely unpaved and new houses were beginning to appear from bush land.

Before I went to school, my best friend was an 80-year-old man named Charlie. He lived on the hill above our house. Charlie and his wife Bella were great gardeners. Over many years, they managed to build terraces. It was Bella's hobby, constructing the stone walls between each level. Every year they planted vegetables, and their yard featured berries: goose berries, raspberries, strawberries, along with currant bushes and crabapple trees. The centrepiece in all this was a large pond full of goldfish. Charlie liked to bask on the edge and feed them bread crumbs by hand.

Charlie bought things at auction and resold them through classified ads in the newspapers. His garage and basement were filled with curious gadgets. Sometimes he'd have an old car or a newly painted boat for sale on the boulevard. I liked Charlie because he talked with me about important things.

Bella reminded me of Mrs. Santa Claus. She kept her grey hair in a bun and wore two or three sweaters in the house. Although she always knew it was me at the door she acted pleasantly surprised whenever I arrived. "Well, you come right in, Charlie's in the basement." There I was, in the hotbed of good cooking. "Care for a scone, dear?" she'd chirp. The more I ate the bigger her smile. After a chat about the neighbourhood she'd send me down the narrow basement stairs.

Bella was a Baptist, she abhorred cussing or coarse language. Charlie had a mouth like a sewer pipe. He said all the bad words and used them in amazing combinations. I tried some of his expressions out at the dinner table. My mother looked at me and said: "My God, he's worse than your father." Bella had learned to tune out Charlie's bad temper and seemed not to hear his obscene outbursts. The mention of John Diefenbaker turned him inside out. Once, when he heard the Chief's voice on the radio, Charlie said, "I wouldn't piddle on the man's wingtips if his socks were on fire." I pondered that one for a long time and used it to great effect in grade one. However, if Charlie slipped into profanity when conversing directly with Bella she would shoot him a glance that could wither glass. He would flee back to the basement to fidget with junk appliances or lawn mowers. I'd sit on the chopping block and listen to his cursing until he cooled down.

Charlie told me stories about his years as an engineer on the transcontinental railway. He wore a railroader's hat and talked about guys with names like Slim, Snuffy, Duckweed, Waldo and Turkish Tom. He made yesterday sound better than today.

"Rewiring small motors takes brains, hold this." I'd hold the ends while he mopped his brow with a red polka-dot hanky. He began grouching about the fish disappearing from his pond.

"Damned cats! Do you think it's Old Lady Whitworth's Persian?"

I'd change the subject, bringing up Mr. Diefenbaker again, and he'd turn blue. On Sunday mornings when Bella dragged Charlie to church, my brother and I were catching his pets on shiner hooks baited with dough-balls.

Charlie was well-known for being stingy. When people called about the things he had for sale he would scratch his head and swear he forgot to get change. Bella was cheerful. She'd interject: "Oh, I have some change upstairs." She'd go into Charlie's room and take coins from quart jars on his dresser.

Charlie liked to conduct most of his business in the garage.

"Come out and visit the girls with me."

The garage was an exciting place. Charlie had a dozen mannequins he bought at the closing of a dress shop. They stood around naked in mannequin poses, arms and legs wrongly placed in the context of the figure. When Charlie made a sale he waltzed around with one of his inanimate women. "If only Bella could see me now."

Even then I could see Charlie was in love with his own sense of humour. It vanished instantly when things started going wrong. His tongue would begin to travel in circles around themes of anatomy. I didn't know what he meant but it sounded interesting. I went into the house to ask Bella. She gave me a glass of milk and went out to the garage to have a word with Charlie. I heard her clear as a bell, "Charles, you are a pig!" and the whacking sound she made with the broom.

"Kid, if you want to hang around you're gonna have to shut up sometimes," he remarked, locking the garage doors. "She's just jealous of my girls. But don't you go repeating that to her."

"Promise I won't," I said, wondering what girls he meant.

"Now I'll teach you something useful. How to sell a bum lawn mower to a sucker."

The caller was Reverend Hipp, the local Anglican clergyman. He had ridden his bicycle down from the church. He wanted to see the motorized lawn mower Charlie had advertised in *The Vancouver Sun*. I was always a bit terrified at the sight of Reverend Hipp. He was long and weird looking, with a thin neck and a small, bobbing head. He had several shiny bicycle clips on his grey trousers and he wore sturdy brown brogues.

"You're not one of those nasty little boys who play football on the church lawn are you?" Never having been close to a clergyman before I couldn't take my eyes off his collar.

"He's too young," Charlie intoned. "Now sir, this fine piece of machinery was previously owned by a retired gentleman on Boundary Road."

Bella opened the kitchen window and invited Reverend Hipp in for tea. Charlie was furiously chewing on his false teeth.

"We're too busy, Bella," he growled. But Hipp was already climbing the stairs.

I ate a dozen hermits while Bella and the Reverend discussed missions in Africa. Charlie offered facts and figures on blade sharpening, fuel economy and the prices of new mowers. I kept my mouth shut.

Bella said: "Now I know Charlie is at his best when it comes to getting a bargain. After all, it's for the church."

The words seemed to stick into the wall. Charlie's face began to twitch.

"Charlie has a trailer and not much to do, so he can deliver it later in the week."

The Reverend pumped his hand and blessed his heart for the donation.

I noticed Charlie wasn't dancing.

Charlie and Bella had a comfortable veranda overlooking our house and the panoramic mountains. One day I found him on the veranda hunched over a table, peering out the window. "Look what I've got," he said. He had purchased a vintage First World War sniper's rifle from a man who lived on Capitol Hill. It came with three water-damaged cartons of ammunition. He balanced the gun on a pillow resting on the table and was spying at the neighbours through the scope.

"Want to have a look?" He stood and gave me the chair. I

climbed up on it and crouched with my knees under me to make myself tall enough. I put my eye to the long slender scope. Charlie had set it up so the scope was directed at our kitchen window. My father was seated at the table reading the newspaper. His five-year-old son was looking down the barrel of a high-powered rifle, the cross hairs were centred on his head.

Charlie cackled. "Pretty sharp, huh? Think I'll use it on those damn cats."

I went home to tell my Dad how neat he looked through Charlie's scope.

Charlie and Bella were yard proud. They built a sturdy wire fence around their property. It afforded a decent amount of protection from intruders. They had a bed of multicoloured petunias running along the street side of the property. The problem was dogs. They enjoyed pausing to do their business on the boulevard. Charlie blew up in torrents of venomous language whenever he spotted one. "Damn dogs, worse than cats! At least cats bury it. Dogs and politicians, damn world is full of 'em."

Charlie became obsessed with getting even with those dogs. I didn't think it necessary. "I like dogs," I said.

"So do I," he replied, "Well some dogs." Charlie was digging a trench from his basement out to the fence.

"What will Bella think?" I asked.

"We know what Bella will think, don't we?" he said, rolling his eyes behind his strange-tinted yellow glasses.

Charlie had decided to run a wire from his electrical box out to the fence. "It'll just give a little jolt, they'll tell their friends and no dog will dare crap on my petunias again."

"But not my friends," I pleaded.

"Okay, I promise, not your friends." Charlie added a long, thin metal strip along each fence section. "It'll just be a little reminder. Do it on your own lawn!"

I waited by the basement window. Charlie was determined to try his deterrent. In the afternoon a Doberman that we had never seen before came on to the boulevard. "You sure it's not one of your friends?" he snickered.

The dog wandered through the petunias and lifted its leg against the fence. It shot a huge stream on to the wire. Charlie pulled the handle, the basement lights dimmed. An enormous flash engulfed the fence, white smoke drifted off the dog.

"Whoops," he said. The Doberman was on its back, twitching, legs straight up in the air, just like in the cartoons. Its tongue stuck out of its face like a sausage. The smell of burning hair wafted on the breeze.

Charlie was running for the wheelbarrow to cover the body.

"Jeezuz, it was an accident, could happen to anyone."

Luckily, Bella had walked to the Red & White store.

"You go in the house and play with anything you want."

Charlie was frantically digging in the garden between the garage and the lane.

"It'll be our secret," he rasped. "Just you and me, our secret. What do you say?"

By the time Bella got home Charlie had buried the dog. No ceremony.

"Our secret huh, kid?"

I was good at keeping secrets. A few days passed and Charlie was letting me run every mechanical device he had.

"Pretty soon I'll teach you how to drive the car. Would you like that? I bet you would."

I was wondering if we shouldn't say a prayer or put some flowers on the grave. Charlie thought better to keep it low-key.

"Soon you'll be getting your own car."

We were sitting out by the pond minding our own business. A man walked down the boulevard. "You haven't seen my dog, have you?" he asked. "He's a male Doberman."

I blurted out, "Charlie, remember the electric dog?"

His face grew ashen, but without missing a beat he replied, "Oh, that electric dog. I sold it in the auction last week."

TERROR TIME

MY FIRST REGULAR OBLIGATION IN LIFE was the dreaded daytime I did at Cambridge Kindergarten. It was like being in jail. The warden's name was Mrs. Markwick. She was a hideous old crone with a wart on her huge nose. She was nastier than the witch in *The Wizard of Oz*.

There were about 20 baby boomers in attendance at the white clapboard academy on Cambridge Street in North Burnaby. Our mothers were completely entranced by Mrs. Markwick, they thought her an eccentric but lovable woman who would get us ready for the rigours of grade one the following year. She had a way with young women. They trusted her as they would the family doctor.

"Little Robert is a bit unsure of himself, I'll soon help him out of his shell." Little Robert had a stutter and was terrified of Mrs. Markwick so he sat in silence in the corner and learned to become almost invisible. Alas, whenever Mrs. Markwick rediscovered his presence, three or four times a week, no matter what the activity, she would freeze and begin reciting some horrible rhyme enunciating the words with precise emphasis. "Peter Piper picked a peck of pickled peppers." Robert would shrink in size and begin stuttering the same rhyme. She would stop him in mid-stutter to scold him and begin again in earnest, mouthing the words as delicately as a horse might eat an apple. These torturous lessons would last for five minutes. By the end of the term poor Robert had stopped speaking entirely.

Our activities consisted of painting, colouring, cutting and pasting, followed by a story and then a nap in the mid-morning before we got on to our serious work. We handled our paste and paints like the little ladies and gentlemen we were supposed to be. Woe betide any slacker who knocked over the glue pot. We endured our pseudo-naps in order to shut out the spectre of grief that haunted our beings. Mrs. Markwick had eyes in the back of her head.

The bulk of our mornings was spent banging away on triangles, sticks, bells and tambourines. Mrs. Markwick directed the Cambridge Kindergarten percussion band while playing the piano with one hand. We were trained to cease our cacophony whenever she brought her free hand down in a swooping motion.

In October, Mrs. Markwick announced that we would be having a Hallowe'en party, with prizes for the best costumes. I let my mother talk me into wearing my brother Jimmy's old sailor suit. It was a heavy wool nautical outfit similar to the ones worn by Russian sailors in the newsreels. I had to go to the bathroom in the worst way. In the custom of our routine I stuck up my arm with one finger showing. It was a simple system, one finger for one thing, two for the other. Mrs. Markwick chose to ignore me, as she often did. Late into the percussion band session I was periodically pleading for relief with my waving arm and hysterical finger. No luck; she continued to direct us through another five songs.

After a second rendition of "She'll Be Coming Round The Mountain," Mrs. Markwick brought us to a crashing halt. I made a run for the bathroom only to find myself fourth in line. I stood on one leg and then on the other, a human imitation of the question mark. My resolve lessened, there was nothing I could do but let go and pee in my sailor suit. Its heavy navy wool fabric soaked up the liquid like a blotter. However, the torrent was unabated and soon I was standing in a good-sized puddle. Mrs. Markwick went berserk. She gave me a hard pinch and lambasted me with ridicule. I was ejected from the party. I walked home, a soggy sailor wrapped in shame and rage. I knew I had been set up. The wool chaffing on my legs made a rash of my pride. I was being prepared for life by an expert.

The following September, in 1955, I started school. My mother bought me my first pair of Leckie boots. They had metal clasps along the laces so they could be cinched up. I tried to wear them out by kicking everything and dragging them on the pavement when I rode my bike, to no avail. They were nearly indestructible. In the years to come, a new pair of Leckie boots was the omen that summer was over and a new school year beginning.

I attended Gilmore Avenue Elementary in Vancouver Heights. The main school building was an imposing rectangular red brick structure. The inside walls were painted institutional colours; slime green and mock banana yellow. The school grounds were surrounded by rows of deciduous trees, mostly horse chestnuts and maples. We lined up in the basement and the teachers marched us through the halls to our classrooms.

Our principal, Mr. Brown, was a piece of galvanized steel. He had eyes like a bird of prey. In his early sixties Mr. Brown wore charcoal suits that matched his enthusiastic shock of grey hair. He had the body of the young Jack LaLanne. He purposely exhibited his physical fitness by taking flights of stairs like a gazelle. No one ever attempted to kick sand in his face. Mr. Brown was judge of the court of last resort. The routine wallopings that the teachers administered were child's play in comparison with those of the master. Whenever he personally delivered corporal punishment with the strap, the whole school took on the atmosphere of a prison awaiting an execution. The sound of the blows and the wailing of wayward pupils echoed through the walls like a broadcast from God. The poor punished wretch would be out of action for days. Anyone who went back for seconds was of unsound mind.

Mr. Brown had a confederate who helped him keep order by

surreptitiously spying on students and teachers. Mr. Johnson the janitor, a tall brooding man who had a facial resemblance to Lon Chaney Jr., skulked around the school looking for trouble. He pussy-footed in the halls pushing a wide duster that was no more than a pathetic prop. He was really eavesdropping, gathering more dirt for the corporal laundering.

Mr. Brown spoke directly to me on only two occasions. The first time, a motorist reported me for bad bicycle riding. I was racing back to school after lunch weaving at top speed between cars on Oxford Street. A peanut butter salesman followed me in his car. He managed to ferret out my name from kids standing beside the bike racks. He marched into the principal's office and blew the whistle. Mr. Brown called my name on the PA, and everybody knew I was done for. My friends were already afraid to make eye contact.

I stood before him trembling, my knees clacking like castanets. I admitted my guilt instantly. It probably saved my life. He warned me never to come back before him under any circumstance and banned me from riding my bike to school. I felt like the luckiest guy on earth. I danced a little on the way back to the classroom. My fellow students were in awe of my escape. After school, I went looking for four-leaf clovers.

Unfortunately, a few weeks later I blotted my record. Before school, at lunch and after school we were allowed to take out one soccer ball. It would accommodate a game involving a hundred or more kids booting it up and down the field. There were some dazzling dribblers who could keep the ball for half a minute. Our neighbourhood produced some of the best soccer players in Canada. Occasionally, a budding rugby player would pick up the ball and run with it until he was gang-tackled on to the dirt field. I was caught up in the excitement of the game and I chased the ball into the out-of-bounds area. I turned and tried to hook it back on to the playing field, but mis-kicked and blasted the ball straight through Mr. Brown's second-floor office window.

I stood alone in absolute disconsolation. The crowd evaporated into little knots of onlookers. There was nowhere to hide; in any case, Mr. Johnson, with his X-ray vision, would have already spotted me. Mr. Brown's head and shoulders soon appeared in the gaping space where the window had once been. He gestured to me with one finger. I walked as slowly as possible up the staircase wondering if I should make a break for it. He was waiting on the landing. Since he was faster than a kangaroo, I accepted my fate.

He grabbed me with one hand and lifted me until our faces were two inches apart. I could smell the salmon sandwich he had eaten for lunch. His eyes were rolling like a pair of dice; from close up, his hair was an intricate pattern of steel wool. I was thinking about passing out. His lips were barely moving but he was talking in a loud voice about flying glass and things that go bump in the night. I was staring at his gunmetal eyebrows and the map of the Amazon River that lined his face. There were curls of wire growing from his nostrils.

I was saved by his imminent appointment with the PTA committee. They were darting about beneath the hall clock like a covey of quail. Mr. Brown opened his fist and I fell in a heap on the floor. He greeted the committee with a wolfish smile and in a sweet voice asked me to wait for him in his office. I stood beside his large oak desk preparing myself for a flogging. A bright new picture of Queen Elizabeth II looking stern glared at me from the wall. I looked around; there were shards of glass lying about and I began to try to think of a little prayer I might say.

The deflated soccer ball had landed on top of the filing cabinet. A brisk wind was blowing through the room. I tried to remember the methods for avoiding the worst of the pain that were often discussed on the playground. I couldn't think of any. My shirt front remained in a clump from the strength of his grip. I couldn't stop thinking about the curious hairs that were sticking out of his ears.

After several minutes, I heard voices in the outer office and I prepared myself for his return. Mr. Brown was still occupied by the do-gooders from the PTA. He loomed in the doorway like a panther balancing on a steel spring. He clapped his hand on my shoulder and I became slightly paralyzed down my right side. He instructed me to report to Mr. Johnson in the furnace room for sentencing. He released me and I walked past the flock of parents, secretly wishing them all the best. I was out of his clutches, my heart was singing.

Mr. Johnson, smoking a cigar, was playing poker with his floor sweepers. He stared at me for a few seconds with his sunken eyes. He knew I had more lives than I deserved. He stood up, his head touching the pipes in the ceiling, and handed me a large white tin pail. I was to pick up garbage on the school ground everyday after school for one week. I was thrilled. There was never a better candidate for a more appropriate job. I worked like a fiend, picking up lunch bags, discarded fruit, cigarette butts, candy wrappers and every bit of offal that I could find. I enjoyed the taunts of my fellows, I implored them to laugh at me and call me names. Every now and then I would glance over my shoulder and see Mr. Brown's grey muzzle looking from an upstairs window; I was happy in my work, the pail was my refuge.

A MUTT NAMED JEFF

BEING A KID WAS MY FIRST JOB. My two brothers and I had one thing in common. We went everywhere with father in his green International one-ton flat deck with dual wheels. The turn signals operated manually. By pulling down on a handle the driver signaled his intention and a direction pointer dropped like a salute from the side of the vehicle to warn traffic of the impending turn.

Father was in fish. He bought it, sold it, processed it, stored it under piles of flake ice or in cold storage. He hauled fish from the Fraser River. He fished crabs with Hank Lougheed on the crab boats they tied up to the old man's wharf a few miles up the Nikomekl River from Crescent Beach. He hauled crabs daily from Boundary Bay and White Rock to Campbell Avenue Fisherman's Wharf. He sold fish in Chinatown and to cafés and fish and chip joints as well as swank restaurants. He unloaded draggers filled with grey cod, ling cod, lemon soles, red snappers and rock cod and sold the fillets from them to frozen food companies or chain stores. He exported salmon to Europe and imported frogs' legs from Mexico and smoked eels from Holland. He financed seal lion hunting expeditions, sold the carcasses to pet food companies and sent the skins to a tannery in Liverpool that made aprons for blacksmiths. Every holiday season he made 1500 gallons of pickled herring that he sold in five-gallon white plastic pails to fancy restaurants. Father was a going concern and since we travelled with him often, we became habitués of fish companies, reduction plants, smokehouses, and canneries. We knew all the stops between Fukiyama the egg man, scurrying around his caviar factory, to the plaster lions at the end of the wharf at Queen Charlotte Fisheries.

To complete his fish profile: father was also an avid sports fisherman. When he wasn't working long hours at the docks he was fishing for steelhead, trout or netting smelts or trapping crayfish. The back of his truck usually carried a rowboat or a punt.

In the fall he brought along his old Greener double barreled 12-gauge with automatic ejectors and he hunted pheasants and ducks on the foreshore in Ladner or at Boundary Bay. In his ingenious moments he rowed sedately down the Alouette River or the Nicomekl, trolling a spoon for cutthroat trout while his shotgun rested against the stern ready for mallards jumping from the grass or high flying pin tails. On Saturdays we towed two punts loaded with decoys behind our 16-foot clinker built, as we took turns rowing down river into the foreshore at Boundary Bay where we set out two large rafts of duck decoys and shot over them for the day. Father was firmly against outboard motors. No matter how hard we tried we could never convince him of their usefulness. His fishing and hunting excursions were sacrosanct. Noisy outboard motors drove him into paroxysms of rage whenever one intruded on the sanctity of river or lake.

We were a dog family by definition. Father admired a good hunting dog. He also loathed cats with a passion that bordered on unreason. He peered out from the windows in the morning hoping to catch one digging in his garden. He was known to employ slingshots and B B guns in his determination to rid his yard of feline intruders. He had a big green thumb. His roses were monumental. The secret was the cod fish offal he hauled home from the fish dock. He buried a carcass under everything he planted. Even a four year old could figure out why every cat for five miles around came to dig in our garden. Dead fish begat lush roses and fat cats.

Father's pride and joy was an American Springer Spaniel named Jeff. He had more energy than 10 ordinary dogs. Jeff loved to hunt as much as my father did. In time he became the consummate gun dog who performed well retrieving ducks from saltwater shoots over decoys or fetching downed blue grouse from thickets on mountain sides. Jeff's speciality was flushing pheasants from heavy cover. Occasionally he emerged from a corn field with a live cock pheasant in his gentle jaws. He was observed leaping and catching a pheasant in mid-air. Father's relationship with Jeff taught me many lessons about the human condition. They were a team. They hunted together on the foreshore at Boundary Bay, on the dikes that lined the Nicomekl River, in the fields near Pitt Meadows, at Burns Bog, Pigeon Cove or Burke Mountain. In the field they had an impeccable relationship. The problem between them was rooted in our home life.

Father's pathological hatred of cats (which in my adult life I have decided was a fear of cats), was instilled into Jeff while he was still a malleable pup. Father had the habit of siccing the dog on any unsuspecting cat that might have been doing its business in his raspberries. Whenever he saw a cat Jeff changed character immediately and turned into a lethal streaking attack of rage. He not only put the run on stray cats but he became proficient at killing them in a matter of seconds. His method was to get them before they could make a stand. He would grab the cat by the scruff of the neck while travelling at full speed and shake the life out of the poor thing. Not many of our neighbours had cats. Without the distractions of cats, Jeff was a gentle dog. It was never clear to me whether it was the dog's guile or father's charm that kept Jeff from a death sentence. There were many instances when irate cat owners demanded satisfaction. The old man lessened their anger by buying them a new pet or delivering a supply of fish to help reduce their taste for revenge.

The worst incident occurred at Easter in 1957. Rabbits being cute and furry with four legs were in the same category as cats. They drove Jeff into spasms of blood lust. The Domijans, who lived up the street, bought their children a fluffy white bunny as an Easter surprise. Easter Sunday Jeff went right through the wire cage and dispatched the creature with the skill of an assassin.

The situation was exacerbated by the fact the Domijan daughters had just returned from church in pristine Easter outfits. They were standing beside the enclosure feeding tidbits to their adorable pet. The dog may as well have done his dirty work in broad daylight before a choir of angels. Mr. Domijan was almost haemorrhaging with anger when he accosted father. A pall settled over our house. Jeff seemed to sense the mood and quietly curled up under the kitchen table. We were outcasts for about a week. Eventually threats of death by shooting on sight subsided and the whole scenario faded away. Jeff was safe again. The old man cooled it for a month, relying on his slingshot for skirmishes in the cat wars. I wondered if there had been a payoff to restore the *status quo*.

Jeff was my father's best friend and his worst protagonist. Theirs was a complicated relationship. Father loved to hunt with this dog and Jeff, in turn, responded by being a keen hunter. Father could not bear to part with Jeff because he knew deep down inside that he had ruined Jeff with his own prejudice. Jeff, being no slouch, had a couple of ways of paying him back. Often father would stop and chew the fat with a farmer. A great talker, he usually had no problem getting permission to hunt on the farmer's land. Jeff sniffed the farmer's dog, looked calmly at the domestic ducks and geese without a twinge and stood mildly while two or three dozen chickens pecked at the barn yard. He was a solid citizen if confronted by a crabby Holstein bull, a flock of sheep or a solitary ornery goat. However, he stiffened and went absolutely berserk if there was even a hint there might be Bantam chickens nearby. The astonished farmer would witness the transformation of this noble Springer Spaniel from Dr. Jekyll to Mr. Hyde. After a few startling experiences, Father learned to recognize the signs, and he was usually able to grab Jeff and put him into the truck cab before he massacred again.

Jeff was a friendly family dog who liked people and enjoyed the companionship of his own kind. In our minds his virtues outweighed his failings. However, he was adept at disappearing from view and prone to taking off for unknown parts about half a dozen times a year. This rankled the old man who expended a torrent of profanity at the thought of his hunting partner being on the loose. These lapses of concentration upset him since Jeff often got into trouble during these innocent forays. While he was having fun chasing a bitch he would invariably encounter a pussy cat.

When Jeff disappeared for five days my brother Howie and I were beside ourselves with worry. Every night after supper we drove up and down streets with father in his flat-deck fish truck. We stopped here and there peering into yards and searching the bush land on the edge of Confederation Park. On the fifth night driving down McGill Street we noticed a small group of people standing on the boulevard in front of Mrs. Kubiak's house. We slowed down and attempted to see what the people were looking at.

"There's Jeff!" Howie exclaimed.

It was Jeff alright, *in flagrante delicto* with Mrs. Kubiak's champion white poodle. Jeff had turned around in the act and he and Mrs. Kubiak's Froo Froo were firmly attached by the sexual organs while each attempted to run in the opposite direction. A group of neighbourhood women were transfixed into a state of silent voyeurism in the face of this remarkable situation. Father gasped and muttered as he stepped on the gas and pulled away.

"Aren't we going to get him?" I asked.

"Nah, he's having a good time."

"How's he having a good time?" I asked.

"Maybe I'll cruise by after dark," he answered.

I persisted, "Doesn't look like he's having much fun."

"Why don't you just leave it alone. He isn't going anywhere," he said pulling up in front of our house.

"Did you see that poodle's nice haircut?" I offered.

"No I wasn't looking at its haircut," he said as he stomped into the house.

In the morning Jeff was fast asleep on the back porch. He looked a little worn out. At school that day Bobby Leech came up to me and said, "That flea bag of yours is some stud. He got stuck screwing Mrs. Kubiak's poodle."

"Is that what they were doing?" I asked.

"Of course, what do you think they were doing? They finally separated when Mr. Kubiak turned the hose on them."

I was in shock. I had no idea. I went home.

After supper I asked father why he hadn't told me.

"Well, it was pretty obvious," he snapped.

"Besides, now you know."

It all added up to one thing. I had actually witnessed Jeff making it with Mrs. Kubiak's silky white super star. Mother looked up and said, "In my opinion, Jeff has good taste when it comes to female companionship."

Father was preoccupied. I think he was expecting to see Mrs. Kubiak at the front door looking for compensation for the desecration of her beauty queen. It didn't happen. I went another few years before I learned that human beings did not have sex in the same fashion. I would look at my willy and wonder how the heck it would ever be able to accomplish such a peculiar gymnastic manoeuvre.

NORWEGIAN RATS AND ALLEY CATS

THE FISH COMPANY my grandfather, John Safarik, started in 1917 with his partner William Steiner was called Vancouver Shellfish & Fish Company. It was located in a fish shed on Campbell Avenue Dock at the foot of Campbell Avenue behind the Rogers Sugar Refinery on the Vancouver waterfront.

During the '50s in our elementary school years my brothers and I hung around on the fish dock as often as we could. My father, Norman, who ran the company, practically lived there so it was a simple matter of going with him whenever it was convenient, which was most of the time. My brother Jim, who is six years older than me, started working at the company full time when he was 15 and stayed in fish his whole working life. My younger brother Howard, who is three years younger than I am, started working at Van Shell full time in his early 20s and still spends his days wheeling and dealing fish. Father, who turned 88 on August 5, 2006, still goes to work everyday. He has 75 years experience processing and selling fish. Van Shell which has been in existence since 1917 at Gore Avenue and then moved to Campbell Avenue in 1924 is still in business, at a different location since Campbell Avenue was tragically decommissioned and left in limbo in the early 1990s.

Father worked at the company during the weekday business hours as well as in the evenings hauling crabs from Boundary Bay or fish from the Fraser River. Boats of different sizes came in at Campbell Avenue at all hours during the week nights. They might be trollers or gill netters with salmon, cod fisherman, crab fishermen or the Dane in his small boat with a catch of smelts from English Bay. The large boats; seiners, draggers, or packers usually timed their arrival for early morning at the beginning of the week. Hatch covers came off before first morning light and 100,000 pounds or more of fish would be unloaded by noon. The draggers who fished for the Fishermen's Cooperative came in loaded with ground fish (bottom feeders). Fish and shellfish that didn't come by boat came by truck from every part of the west coast in Canada or the United States. Live carp from Washington State were kept alive in a big plastic swimming pool that was set up in the middle of the main floor. Chinese merchants and Jewish matrons lined up to purchase the lively carp that swam around splashing and cavorting. During the week, fish was being loaded, unloaded, processed, frozen, shipped to local customers as well as to customers across the continent and around the world. Father was obliged to go down to the wharf on the weekends to unload boats or to ensure that the ice plant was making ice and to ice down the fresh fish that was stored on the floor in piles under receding blankets of ice. An ice machine on the second floor of the ancient fish plant made flake ice that piled up on the cement floor below. Depending on the weather and the air temperature, it was often necessary to refresh the fish that were being held over for the following Monday morning by shovelling a ton or more of ice onto the piles.

When I was small the waterfront was a kaleidoscope of wonders. I sat in my father's truck watching the world of every nationality pass by. When the whistle for coffee breaks or lunch sounded the workers filed out like lemmings from the various fish companies headed for the coffee shop or washrooms. They filtered back a few at a time usually with cigarettes in their hands and stopped before they reached the entrances to take a couple of final deep drags before going back to work. The filleting crew at Van Shell were a mixture of European nationalities including Norwegians, Finns, Icelanders, Italians and Croatians as well as Japanese, Chinese, and Aboriginals, including Iroquois from Ontario. The foreman was an Icelandic Canadian named Gunner. The crew that made crabmeat was run for about 40 years by a Scottish woman named Nancy and included Italian, Croatian, and Chinese women.

The tiny Japanese men who fished shrimp everyday in Vancouver Harbour or out by Bowen Island came to work pulling wooden wagons, the kind that children played with. These small wooden wagons were perfect for transporting the shrimps from their boats along the uneven dock to the plant to be processed each day. My favourite shrimp fisherman was a smiling joker named Hirokita with gold in his teeth. He gave me Japanese crackers, pickled salmon noses, exotic candies, or strange pieces of fruit that I had never seen before. They fished on weekdays and brought their catch into Campbell Avenue and unloaded it and crews of Oriental women picked the shells from the meat. Piles of shrimp were cooked in large metal baskets that were lowered into steam tanks, divested of their shells and were tightly packed into 50-pound silver aluminum pans and were stored over night on ice in my father's plant ready to be quickly sold to the fresh fish market along with the tons of crabs that were cooked in a similar manner and were shucked and made into crabmeat that was packed into similar silver pans.

In the early morning before light had streaked through the blackness the peddlers were arriving to look over whatever catch had come in from the night before. One of the most intense of these mostly oriental businessmen was a Chinese man named Sing Lee who owned an extremely successful fish store in Chinatown. I thought he was ancient when I was five years old but he still looked the same when I was twenty-five and he was just as spry. He plied me with White Rabbit candies and gave me two bits to help him pick out his fish. I always looked for him among the throng of peddlers who were pulling fish out from the piles of ice. One day before I was old enough to attend school, Sing Lee in a strange mood got an impulse and picked me up and carried me to the edge of the wharf and held me out 30 feet in the air over the open green water. He meant it as a joke. However, the experience terrified me and the joke backfired. When he put me down I ran for the safety of the fish shed and hid in a corner by the staircase so I could flee upstairs if he came near me. My grandfather, normally a good-natured Czech who wore thick glasses and spoke English with an accent, was not a man to be trifled with. He went out on the wharf, grabbed Sing Lee by the coat, and held him out over the water to see how he liked it. That was the end of that.

Also in the early mornings men and women in white coveralls, who were members of the United Fishermen and Shoreworkers Union, pulled on huge rolls of white parchment and wrapped the shrimp and crabmeat into 5- and 10-pound packages that they carefully weighed on the Toledo Scales that hung on hooks above metal tables. These packages were destined for the restaurant orders that were piling up on the cement floor in boxes on skids. These would be loaded onto the backs of delivery trucks that set off in the mid-morning with their loads of exotic fish products. The rest of the day was spent putting up the out of town and foreign shipping order that left by truck late in the afternoon.

The company had a vast inventory that included every kind of salmon (smoked, fresh, frozen), soles (lemon, Skidegate, witches), ling cod, grey cod, red snappers, ocean perch, rock cod, halibut, sturgeon, flounders, black cod, sword fish, maui maui, tuna, turbot, eels, turtle meat, smelts, carp, herring (salted, pickled and kippered), crabs, prawns, shrimp, oysters, clams (little necks, Manila, geoducks), lobsters (Atlantic, Cuban, Australian), mussels, scampi, crayfish, frogs' legs, monkfish, octopi, squid, dulce, caviar, and anything and everything else that came from the oceans, rivers or fresh water lakes. The company had no problem selling 1500 pounds of fresh crabmeat, treated like gold, every weekday to the local trade. The main downtown delivery routes covered the high-class restaurants and hotels that did business with my father's company. The Hotel Vancouver, The Devonshire, The Georgia Hotel, Trader Vic's, Monty's, The Fish and Oyster Bar, William Tell, The Vancouver Club were served by a pair of wisecracking Dutchmen named Tommy Meyers and Pete Snook who worked at Van Shell as long as I could remember, along with the foreman Harold Thompson and his assistant Johnny Bickle. Some workers' names I have forgotten, but I still remember Big and Little Annie, Maria, Agnes, Rosemary Fong, Nancy Speares, Gunnar Stevenson, Tat Hamaguchi and Stanley Kong.

Every June when school let out my brother Howie and I headed to the dock. We wandered among the trucks and boats watching fish being unloaded, nets being mended, or boats being scraped or painted. When the tide was right we fished for shiners from the lower pier where the fishing boats tied up. Sometimes we stood in our rubber boots in the blood and fish guts that piled up on the cement floor from the crew that was gutting salmon. We toiled among the piles of innards and stripped the long columns of orange salmon eggs and white milts and tossed them into Fukuyama the egg man's cans. He bought the eggs which he turned into salmon caviar and the milts. In those days standards were much different and a great amount of the gore, that was not kept to sell as scrap, was swept with the blood down the drain holes in the floor and became food for the huge number of Dungeness crabs that lived in the harbour.

When we weren't fishing, throwing ice balls at the sea gulls, rubbernecking at the various crews around the wharf who were unloading boats, watching the filleters upstairs on the second floor cutting ground fish or helping out downstairs we made fish boxes in the box loft. A couple of times a year a flat deck arrived loaded with box lumber that was stencilled with blue writing and the Van Shell crab logo. At that time wooden boxes of different sizes were employed to hold fish and ice that were shipped by truck, rail or air freight to different cities in Canada and the US. This was an era long before cardboard and Styrofoam became popular. The box lumber came in different sizes that were strapped onto pallets and lifted with forklifts into the box loft. My brother and I and a number of our neighbourhood friends who we recruited were employed to make boxes for shipping orders. We got paid 10 cents for a 50-pound box, 15 cents for a 100-pound box, and 20 cents for larger ones. The lumber was held in a jig we while we hammered nails into the ends to hold them together. Finished boxes were piled on skids waiting to be lowered down onto the main floor and then filled with fish and ice and tops were placed on them before they were nailed shut and loaded on trucks and hauled away. We made just enough boxes to stay ahead of the demand and the work provided us with the pocket money that we needed to blow at the Pacific National Exhibition later in the summer.

Strangely my memories about Campbell Avenue are some of the earliest memories I have about my childhood. In my middle age, some vivid chapters stand out like beacons from the distant past illuminating people and places that have long passed into the personal history that every person remembers parts of in the various decades of their lives. My first memories of Campbell Avenue are of being a preschool kid who often went to the wharf early in the morning with my father and helped him pull back the huge sliding doors that opened on railway tracks above metal riveted ramps that joined the wharf to the cement floor. My father, grandfather and some of the workers went gingerly around the plant to check on the rat traps (oo mink traps) that were invariably gone from their places but were easily found again by following the chains that were attached to them. The waterfront which contained foreign ships, fish plants, grain elevators, a sugar refinery and all manner of processing plants was infested with Norwegian rats of every size. Every morning each of the traps set the night before would contain either a dead or a very live rat caught in some kind of awful compromised position by its legs or some part of its body. Reeled in by hand on the end of the chains that went under totes and into corners the rats were dispatched with the stout end of a fish pew. I was fascinated by how they reacted to being caught as if whatever dignity they possessed had long fled their still living carcasses. A few were defiant to the end but most simply seemed to stiffen up and begin to die before they even felt the final killing blow. It was as if the man with the pew was using a coup stick rather than club. He counted coup with a token blow and the rat immediately turned toes up. The company was bountiful with fish and in turn was plagued by the hordes of rats that came to dig in the ice and feast on whatever fish they could manage to expose.

Eventually somebody got the idea of introducing alley cats into the scenario in order to reduce the number of rats. It seemed a natural solution to a serious problem. After all, cats were devoted enemies of rats which they dispatched with great relish and it seemed that an increasing population of cats would be preferable to an infestation of ugly, filthy rats. The fish companies at Campbell Avenue bought into the plan and soon every company had a few cats patrolling their premises. At first this plan seemed to be working as initially the rat problem seemed to decrease dramatically. However it was only a short-term solution to the problem.

The cats took a toll on the rats but soon developed a much more sophisticated diet. They were happier to eat fish rather than rats. Soon the cats were breeding like mad and the box lofts and attics in the fish plants were filling up with litters of kittens. The rich diet of fish without other components soon saw the generations of cats mutating into astonishing forms. Standard alley cats were transformed into elongated felines with small heads and fierce mouthfuls of needle sharp teeth. Literally the iodine enriched cats became fearless fighters who were virtually unafraid of people. Employees began to complain that they were afraid to go into the box lofts for fear of being attacked and mutilated by half mad cat replicas that had taken over the top floors of the fish plants. The great fish sheds were all attached to one another, thereby creating a linked environment that allowed the cats to survive in vast dark areas that were mostly used for storage. In the morning when the big doors on the fish sheds slid open, instead of rats in traps, the workers were greeted by circles of cats that had pawed their way into the piles of fresh salmon. They were now gorging themselves on the choice parts, having spoiled the rest of the fish. These cats were loath to move away from their breakfasts and began to become aggressive in their behaviour. Losses to rats paled in comparison to the toll of product that the ravenous cats were taking. Large areas in the various sheds were off limits because of fierce, crazed felines protecting their litters. In the meantime, the rats had begun to return in numbers since the fish-gorged-cats were not so interested in chasing them. The organic solution to the problem, introducing a predator to reduce a pest became a total failure because in the process the problem became a lot more complicated than the simple solution to solving it.

On a cool, fall Saturday morning a group of men drinking coffee assembled on the wharf. Armed with shotguns loaded with number six bird shot they put miner helmets with spot lights onto their heads and proceeded into the fish plants. Moving slowly through the various floors of the great fish sheds under the massive beams and high ceilings they flashed their headlights and spent the day blasting cats into oblivion until there were virtually none left. I sat outside on the wharf in my father's truck looking at my Mickey Mouse comic books while the guns blasted the air. Now and then a few of the men came out to stand on the dock and have a cigarette and cool their shotgun barrels that were too hot to touch. That was *finis* for the cats on the fish dock. Occasionally, I encountered an alley cat sniffing around the garbage bins on the wharf but none of those dared try and move into the buildings. Nobody seemed to mind a few cats wandering here and there on the wharf but the generations of mutating felines were history.

The rats never recovered in strength of number after the cats were eradicated because shortly thereafter a poison called warfarin, a water-soluble anticoagulant, was introduced on the waterfront. The legions of rats that came off foreign ships visiting the harbour and that thrived in the grain elevators, sugar refinery and in the fish and other processing plants that existed in the inner harbour became a rare sight on Campbell Avenue. The hundreds of rats of my childhood become non-existent.

I didn't encounter another rat on the fish dock for over 10 years, until I was a teenager assembling wax cartons in the box loft. I was on my way up the third floor stairway when I encountered a smallish rat in the middle of the enclosed staircase. It sat up on its haunches and made eye contact before it suddenly bolted and ran down the stairs past me and disappeared into the huge piles of flattened wax cartons that were stacked on skids. I figured maybe this rat had found a home feeding off the discarded food that was left behind at noon hour when some of the workers sat upstairs in the dressing rooms eating their lunches. I went down to the cupboard on the first floor and fished out an old rusty mink trap that was attached to a rusty chain. I climbed the stairs into the box loft and set the trap with part of the peanut butter sandwich from my lunch bag as bait. I nailed the ring on the chain to the wall and bent the box nail over it so that the trap was firmly anchored.

Late in the afternoon I went to check the trap and found it missing. When I followed the chain I discovered the rat caught in the trap, hiding behind the metal stapling machine with the foot peddle that was used to staple wax cartons. I slowly yanked it out into the open and saw that the rat was caught by one leg high up on the shoulder. Before I could manage to hit the rat with the end of the fish pew that I held in my free hand it looked at me and suddenly began to stiffen up and die right in front of my eyes. Within a few seconds the rat was dead and *rigor mortis* set in almost instantaneously. The rat knew it was done for and had gone "gently into that good night" without so much as a squeak. I felt its voluntary death was a ceremonial act that summed up the symbolic relationship between us. We were linked by our own needs and our own histories; the mutual histories of our ancestors' survival. I was reminded that there would always be another rat to catch.

BRIDGE TO THE PAST

IN MY OLD NEIGHBOURHOOD, Vancouver Heights in North Burnaby, the most significant monument was the old Second Narrows Bridge. It carried a lane of traffic in each direction and train tracks ran down the middle. There were toll booths on the North Shore side; it cost 20 cents to make the return trip by car. Traffic stopped when trains moved on to the bridge from wooden trestles.

Massive grain elevators and a rail yard sprawled southwest of the bridge approach on Cassiar Street. The bridge, controlled by a man in a shack perched in the girders, opened to let shipping pass through the narrows. Depending on the tide, even a tow boat, a fishing boat or any craft with a tall mast forced the bridge open. When the warning bells sounded, traffic halted and the middle of the bridge groaned open, tilting each lane into the air.

We often travelled across to the North Shore in my father's upside-down bathtub Nash, an efficient, if odd-looking car, with luxurious fold-down seats that could sleep a family of five if the kids were small enough. We went berry picking on Grouse Mountain or fished for trout in the deeper pools of Seymour Creek. Sometimes we gathered fire wood on the foreshore, where Hooker chemical now stands. The harbour teemed with pintails, mallards and green-winged teal zipped along the inlet. In the fall my father would bring down a few birds with his double-barrelled Greener shotgun. The din of seals and their pups barking along the beach faded away in the mist rising from the water.

In 1956 I was eight years old and already a veteran fisherman. I fished with my brothers from the sidewalk on the bridge, dropping our large baited triple hooks with suitable weight down into the boil. The narrows was a treacherous piece of water fraught with rip tides and churning cataracts. Our lines dropped 20 or 30 feet before entering the water. We made our own weights from lead line my father brought home from the fish dock. We cut it into sections and melted it away from the rope in an old frying pan on top of a Coleman stove, pouring the shiny hot lead into moulds. We used 100-pound test halibut line wound on grooved pieces of plywood, pulling it in or letting it out by hand. Our hooks were baited with clam meat or sea worms found under rocks on the beach.

My brother Jimmy is a person I have admired all my life. We are basically opposites. He can build anything and has always understood how mechanical things work. I am a klutz, unable to fix or run anything. In childhood I was the gofer on his construction projects. He built us a "bug," our term for a soapbox derby car. It had a steering wheel, brakes, pipes for axles, and real ball bearing wheels. We lived on a steep hill and our bug went like a streak — nothing in the neighbourhood could match it. Jimmy weighted the front end for more speed and eventually he flipped into the ditch, breaking his arm. One Hallowe'en, Jimmy made a bomb from gunpowder and other materials. He took it into the bush and buried it in the ground in a pipe with a plug of road tar. It blew out half the windows on two streets. He was also good at making home brew from beets, which he hid in a bucket in the closet of his basement room.

I helped him deliver his papers. After school we went to the shack on Oxford Street and loaded our bike with two sacks. We had the most unusual route in the entire city. We delivered *The Vancouver Sun* to the squatters who lived in shacks built on stilts in the mud at the Burnaby side of Burrard Inlet. We followed a trail down through the bush beside the Standard Oil refinery. Occasionally, we would glimpse deer in the clearings or find fresh black bear tracks in the mud. We pushed the loaded bike along a path beside the railway tracks. Huge rafts of sea ducks clustered along the shore. We fired our slingshots at the glass insulators on the power poles and kept our eyes open for railroad cops. When the train whistle sounded, we moved over to the bush side of the tracks. Sometimes we put coins on the rails and carried the flattened specimens home in our pockets.

The squatters were not considered entirely respectable citizens by some of those living in more conventional housing beyond the bush. Most of them were eccentrics or artistic types. One old guy raised sheep and others kept domestic animals ranging from pigs to parrots. Our favourite subscriber was named Doc. He had a business card that read:

Dr W. W. Watson

Paraphysical Investigative Bureau

We usually encountered Doc on his way home from his office in Vancouver. He walked along the tracks at about the same time everyday. He had the uncanny ability to read a book while his feet automatically found every second tie. I tried walking like that for years, usually stumbling after thirty feet.

Doc would invite us in for a cup of tea and show us his latest gadget. We liked it when he opened his window on the harbour so we could watch the seals and look for exotic birds. He had several machines that ionized things or caused sequences of weird flashing lights. Once he encouraged me to hold the handles on a strange box that had wires and fuses and a gauge. I grabbed on with both hands and got the shock of my life. I had Don King hair for about a month.

The row of shacks built along the inlet extended for three miles from the refinery to the Second Narrows. When we reached the bridge we climbed on to the railway trestle and pushed our bikes along until we reached the deck. After that we climbed a steep series of hills from the bottom at Cassiar Street up to Boundary Road. When we reached the top I sat on the handlebars and my brother pedalled for home.

My younger brother Howie and I were like the chipmunks in the cartoons. "After you, I'm sure." "No, I insist, after you." Or we fought like the Battling Bickersons. He had pure white hair, wore a captain's hat, Cowboy Bob boots, and a leopard skin-patterned cloth bag on his belt. We spent hours fishing on the bridge. We caught cod, flounders, dogfish, and the odd small salmon. Occasionally, a fat Dungeness crab (the narrows were loaded with them) would hang on to the bait.

One slow summer afternoon we had the heavy line out in the chop. We tied the line on to the bridge railing while we settled down to eat our lunch. There was a sudden strike. We grabbed for slack and gave the line a good jolt. We had it, whatever it was, hooked solidly. A crowd gathered to watch us walk up and down the sidewalk, straining with the line over our shoulders, trying to gain a few feet. The battle went on for two hours. There was speculation about what might be on the end of the line and how we were going to land it. Some kid nearby guessed it might be a 50-pound ling cod. Another suggested it was a big salmon. "No, that would come to the surface," we grunted.

About the time we were betting huge halibut, the line went slack. We pulled it in, listening to voices saying, "Oh, too bad, it's gone."

It wasn't.

The line tightened and shot through our fingers. We tore our shirts to provide protection for our raw palms. It was too late, the line ran all the way out, stretching from where it was tied to the railing. We could only stand at the edge and look down. A ray with a vast span came to the surface. We had snagged it in its back. It turned over, slashing the water with enormous wings. The line ex-

ploded with the sound a .22 calibre rifle makes. Our intended dinner was gone.

"After you," I said.

"No, after you," he insisted.

We were sharing a big fish story.

By the mid-1950s a new bridge was planned for the Second Narrows — a stupendous, state-of-the-art high bridge to arch trium-
phantly over the inlet. It would be built just west of the existing
bridge. The neighbourhood was on the move. Our monument was
being replaced by something with big shoulders. We figured we'd
need one hundred feet of line to get down to the water from this
monster.

In the summers we went to our favourite and only convenient
swimming spot. It was named Windermere Pool and was located in New Brighton Park across the street from Exhibition Park
racetrack. It was one of those old cement-walled jobs that let sea
water in with the tide. It had a pill box you could swim out to and
dive from. Whenever we got bored or the pool was too crowded,
we swam out to pilings offshore in the inlet. The lifeguards went
crazy ordering us to swim in the pool. We jumped in upstream
to allow the current to carry us while we swam furiously for the
pilings and their make-shift diving boards. Once we reached the
pilings, we could dive at will and bask on the platform in the sun,
thumbing our noses at the chickens on shore. Truth was, the water
in the open inlet was so cold, by comparison with the sun-heated
shallow waters of the pool. We were really gathering strength to
make the return swim.

Afterward, we ran around with our towels trailing behind us like
so many versions of Superman. We played soccer on the field or
lashed each other with seaweed bullwhips. We lay in the sun on
our towels chewing on long stems of grass. The conversation always
came back to the new bridge going up before our amazed eyes.

"How in the world did the bridge end, extending from North
Vancouver, hold itself up?"

It jutted well out over the inlet and it was covered with trucks, machinery and workers. It seemed to defy logic; we wanted to learn the secrets of the modern world.

On June 17, 1958, I was 3 months and 10 days short of being 10 years old. We had no real park in our neighbourhood but there was a reservoir on several acres of bush land. We had a ballpark on the grassy corner at Trinity and McGill. There was a mythical outfield fence, really a steep bank, that dropped to the road. Hit it over the bank in the air and it was out of the park. The game lasted all summer. We kept statistics. I was pitching to Ron Villman. He was a slugger and, even though it was early in the season, he had 40 round-trippers. The ground began to tremble, followed by a sudden, indescribable noise. "Earthquake," we thought, "maybe the bomb."

We rushed to the edge of the field. Mr. Zunti, who had been re-shingling his roof, stood at the peak looking out over the inlet. He turned and yelled to us, "The bridge has fallen." We stood for impossible minutes. Our new monument had collapsed. The game was over.

THE DAY BILLY COOPER LOST AN EYE

It was a day like most days in childhood. I wore ugly black Leckie boots with metal eyelets. I slathered the seams with orange dubbin to keep out the water. It seemed to rain on nearly every school day. I walked or rode my bike eight blocks mostly uphill to school in it and home again. I loved the sound of rain falling on our roof late at night when I was in my bed. I slept on the top bunk, parting the curtains to look at the drops of rain making rivers down the window pane. I never owned a winter jacket. I wore a sweater and a raincoat and rode my bike everywhere. Sometimes I imagined my bike was a motor cycle, a race car, or a horse. When I rode it like a bucking bronco through the puddles it threw water right up my back. When I drove a racing car I left rooster tails on every street. The only sound I loved more than rain drumming on our shingles at night was the sound of the freight trains that passed below our house along the edge of Burrard Inlet in North Burnaby.

My favourite day in the year was Hallowe'en. I could suspend my belief and dress up as somebody else and get away with murder for once. I had a pocket full of firecrackers including the nasty little Lady Fingers that one quickly tossed before the short fuses went off with a real bang. It was no fun having one go off in the hand. I had punks and wicks to light and revelled in the explosions in the fall mornings. I loved the smell of the acrid powder from fireworks and the fog that enveloped the world whispering down around the rain forest like a shroud of mystery. Sometimes it almost obliterated houses and buildings and covered up cars crawling cautiously down side streets. There were years the fog stayed around for several weeks until one felt it was a permanent condition of the environment. Horse chestnut tree leaves fell into the ditches and accumulated in the drains like pieces of soggy paper. We made conkers of the chestnuts and whacked away after school trying to obliterate the opposition. A foggy Hallowe'en was best, then we could raise hell and do it in relative anonymity. Soaping windows, tipping garbage cans, setting off fireworks and scaring all the smaller kids to death was our child's play. We slipped away in the fog only to reappear again as scary monsters or trick-or-treaters.

We played baseball in the summer every day. Some version of baseball, whether it be teams, scrub, American Ping Pong or 500 as well as Little League at Willington Park. We played a game called "peggie" in the alley with broom sticks and "kick the can" on warm summer nights when there was a gang of kids with nothing to do. In the fall we played football at the reservoir field on Trinity Street. It was either a vigorous game of touch or a full fledged game of tackle that sometimes resulted in bad feelings and injured bodies. When there was only my brother Howie and I, we played tackle in our hilly backyard on frozen ground with one end zone across a sidewalk and the other being a grassy bank leading down to the road. We took turns hutting the ball and then attempting to tackle the raging halfback who was rampaging across the yard. I played minor league football at Adanac Park for a team sponsored by a furnace repair company. We wore uniforms similar to the Winnipeg Blue Bombers. When it got colder we played road hockey in front of the Delasalle house on Yale. Their father was a rich lumberyard owner. Pat and his brothers had hockey nets that could be dragged onto the road. It hardly ever snowed where we lived so we played road hockey on pavement. Our sticks wore down until the blades were little more than long splinters. We used a tennis ball that soon lost its fuzz. A slapshot off a part of the body left a nasty red welt. The Delasalle boys (possessing an array of sticks that would have made a pro team jealous) played ice hockey at the North Shore Winter Club and could blast the ball like a bullet. The few of us who played minor hockey at the Renfrew Forum (where the old WHL Vancouver Canucks played) were used to getting by on one stick per season. We thought slapshots were high risk ventures. A few times every season we got out the roller skates and played end to end Stanley Cup finals on the pavement that covered the ground around Gilmore Avenue Elementary School. Every few years it got cold enough long enough to freeze the local ponds and lakes. We played hockey on the frozen bowl on the PNE grounds where they held the logging events in the summer or we took the long bus ride to Stanley Park and we stayed all day playing hockey on Beaver Lake. If we were lucky somebody's father might drive us out to Deer Lake and we'd play there. Below-zero weather never lasted long and most of us remained pretty bad skaters. We were the children of rain.

We played soccer as if it was our religion. We kicked the ball around the yard, in the streets, on the boulevards, in parking lots, churchyards, schoolyard, parks, alleys, against walls, off garage doors and fences, in the basement and in the hallways of the house with a rolled up pair of socks for the ball. We played soccer before school, at recess, at lunch, after school, after supper, before bed. My first team was Johnson Shoes and then I went to the Norburn Athletic Club and then to the legendary North Burnaby Legion 148, three time BC Champions and Canadian Champions. We played on Saturday mornings at Confederation Park on Willington in Burnaby our home field. There were pot bellied stoves in the dressing rooms below the caretaker's residence and we piled in to change into our shorts. We lobbied for heat while our coaches gave us a pep talk before we set off to demolish the opposition. We played hard to win. We ran the other teams into the ground and kept on hammering away at them until they folded and gave up the ghost.

Sometimes we got a surprise and they fought back and the dog fight was on. At the end we left everything we had on the field. On away game days we piled into our manager's and coaches' cars and headed off to South Burnaby or East End Vancouver, Coquitlam or New Westminster, or North or West Vancouver. We played cup games at Central Park in Burnaby before Swangard Stadium was built. It was the class field in Burnaby for important matches. We practised two nights a week at a school gym and we played League games on Saturdays and exhibition games on Sundays.

Callister Park in East End Vancouver was the soccer player's mecca. In 1968, North Burnaby Legion 148 managed by Scotty Kemp and coached by Doug McDonald and Larry Wilson, won the Canadian Championship on the hallowed grounds beating Etobicoke for the national title which we had lost the year before in Montreal on a field that was under water. These men taught us a great deal about ourselves and the concept of team. Over the years they spent hundreds of hours teaching us the finer points until we were a well oiled machine capable of holding our own against the teams from the senior men's leagues in training games to prepare us for slaughtering the opposition in our own age level. But we learned the game playing it endlessly in backyards and city parks or on boulevards in the forum of our own peers who lived in the houses in our own neighbourhoods.

We played well over 50 games per season from September until the first of May and we loved playing in the rain. Sometimes in bad years if the rain was too severe for a long period or when the fields were captured by snow and ice the various parks boards would close the fields. Let it rain, it made no difference to us. Games on the pristine turf or games in a mud hole in a drenching rainstorm were the same high. We played for the love of it. Limping around all week, taking it easy at practice in order to make it back on the field the following Saturday morning. There were broken toes and the odd broken nose and even the odder but tragic broken leg. There were different kinds of breaks; the stiff crack like a gunshot that promised a compound fracture and a screaming victim soon deep in shock; or the dull thud of boot biting into the turf and a man down wallowing like a wounded horse in the mud and another cracked bone. Cleat marks on thighs like calligraphy and bruises from a shin hacking stood out on flesh, were grim reminders of the game, a litany that graphically illustrated the axiom of no fun without a little pain.

Everyday was like most other days in childhood. I went to public school, Gilmore Avenue Elementary in North Burnaby, to be precise. Other kids in my neighbourhood went to St. Helen's, the local Catholic Parish School. Gilmore Avenue Elementary had a couple of dirt fields behind the school that were surrounded by trees and a wire fence. St. Helen's had very little playground area and no field. Students from this school took their physical education classes at the field on the local reservoir. This reservoir area between Trinity and Eton Streets in North Burnaby contained a reservoir and a pumping station on a large area of relatively undeveloped land. Tennis courts had been built on top of the reservoir itself next to a pebble and dirt soccer field. The north east end of the property contained an additional grassy area that was almost a soccer pitch in dimensions. The main dirt field was edged by trees and there was a large area between the two fields that was sunken ground. This lowlands valley was perpetually covered by a vast forest of broom plant. A small creek ran out from a culvert and cut through the valley until it entered a culvert again on the east side.

The fields in the Reservoir were not adequate to allow organized sporting events. Basically they were rough fields carved out of bush land in order to provide recreation to the neighbourhood. It was land that's use was outside normal jurisdiction. It was not in the possession of parks boards or the education departments. It was no man's land and the law of the jungle prevailed. At the south east corner of the property *The Vancouver Sun* paper shack was situated. Here the rules and conduct of the paper shack were in order. Nobody stepped out of line without getting an earful from the sub manager. Kids who were unfamiliar with paper shack culture seemed to automatically know enough to stay away. Offenders who broke the rules were subject to the discipline of the straw broom or were tossed into the perpetual pond-sized-puddle that accumulated on one side of the shack. From the higher elevation on the dirt field the acres of broom plant stretched out like a dark green carpet across the lowland centre of the property. The wild mini-forest of broom turned the whole valley yellow when it bloomed. Kids built forts and made secret trails. They pushed planks across the creek and dug clay from the steep banks and wove the broom plant into elaborate hiding places.

The upper dirt field that we dubbed the "soccer field" had no goalposts. We counted goals scored when the ball was shot between a pair of trees at each end of the field. On one end of the field there was a backstop and the field was measured out in the dimensions of a baseball infield. When school was out there was a game of scrub there about 12 hours a day. During the school year St. Helen's and Seton Academy, a nearby girls school, used that field for their PE classes and for games against other Catholic schools. The students from St. Helen's would arrive after school for a big game against another school; boys wearing their powder blue shirts and dark blue pants. The girls were attired in navy blue jumpers. It was only when the nuns, severe in their black habits, arrived that we would relinquish the field after they berated us for being nasty little boys. Some mouthy kid always made a speech about possession of the diamond being nine points of the law but it never worked, we were always driven off. The nuns coached, umpired and patrolled the grounds keeping the kids who were watching in order. Sometimes the nuns came out by themselves, still dressed in their formal black attire, with white wimples and dangling crosses. They played catch and then took to the diamond, gracefully whipping the ball around the horn and playing a spirited game that saw them stealing bases and sliding into home. They could hit and throw and field grounders like vacuum cleaners and they razzed each other just like ball players in the Industrial League on Powell Street. After a few innings they packed up their well worn gear in old canvas bags and left laughing covered with dust and grime, chattering like school children on holiday.

The lower square-shaped grassy field on the north east corner had no goalposts or backstops. It was the training ground for the real athletes in the neighbourhood. Here the ball games were serious business that went on all day and lasted well into the evening of summer nights. Devoted soccer players met here on weekdays after school for titanic games of four on four or five on five. It only took one kid with a ball and another with the inclination to join him. Here tackle football was played because the clumps of poor quality grass somehow allowed the pasture-like surface to resemble a football field. The games were played by boys of all stripes. The public school and Catholic kids played together on the organized teams in various leagues and here at the most base grass roots level. Friendships and competition in the sporting world went far deeper than religious or social differences. Though at various times through the years the nature of the larger community was sometimes played out on the reservoir bush lands. Rudimentary playing fields taught each individual player a thing or two about a bad bounce, an unbelievable catch, or a pile driving tackle into half-frozen ground.

The day Billy Cooper lost an eye was like practically any other day of the school year. The older boys played soccer on the killing ground, the school field that was nothing more than a large patch of dirt with the odd rock erupting up to the surface in the rain. Girls and the younger boys played on the paved ground in front of the school where skipping games, hop scotch patterns and tether ball predominated. It was the times. Runty W. was agitating some of the older boys. He and his few closest friends, by grade six, were already well-suited for their future lives (that would largely be spent in penal institutions). They were recruiting on the school grounds demanding that the boys follow them to the reservoir, after school, to take care of the "Catlickers" as they called the Catholic school kids. Runty and his boys had moved into the reservoir for entertainment. They terrorized kids in ways only they could imagine. They raided the St. Helen's students when they were playing scrub on the diamond or were building forts in the broom plant wilderness. They trashed the forts, slapped younger kids silly, and developed a serious animosity between themselves and the St. Helen's student body.

Runty came from a disastrous environment. His two older sisters were real beauties. By grade eight they were fully developed tarts with short skirts, padded pointed bras and acid tongues. They attracted older men, usually bikers or large hairy dudes with bulging jeans and skin tight tee shirts. Guys with a pack of cigarettes rolled up in the tee shirt material on the upper arm. One of the sisters, while still of high school age, was sitting in a car in the East End with her drug dealing boyfriend when he was assassinated for a heroin deal gone bad by a shotgun blast. It was fired at close range at his head through the side window of his jalopy. She walked away without a scratch. Runty, who later in life ended up in the BC penitentiary for committing horrible crimes that included armed robbery, kidnapping, and rape, was a pint-sized bully who had cultivated a few goons with low values to be his assistants in life. They patrolled the neighbourhood looking for opportunities to raise real hell, not the junior league stuff the rest of us pulled off. The boys who played sports had no problem with Runty and his pals because we knew how to deal with him and because he half-respected athletic ability. Once Runty tried to take my lunch money but he was small. It was relatively easy to fend him off. Almost by accident I punched him in the face harder than I intended to and his nose bled like a stuck pig. He needed henchmen to help him live up to his ambition. It also became apparent to Runty that it wasn't a good idea to try and bully kids who had older brothers at the junior high school.

The day Billy Cooper lost an eye was the day Runty W. raised an army from the ranks of school boys from Gilmore Avenue Elementary. "Bring your hockey sticks and your baseballs bats," he implored as he and his associates riled up the boys by urging them to join in cleaning out the "Catlickers." They needed to be taught a thing or two before they got too confident thinking they were entitled to the reservoir.

"Bring slings and slingshots, bows and arrows, knives, clubs or hammers," he cried. "Rally in front of the Oxford Market at four o'clock for the march up to the reservoir to beat the crap out of the 'Catlickers'."

Runty and his pals were banned from the Oxford Market because of shoplifting but he wanted to meet there so he could send somebody into the store to steal him a chocolate bar and a coke. Runty W. had made himself a blackjack by pouring lead into a piece of rubber hose that had a leather thong on one end so he could wrap it around his hand. His friends had pounded nails into the blades of their hockey sticks until they were bristling and the 50 or so boys who turned out were largely unarmed, but some brought hockey sticks and others had slings and slingshots.

They set off three abreast on the seven block walk to the reservoir picking up more recruits along the way. My friends and I were already playing soccer on the grassy field when we saw the snaking line of armed kid-desperados approaching the reservoir. We had been watching for them to see if they would really show up, some kids thought Runty was full of bull and that nobody would follow him. We were wrong. Soon he and his followers were occupying the ground close to the paper shack while a crowd of St. Helen's students were on the higher ground on the bluffs on the other side of the broom plant forest. Shouts and taunts went back and forth between both sides and people began to throw rocks but the distance was still too great. Runty W. was making up a plan, he urged the boys with slings to unlimber and start hucking rocks at the crowd in blue that was gathering on the bluffs.

Some of the boys playing in our soccer game decided to move closer to the action to see what was going to happen. We picked up our ball and moved along the edge of the reservoir on our way toward the paper shack. Billy Cooper saw a few of his friends in Runty's army so he moved forward to speak with them in the hope he might talk them into leaving before they got into trouble. Soon, both sides were firing deadly rocks way up into the clouds across the field of broom. These heavy missiles came down with a vengeance and landed in the mud with a whumping noise or crashed into the trees. Soon the crowd on both sides began to get agitated as the missiles began to find the range. Billy Cooper had decided to jog back to our position about a hundred yards north of the Gilmore Avenue crowd. When he turned and looked out over the broom plants he was suddenly and rudely knocked to the ground by an rock that had been fired by someone with a sling on the far bluffs. A crowd gathered around him and someone ran to the nearby houses for help and soon the fire department and police arrived and then another police car and an ambulance appeared at the scene. Billy was being attended by two women from the neighbourhood. They wrapped him in a blanket and hovered over him before riding away with him in the back of the ambulance.

Both sides were still mustered in the reservoir. The sight of poor Billy Cooper going down under a stone brought a severity to the moment. Before long, Mr. Hodgson, the Principal of Gilmore Avenue Elementary School, arrived in his red and white Studebaker and he immediately took charge. Mr. Hodgson, a short stocky man with a frilly haircut, took no prisoners at the best of times. He marched around the scene with an RCMP officer and ordered ring leaders and members of the mob to surrender their weapons. He had a little notebook in hand and he wrote down names and he accumulated information while the disarming went on. We stood in a clump on the far edge of the field and he strode the distance over to us to find out what we saw. We told him. He knew we weren't involved. The RCMP officers loaded the weapons into the trunks of their cars. Mr. Hodgson ordered Runty W. and his thugs into a marching order and gave them instructions to follow him the seven blocks back to the elementary school. He drove his red and white Studebaker slowly while the children's army followed solemnly behind on foot like a funeral procession. They were headed for trouble, we had no doubt about that. Mr. Hodgson was a legend with the strap. Although short in stature, he was built like a brick with a pigeon breast and according to rumour he administered punishment that was right out of this world. I was lucky I had no occasion to find out.

I went home to tell my mother about what had happened. When the Cooper family car returned home late in the evening from the hospital, mom went across the street to find out how Billy was doing. She came back in tears. The Bantam hen's egg sized rock that hit Billy Cooper square in the face while he was looking up at the bluffs had completely destroyed one of his eyes. He would never have the use of it again. Billy also suffered a severe head injury. It was several weeks before he finally returned home. It was over three months before he resumed going to school. The first day he came back we tried hard not to look at his glass eye. Nobody had the courage to talk to him about his ordeal.

Runty W. and his few pals were booted out of school for a few weeks. When they returned they never attended regularly. Most of them had already failed a grade or two along the way and it wasn't too long before they turned 15 and were long gone from the educational scene. I followed Runty's exploits years later when he escaped from the penitentiary and went on a rampage commandeering cars and raping his victims. I often wondered how in the world a budding thug like Runty, who would sink his whole life into the morass of criminality, could have inspired a bunch of normally peaceful city kids into getting themselves involved in what was nothing more than a race war with a bunch of kids like themselves, only with a slightly different religious point of view. It made me blanch at how the causes of disharmony and hatred could be so easily motivated by the forces of darkness. How, on a perfectly arbitrary school day, basically the same as any other day, a drama could unfold, making it the day Billy Cooper lost an eye.

ANONYMOUS

AT AN EARLY AGE I WAS AN AVID READER who devoured piles of library books early in the mornings before I went to school. Just before dawn, waking from the sound of my father stoking our coal burning furnace, I would go into the living room and lie on the rug and read with my feet against the heat register.

Every Saturday afternoon, my mother took me to the McGill branch of the Burnaby Public Library that was situated next to Eagle Motors on Hastings Street not too far west from Willington Avenue. The old building had children's books on the bottom floor while the adult books that I longed to read were on the second floor mezzanine. Sometimes I snuck upstairs and shelf-read the books looking for titles that I wanted to read. This got the ire of the librarian on duty who would tap me on the shoulder and tell me that I should be looking for books on the floor below. One day in frustration I asked mom if she would speak to the librarian so that I could check out and read the adult books. She took me to the counter with her and we approached the same woman who had chased me down the stairs. Mother politely informed her that she wanted me to have complete freedom of the library. I couldn't believe my ears when the frowning librarian acquiesced. I was free to go upstairs whenever I felt like it and I used the opportunity to keep checking out the titles.

My reading habit got to become an important part of my life. It provided me with an abundance of enjoyment. I read in the mornings before school and at school, whenever I got the opportunity. If the class got unruly when the teacher was out of the room for some reason I merely put my fingers in my ears and read from the book that I balanced on my lap. I learned how to appear to be attentive while I was reading from the book I had wedged between my stomach and the front of the desk. It was good practice. Several years later I wrote my first book of poetry, *Okira, Selected Translations From The Text Of,* writing the poems into a notebook balanced on my lap during the lectures of a Commonwealth Literature class I was taking from Bruce Nesbitt at Simon Fraser University.

At recess or lunchtime, if it was too cold or wet to play soccer, I went to the school library to check out books and then read until the bell. I had a scam going.

Whenever I got a detention, I'd ask the teacher if it was possible for me to read during the time of my sentence. Sometimes they said no and ordered me to write lines or sit with my hands behind my back but usually they allowed me to read. When they did this I felt a small twinge of victory inside. I loved reading and being allowed to sit quietly in a room and read my book without being disturbed for any reason was my Shangri La.

Unfortunately, I was not a good student outside of English, geography, and social studies. Math and the sciences failed to keep my interest. In the evenings I barely kept up my homework in those subjects. Instead I opted for reading a Hornblower novel or the White Company or a book about Marco Polo or a volume about explorers in South America in the 16th century. There was a five-foot-tall brown bookcase in our basement full of books that soon fell under my gaze. It contained mostly atlases and nonfiction books about Canada and particularly British Columbia history but also held a substantial number of novels, including *The Egg and I, How Green Was My Valley, For Whom The Bell Tolls, All Quiet on the Western Front, The Last of the Mohicans,* as well as volumes by Daphne du Maurier and Robert Ruarke, including a particularly graphic novel about the Mau Mau period in Kenya. In this bookcase I found a memoir about her time in Africa by Margaret Laurence and a copy of *The Stone Angel.* Mom was a fan of the Los Angeles Dodgers, the Toronto Maple Leafs, and Margaret Laurence. I also remember her enthusiasm for the featured stories in *The Star Weekly* which was delivered to our home. From those august pages, I became a huge fan of Hugh Garner and Prince Valiant. Mom also had a tradition of giving me books for my birthday and also at Christmas. Her sister, my aunt Lois, also gave me books whenever a present was called for. I still have most of the volumes she gave me through the years, including editions of *Black Beauty, Wind In the Willows, The Jungle Book, Oliver Twist, The Leacock Roundabout* and poetry books by Keats, Earle Birney, Dylan Thomas, and Leonard Cohen.

I started to write poetry when I was about 12 years old. By the time I got halfway through junior high school I was absolutely hooked. My mother liked to do crossword puzzles and write limericks and play around with word games and anagrams. Sometimes I joined her in these mutually interesting time-passers. Late at night in bed I tuned in a radio station from California that played Bob Dylan tunes. For the first time I heard the haunting voice of Joan Baez and the poetry of Lawrence Ferlinghetti and Kenneth Rexroth being performed by the authors with jazz accompanists recorded in front of live audiences. I had an egghead friend named Robin Kelsey who knew a lot about contemporary folk music, jazz, and the alternative society that was beginning to develop a large audience among university students. His older brother had gone off to march in civil rights demonstrations in the southern United States. Robin influenced my taste in literature and taught me how to play chess during noon hours at the McGill library branch, that by this time had moved to a brand new location down the street from Burnaby Heights school across from Confederation Park. By the time we reached Burnaby North High School, which was a monolithic school with 2000 grade 11 and 12 students (from several feeder junior high schools), Robin found students to hang around with who were way more advanced than I was. He was a brilliant student who always achieved the highest grades and won most of the academic awards. Unable to hold my own with the sophisticated academic crowd that he preferred to hang around with, I got more serious about my jockish pursuits.

My grade 9 teacher at Burnaby Heights Junior Secondary, Mr. Foulds, noticed that I was displaying more than a passing interest in writing poetry. One day during English class he asked me to drop back to his classroom at the end of the day. I was miffed. I hadn't done anything wrong but I figured he must have fingered me for some petty detail. During that morning in English class we had been discussing our favourite poems in the class textbook. Of course, nobody but me had a favourite poem; most of the students, especially the boys, abhorred poetry. I spoke up and said that easily my favourite poem in the book was called "The Shark" by E. J. Pratt, who happened to be a Canadian. I was fascinated by the use of language and the economical way Pratt expressed himself. It was so clean and vivid. The diabolical force moving leisurely through cerebral water. I could virtually see that shark in my mind's eye swimming around in that harbour — its fin "stirred not a bubble." At the end of the day I turned up at Mr. Foulds's classroom ready to clean brushes or try and convince him to let me serve out my sentence reading my book. Much to my astonishment, Mr. Foulds, who looked exactly like the bust of Voltaire in our junior high history textbook, reached out and handed me a hardcover book. It was the *Collected Poems of E. J. Pratt*.

"I want you to have this book," he said, "because after listening to you today in class discussing how much you liked Pratt's poem I have no choice but to give you this copy I picked up a few years back because I'm sure it was meant for you."

Mr. Foulds was acknowledging that he approved of the fact that I was scribbling poems on the margins of all my notebooks and binders. One morning Foulds was giving us an inspiring talk about Jonathan Swift. I was kind of spaced-out wondering if Mr. Foulds took after Voltaire's nature as well as being a dead ringer for him. I speculated on whether Mr. Foulds, like Voltaire, drank 40 cups of coffee per day and if he did how in heaven did he hold his bladder for so long since he never left the room. I was doodling on the margins when I came up with the following lines:

History's snail crawls
along time's turnpike
leaving an indelible slime
as nature's visible
impression of man

A few days later I gave it the title "History" and signed it "Anonymous" and dropped it into the school annual's letter box. Near the end of the year when the annuals were handed out I opened my copy and perused the pages. There before my eyes in the "art section" was the pessimistic poem I had written earlier in the year and forgotten about. It was attributed to "Anonymous." This was the first publication in my lengthy writing life. The fact it appeared under the by-line of "Anonymous" had nothing to do with it. I wasn't looking for recognition but only for some little sign that gave me the confidence to keep it up. The fact that somebody liked my poem enough to print it was enough for me. The poem, good or bad, had a life of its own, apart from me. That was an important lesson.

I listened to a few of the kids from the annual staff sitting around the library speculating on who had written that "snail poem." I was reading a thin biography of Babe Ruth while I eavesdropped on their conversation, taking great delight in their lack of information about "Anonymous." I was a jock; a runner and a soccer player who happened to dabble in poetry on the side. I was not the type who would be seen talking with the annual "swells" who were the brightest academic students distinct from the brightest street smart students who would have nothing to do with the annual and did as little reading as they could manage. The annual crowd revelled in gossip and prided themselves on knowing everything there was to know about everyone but they couldn't figure out who "Anonymous" was. Writing for me was a pretty secretive enterprise. I enjoyed it on my own because that was easier than trying to explain my interests to those who did not share my enthusiasm. I coughed a few times and stretched my legs around the chair leg. Finally, I asked them if they could keep the noise down a little since they were interrupting my concentration.

Later my small triumph in gaining a measure of respect in Mr. Foulds's English class was somewhat tarnished when Mr. Bloom, who taught art and typing, told me I wasn't deemed a strong enough student to be allowed to take Art 10 the following year.

"I'm afraid you don't display enough talent for it," he said.

"Next year, in grade 10, I'll be teaching a small select class of the best students. Why don't you think about taking extra shop or typing?"

I was in shock. Art was my favourite subject. I loved to draw and paint and I got giddy at the displays of artists' materials in art supply stores or hobby shops. I was typing my poems, with two fingers, carefully on blank sheets and cutting them down into pages and stapling them into folders or between wrappers that I illustrated with felt pens, water colours, or poster paints. I made potato prints and decorated brown butcher paper covers that I gave French flaps, although I had no idea what they were called. I got a lot of ideas in art class and I took the opportunity to work with the materials and equipment at school.

I was mortified. Some of my closest friends shared my enthusiasm for art class. I found it almost impossible to articulate why

Mr. Bloom had decided to shuffle me the Queen of Spades. Some of them thought I should appeal his decision, but I accepted the fact that I was probably pretty bad and that maybe he was right. Who was I to question his opinion? Mr. Bloom, a nice man, was forthright when he looked at me with his watery blue eyes, light careening off his shiny high forehead and matter-of-factly listed my failings, which according to him included: no drawing skills whatsoever, and an awful sense of colour and form. A truthful man. I was blown away. At the end of the term he reinforced his decision by insuring that I got a marginal pass with a C-minus grade.

The next year I took Mr. Bloom's advice and took typing. My parents thought it was a good idea because it might come handy in the future in my gaining employment in an office or obtaining a clerk's job. I was far too embarrassed to tell them that Mr. Bloom had given me the deep six. I settled on typing instead of extra shop because all my good projects in shop got stolen before I finished them or had a chance to take them home. I was also a bit of a klutz, not up to the exacting standards of our electrical shop teacher, Mr. Switch, or those of the accuracy zealot, Mr. Woodrow, our woodwork shop teacher.

There was only one other boy, carrot-topped Bill Story, in the typing class among a bevy of the most attractive girls in the school. Many of them were "business" students who generally had older boyfriends than other girls their own age. They tended to enter the workforce earlier than most, finding employment at a bank or in a clerical situation. I learned to enjoy typing to the rock and roll tunes that Mr. Bloom spun on his turntable as I rushed toward reaching the magic passing grade of 24 words per minute. I grew stronger in typing whenever Mr. Bloom put on Bill Haley, Jerry Lee Lewis, or Little Richard. For some reason they seemed to make my fingers dance more quickly across the keyboard. I coughed and choked under the constant bombardment of hair spray but I made the grade. The immediate downside of the deal was that I began to suffer horrible allergic attacks because of the hair spray that the typing class girls used liberally on their bouffant style hairdos.

In the short term, typing failed to fill the void of my terminated art class; however, learning to type has been a godsend in my adult life. I have literally spent several hours a day typing for the past 30 years.

Some afternoons I managed to escape from Mr. Stronach's science classroom when he was in the cloak room having a shot of vodka. I roamed the halls, passing the art room, distracting my former fellow art students who were busy working on their assignments and projects. I was a little lost in my mind over the fact that I had been rejected for lack of talent. Art for me was more about enjoying my life by having something to think about that went along with the fantasy poetry life that I had already established. The two processes — writing and illustrating — went together for me.

In later years, it became apparent to me that Mr. Bloom's decision while probably a good one for him wasn't necessarily the right one for me. I became terribly self-conscious about trying to draw or paint. I began to write in cramped, smallish letters. Within a year or two I ceased making any illustrations. I cringed from any conversations about art as an active process. I tended toward becoming a critic because I was not afraid to say what I thought, though there were times when keeping my mouth shut might have been a better option. The pamphlets and thin books that I put together were in non-illustrated covers with hand lettering. In the long term I probably benefited because I put my energy into learning about editing and other facets of the book arts, which dragged me further into the culture of printing, publishing, writing and editing. Perhaps a natural place for a poet to end up. Like the drunk who gets a job in the liquor store.

(It wasn't until I reached my 40s that I found the courage to begin drawing and painting again. I was jolted into action after a personal crisis inspired me into filling up several art tablets with a variety of illustrations — mostly small works — executed with pencil crayons, felt pens, charcoal, wax crayons, or water colours. I followed these up by making a couple of hundred paintings with different mediums on a variety of surfaces including art board, cardboard, canvas, wood and paper. It started on a sleeting winter evening in Montreal, after dark. I had a few hours to kill when I noticed an art supply shop and decided to go in and buy some supplies. I stayed up three nights in a hotel room drawing with pencil crayons. When I got back home to White Rock, I scoured the old blue house that I lived in on the hillside above the pier and found an amazing variety of decent surfaces to paint on. I went to artist supply sales and bought up enough materials to keep me going. I found the time to paint about four hours every evening for about two years and I produced a enormous variety of mental patient art that I gave away or stashed in the closet. I had a hard time turning off the tap so that I could get back to writing. Finally I was liberated.)

During my university days, in the early '70s, I noticed that the student newspaper, *The Peak*, was putting out a poetry supplement. Its student editor was a well-known campus bohemian who had strong opinions about writing and poetry in particular. He was in my English class and I thought he was a bit of a blowhard. He was always pontificating about literary theories such as projected verse. Once I dared submit a couple of poems for the poetry section that my fellow student was editing in *The Peak*. He rejected my poems quickly with a rather insulting letter that suggested I would better to get an education on the more sophisticated modes of writing that had long ago superseded my sad outdated efforts. He had already attached himself like a remora to the snobbish faculty poets who worshipped at the altars of Ezra Pound and Charles Olson through the influence of the charismatic Robin Blaser, a flamboyant man in dress and style who lectured brilliantly, especially on the Romantics and was a central figure in the poetic movement that was known as Black Mountain.

(Blaser, a marvellous poet with theatrical mannerism and a bitchy attitude, had established deep roots in American poetry movements. Long associated with Jack Spicer, Blaser influenced Simon Fraser's academic/literary community in the '70s in a similar way that Warren Tallman had at the University of British Columbia. The Vancouver connection was a literary branch of a wider movement that had enclaves in San Francisco, Buffalo, Toronto as well as in the Kootenays and other locations and attracted disciples into an intellectual and poetic tradition that seemed to have a cult-like intensity for some of its devotees. A coterie of literary young lions were groomed by Blaser and his fellow faculty, who included Ralph Maud, and were regarded as important budding literary figures. The best of them, Sharon Thiesen and Brian Fawcett, in those days, a young married couple from Prince George, have both become important writers. Another, Karl Siegler, probably the most stubborn figure in Canadian publishing, has enjoyed a long successful career at the helm of Talon Books.)

I rushed over to the student bookstore and purchased a pad of onion skin paper, a pad of yellow typing paper and one of bond paper. I went home and started writing poems in slightly different forms. I worked diligently for several nights writing the worst poems I could devise but incorporating certain conventions of style that I figured would hook the editor. I knew what he wanted to read and by the end of a couple of nights' work I could write it *ad infinitum*. I came up with a number of pseudonyms, including J. Albert Camberback, Charlie Cunard, Robert Comely and Donald Duff. Camberback must have been a character I assumed after reading T. S. Eliot — undoubtedly a "Prufrockian" influenced name. During my high school years I often took Eliot's Selected Poems on bus rides and got off at stops and read his poems on park benches. The latter three pseudonym names were variations based on my mother's Irish/Scots family roots. I moved around to various offices and garrotes and typed the poets' works on different typewriters on various kinds of paper. The result was half a dozen different submissions on an assortment of papers, each submission had its own typeface and unique envelope. I mailed my submissions over a number of days from different locations.

A week later I was flabbergasted when I opened the supplement and saw that four of my pseudo-poets — who, by the way, were all terrible writers — dominated the pages with several poems each. They were proclaimed by the proud editor to be among the finest student poets on campus. He marvelled at the depth and excellence of local talent. At our English tutorial he handed out copies of the supplement to the Teaching Assistant and to each student and made an insufferable little speech about his role as editor. Later, on my way from the classroom, he remarked to me that he hoped I had learned something from his criticism, and that if I worked hard I might get a poem in the next supplement. I walked away without comment, I already knew where I was going and the direction my interests were taking me. I was proud of my instant poets because, beyond a doubt, they proved a point to me and I never had to be reminded of it again. I didn't have the heart to tell him my secret. I shared it only with one other person. She helped me package my submissions in the middle of the nights usually after we dropped acid together in her one bedroom apartment on campus at Louis Riel House. In the morning we sat outside on the dew covered deck and watched the new raw light stretching down across the mountainside.

MUSIC IN THE DARK

GESTURE OF GOODWILL

FEBRUARY, THE SHORT MESMERIZING MONTH of winter, fills the rain forest with gloom. Wind hammers in from the ocean, black rain squalls drop torrential cargo. Waves crashing over the breakwater pound into the crab boats. White edges dance on grey corrugated water. The empty Blue House is like a shrine in hell. Memories of the years run through the human dream machine. Night into day, decoded messages, first drafts of unfamiliar texts.

Who knows what causes the roots of alienation to begin growing in the mind? Perhaps, self is the best place to start looking. Troubled self is a complicated dwelling with emotional trap doors and an unconscious double living down the hall. I knew a man who lived in an eccentric seaside town for nearly 20 years. When his dynamics slipped he found himself isolated, unable to find his friends and neighbours. The events in his life had played out like so many scenes in a ludicrous soap opera. He was the last one in on reality. He was already well into his new life, even if he didn't know it. He had become a ridiculous man who crawled too far along the rope to the past and found himself holding a frayed end that he could no longer connect to anything.

Days merged into darker days. There was never enough time to finish routine jobs, although time slowed down and crept along the vines running up the walls of the house. Objects that broke stayed unrepaired. When the phone rang, he was afraid to pick it up. Before he could stop the spiral into isolation, two years had passed. When he went shopping for groceries he scarcely encountered anyone he knew. When he did, lines of communication seemed to evaporate into meaningless chit-chat about the weather. It was his obsession to make it through the bad months of rain. When summer came and the sun was shining in the blueness of the sky, he worried about the end of it and the certain approach of another rainy season.

Every month brought a little more despair. Good weather became bad weather soon enough. Voices lived in the back of his head. He started talking with them. Thoughts became repetitive, questions could not be answered. He remembered back to the crucial months of the past when every gesture of goodwill had blown-up in his face like an incendiary device. How the words from his mouth bounced around the room. His voice damaging the listener until the listener departed. Each day his voice constructed another ladder of gibberish. He climbed up it one syllable at a time. His mind worked overtime trying to think of the right combinations of words that might lessen the barrier. Fences climbed into the air. His head ran in frenzy from the futility of organization and planning. Everything went wrong, his gestures became kindling that gently smouldered, then burst into bonfires of unhappiness.

He went home to his untidy house and pulled the walls in around his head. The garden turned into a weed factory, fences fell over, the lawn became a pasture. The rain came down hard enough to keep the promise in his heart. He began reading books about the great battles in history. Sometimes he saw stars from the window near his bed. He pulled the sheets over his head and stayed unreachable until reassured by the gentle sound of rain flicking off the roof tiles. The train whistle in the distance made him feel like a hunted dog. He covered his ears to forget the sweet sound of steel rolling along steel rails. He could feel the power of it passing through him. The shudder of it dulled the chuckling voice that always seemed to be calling him into another room.

He studied the business cards and brochures he received in the mail. Real estate agents came to the door, offering a quick evaluation leading to instant sale. "Hong Kong money is on the move, there'll never be a better time," they promised. He filled up the afternoons writing letters to the editors of various newspapers under false names. He walked every evening along the beach avoiding people but talking with every strange dog. Some followed for a while. It made him feel better to have such innocent friends. They made few judgements and stayed in the present tense. He went bird watching in the ravines. He watched red-headed woodpeckers whacking hammer heads against rotten snags. English robins, sad fugitives, sat in a laurel hedge bending under the snow. In the summer, a mother hummingbird brought her brood of bee-sized babies down among the wild flowers beside the trail. Blue herons fished along the shoreline, standing dishevelled in the breeze. Beautiful question marks in the margin. He thought they were praying for rain. He wanted it to pour.

It did, through holes left by wind torn shingles. He moved buckets into the rooms, the house seemed damper. When it ran over onto the floor he merely opened the door and let his house run into the street. A passing stranger came to the door. "You seem to have a leak somewhere," he remarked, standing knee deep in current. "You understand these things sometimes get out of hand." It was a clever answer. At last, he thought, I'm gaining a little everyday. It might be possible to open a fishing lodge in the front room. He replaced the couch with a rowboat and began casting buck tails for salmon.

"You have some leaks," he thought. "Yes you do, upstairs, downstairs, all around the house." He decided Sundays would have to go. He renamed Sunday, Allday. He merged the seven day week into one long day of 168 hours. He kept the blinds drawn to delineate daylight and darkness. He stopped keeping track of months. He thought it a bit much to try and redefine the year. It seemed a harsh enough increment. He found the one weekday with no particular month suited his lifestyle. Every month, February. He threw the bones, cut the cards, pulled straws in the hope of rain.

When last I spoke with him he talked about getting up enough nerve to order in Chinese food. I thought his calendar idea rather peculiar but was persuaded by his argument that different folks have differing ways and methods of measuring such things. He asked me if I ever dreamed of driving in an open convertible in a downpour. I confessed I hadn't give such things much thought. I finally understood what he was getting at. Things had gone beyond his control. He went inside the house of self. Life had become like an ingrown toenail. By now it had curled around his mind. His foot was attached to his head. He had become a snail with his house on his back. There is no reprieve from life, the way it hits. Only from the ways of accepting it. He couldn't understand, and, being a sensitive man, he couldn't stop trying.

TWENTY-FOUR HOURS TO

SASKATCHEWAN

PREOCCUPIED WITH THE VAGARIES OF A LIFE on the run, I found myself overwhelmed with urgent paper work. Needing the services of a professional witness, I thumbed the phone book and after several calls found a notary public who could attend to my emergency.

Packing my car (heading for Saskatchewan) I left for his office. I was ushered into Mr. X's private office after spending an hour in an astonishing high-tech waiting room crowded with tropical plants. I was greeted by a large, distinguished looking man in his late fifties who offered me a canvas and chrome chair. After perusing my papers he told me it would cost $40 to stamp his seal on my documents. His wide smile and efficient manner allowed me to relax and realize that my document dilemma was merely one of those small inconveniences of panic that was now passing into legal oblivion. I mentioned that I was leaving White Rock to move to rural Saskatchewan. Mr. X shifted in his chair, stared at me and in a loud booming voice said, "Why in hell would you want to move there? The place is crawling with gawdamn Indians." A momentary sneer passed across his smiling face before it lapsed back into sublime confidence. I picked up my documents and headed for the post office.

By the time I hit the Trans-Canada I had thought of a hundred comebacks, but the truth was his ugly remark had only elicited an awkward response. I wasn't prepared for his mindless racism. He merely wanted to enjoy a little "white talk" with me. You know that off handed nudge-wink way we have with each other. There I was several hours later stewing, thinking if only I had the composure to have told him he was a bigot and that an educated man ought to know better. I wondered if his children shared his attitude.

Later that night, past Manning Park, we had a flat tire. Putting on the pathetic spare tire on a dangerous incline urged me to speed to Princeton to find a gas station before 10:00 pm. I made it in time to see the local mechanic pulling down his doors while his assistant shut off the pumps. Fortunately, my companion's tank top galvanized his attention and between us we cajoled him into fixing our tire. He had a hot date waiting in the Greek restaurant next door. While he had our car in the air he paused to tell us a vicious racist joke about Ben Johnson.

We stood there with our mouths open in shock. He sensed our discomfort in an instant and covered it by telling us a few sexist jokes making it obvious that if Dolores had not been travelling with me I would have been out of luck. He had been working long hours on the three-day holiday weekend and he was fed up with tourists. I couldn't help consider how many other travellers were subject to his despicable racist humour. How many of them had laughed uproariously? It seemed to me he wouldn't be telling his joke with such a flourish if it hadn't been a big favourite with the customers. Now we were on the hoist, so to speak, and his joke had left us frozen in an already chilly night. The garage man's gratuitous sexism was accepted silently by both of us. We endured it for the simple reason that he was the only option in a one-horse town. We could either tell him he was a jerk and continue on our bald spare tire or we could let it pass. The moronic gleam in his eye when he blurted out his jungle bunny humour was too much for our sensibilities. He retreated into safer, sexist territory in order to cover the embarrassment at failing to make us laugh. Once again our lily white faces had inspired confidence in a countryman who took full opportunity to share a little "white-ism" with us. After miles of chewing on the notary I had even less of a response for the garage man. We wondered what happened to black Canadians who got flat tires at night near Princeton?

After driving all night and half the next morning we stopped for breakfast in a small Saskatchewan border town. The owner, recently retired from the military, welcomed us with endless cups of coffee and good cheap fare. He was the talkative type, one of those jolly fellows who has lived and travelled throughout Canada and Europe. The homespun curtains, the warm interior, and his friendly manner were just the tonic after a hard night of driving in the mountains and blasting across Alberta. I told him I lived in White Rock. He remembered spending a week at the beach there in 1960. He and his wife shared the labour of their café. He took the early shift because she liked sleeping in and wasn't much of a conversationalist in the mornings. They loved the Maritimes but had finally discovered their niche in rural Saskatchewan. Most of all, he abhorred big cities. He could stand Calgary and Edmonton because the people were friendly and kind-of-country. While I was munching my toast and peanut butter he remarked, "But not Vancouver, too many Orientals. I don't know how people stand it. I wouldn't go there again if somebody paid me." Dolores and I looked at each other in astonishment. Three times in less than 24 hours we had heard Natives, blacks, and Orientals being put down as if they were disease carrying monsters from outer space. Our blank white faces were bringing in bigots like worms for fat trout. This time I was prepared but he changed the subject and bolted for the kitchen.

On our way through Swift Current we bought a *Globe and Mail*. The Betty Osborne inquiry was going on in Manitoba. The dirty secret of The Pas, 16 years buried, was now out in the open like a festering sore. The rape and murder of a young Aboriginal girl by local boys had been covered up by a mind-your-own business town.

On the same front page the Winnipeg Police Association was trying to prevent an officer from testifying at an inquiry into the shooting of J. J. Harper. Officer Cross mistook a middle-aged man for a young car thief. During the confrontation, it is alleged Harper struggled for the officer's holstered revolver and was shot in the heart. Officer Cross couldn't remember many of the details and his big city police department supporters are afraid he is too distressed to testify. Officer Cross and his fellow policemen enjoyed black humour about Aboriginals and how they should be treated. Now they had a dead Aboriginal man on their hands and it turns out he was a respectable leader in his community. Members of the police force think it would be detrimental to Officer Cross's health if he were forced to appear and explain his role. They are worried that if he were subject to intensive questioning the officer might commit suicide.

Finally, almost 24 hours later, we reached our destination, Dundurn, Saskatchewan, a town of 500 hundred people about 35 km south of Saskatoon. We stopped at the nearby Hutterite colony and bought six chickens, potatoes, and corn. In town, everybody seemed relaxed and content. The rodeo was over. A slo-pitch tournament was going on in the park. The neighbour boy, a kid about nine years old, came over to the car.

"Where did you get those chickens?" he asked.

"From the Hutterites," we replied.

His face screwed up. "My father hates them. They sold our friends three geese. One had a broken wing, another a gimpy leg, and the third got eaten by an owl."

We went into the house and pulled the curtains shut. It had been a long day and night.

IN DARKEST ALBERTA

King Cod the Cheesecake Fairy, Goose Hunting,
Preston Manning, and the Northfield Cemetery

THE NIGHTSCAPE IN THE PEACE RIVER seems scripted by science fiction. Strange fires, markers to a high-tech feudal culture, burn on the compass points. In the morning an exaggerated, bloodshot sun lumbers over the horizon. The sky is overwhelmed by dramatic hourly changes in the weather. Roads snake across the heavy mud. A grid of immense fields of grain covers a sea of oil.

King Cod the Cheesecake Fairy is holding court at the Motor Inn Restaurant in Grande Prairie. It is a question of who outnumber the drug store cowboys — farmers in Cat hats and clodhopper boots, or burly oil field workers? The King is moonlighting with codfish and cheesecakes. He gets laughs with his self-proclaimed name and the off-colour jokes he drops like a pattern of bombs among the breakfast tables. He crams his six-foot, four-inch body into a fiery Fiesta and drives from town to village stopping at each eating place. Blond, good-looking, with a beaked visage he talks the waitress into talking the cook into ordering 24 mixed flavour cheesecakes and a 30-pound halibut.

"You know I might not be back for a month. You must get guys hitting on you. I'm tempted, but too bad I'm married myself."

She knows he knows the general reason for every line in her face. They feel good when he arrives and good when he departs. They buy cakes and fish to avert the dullness in their lives.

Goose hunters are wily as coyotes. Rising long before dawn they head for the pre-scouted destination. They wait for the geese to leave the safety of the lake and head out for the morning-feed. The willow blind is assembled in a stucco wire frame on the frozen stubble. From the air it looks like a harmless bush. Seventy-five larger-than-life goose decoys are ingeniously set out in a manner dictated by the wind. This-not-quite-right bush containing hunters is overlooked because of the inviting flock of decoys and the seductive honking of the goose call — a Faulks number 14. Circling geese will always turn and land against the wind.

When they are point blank with their wings set the hunters let go a blast. Some mornings, when the hunters are most confident, the geese lift off and go elsewhere. The arrangement is repeated in variation in a landscape smouldering with anticipation.

Late in the afternoon, the King and I meet his wife, Queen Cod, at the hotel lobby. She is on the executive of the local Reform Party committee and she has helped organize Preston Manning's political revival meeting later that evening in this very building. By coincidence while we are discussing dinner plans the great man shows up in the lobby by himself. I am baffled; he has no handlers to squire him about. Soon we are sitting with Preston in a booth in the hotel café.

My previous view of the man influenced by watching him on television is completely erroneous. There he comes across like the dullest of the dullards but out in the real world at a chance meeting, he is an articulate charming conversationalist who does not waste time talking about himself. Within a few minutes we are into an inspired political dialogue that is going across the table like a ping pong match. The King and Queen of Cod are mesmerized by the speed of the debate. Preston discovers I am a writer with left wing sensibilities — normally a formula that instantly shuts up right-wingers. It makes no difference to him. He tells me his party is chock full of repenting former NDPers who have seen the light. He seems to be looking inside my head to see if there is a glimmer. I take the opportunity to destroy the very concept of a free trade agreement with the United States in a three minute rant that astounds even me in its thoroughness and sincerity.

"You have good ideas and you're passionate and persuasive in your arguments. If you write like you talk you might have a real future in politics. Give me a call if you want to get involved," he says handing me his card as he leaves us standing in the lobby.

King Cod is ecstatic. "By God don't you realize he was so impressed with your gab he practically offered you a job!" he says as we head out to the parking lot to sit in his fire engine red car and have a few libations and a smoke before the meeting starts.

"You don't get it," I answer. "He's a politician who wants to get elected. He's just doing his job. He wants everybody to like him. Intuitively he knows that pseudo-intellectuals like me dislike him on sight."

Manning wasn't fooled by my glib comments. He figured he might turn me around because in person he's a rational man with a patrician manner who has a likeable personality. He's used to being underestimated. Manning has no charisma on television but he has charisma in one-on-one conversations or when he addresses small groups. He is semi-attracted to those who stand up to his views partly because he gets tired of preaching to the converted. He needs a few token outsiders around to allow him to keep him in touch with his weaknesses. Trouble is, I'm a radical personality without a cause. Too dangerous to have somebody like me around, I'd stab him in the back for a bag of jujubes.

Preston Manning is a slight man with a mouthful of bottom teeth. He doesn't stand out in the crowd; in fact, he disappears almost completely in the sea of heads. In the country of he-men he seems outgunned from the start. The hotel ballroom is filling with supporters. Young Turks from the oil fields glisten with alcohol.

Gold rings and chains gleam against shiny thousand-dollar leather jackets. Wives with too much makeup shimmer in overdressed silk. The majority here are old frumpy couples in grey/yellow hair and casual polyester. King Cod leans over at my geriatric jokes.

"Don't be fooled," he lectures. "Most of the money in Alberta is in this room."

Preston reaches the mike after an interminable introduction by a fat red-faced Dutchman. He grows in stature when he controls the podium. Later I realize it is partly because he is standing on an apple box that has been subtly put in place before his appearance. The rest of it is body language. He begins with a concise articulate history of the Canadian constitution. He speaks quietly forcing people to lean forward in their chairs. A conservative with a grassroots agenda for attaining power, he's in favour of an elected Senate and he approves of the Free Trade Deal.

There is no blood and thunder in his speech or passion in the argument. His schoolboy looks belie a clever speaker. He offers a subtle alternative to the *status quo*; reduce taxes, stop frivolous government spending, tackle the deficit, restore old fashioned Canadian values. Part of his talk centres on Canadian immigration policy, but it goes by so quickly I am momentarily confused by the content and the presentation. I conclude that Preston knows this is a subject that touches a nerve with the audience. He glosses over it. Nothing to risk or gain in the right wing bible belt with everybody already on side. I amuse myself looking around in the crowd pretending I can hear what they're thinking. I think I know what Preston's getting at. It makes me shudder. I make a note to ask a question if I get the chance.

The King elbows me in the ribs, "See, I told you he has the answers. Stop whining about social issues. Money is listening, money hears what it wants to hear."

Preston stands humbly before the applause and then moves into the crowd shaking every hand. I tell him: "You've got a great act but you've got to do some research and find out the exact figures."

He nods, accepts my words sincerely. My eyes fixate on the perfect tiny grey elephant-hide cowboy boots on his petite feet. For the moment I am speechless, and the question I have been harbouring evaporates in my face. Preston moves on, caught up in the crowd, that presses in around him and sweeps him gently across the room in a sea of faces and a windmill of handshaking.

The Northfield Cemetery is on a grid road out of La Glace. It sits on the crest of a field across the way from the best duck hunting pothole in the universe. I wonder if there is quacking in heaven? We park the truck and walk among the head stones. It is a bleak windblown treeless prairie. The graves seem cold and lonely. One plot, framed in by two-by-fours is covered with Astroturf. White yardage lines and hash marks march down field between mini goalposts. In the middle of nowhere in particular, in the Peace River, a scale model Canadian football field marks a lifetime. Snow is in the air.

MUSIC IN THE DARK

After nearly 20 years sailing on a turbulent domestic sea, I found my life wrecked on a sandbar of frustration and sadness. A full year of sleepless nights and the urge to put my neck into the rafters convinced me it was time to change. She was gone to Australia. The kids were grown up, but didn't know it. I was out of control with all gears stripped. Routine chores became hopeless drudgery. Friends suddenly became strangers. Dreams were untranslatable nightmares. My social life became non-existent. T.S. Eliot was right, days were measured with coffee spoons. My head was levitating in circles six inches above my body, the spirit decapitated. I ran away from home, in a way, at the age of 40. Left the fridge full of food, the bills and the taxes paid, went looking for a quieter scene of exile.

Woke up one day in Dundurn, Saskatchewan. My big trees and ocean mist were replaced by flatlands. I was an unknown man in an unforgiving climate. No deluxe beach scene, no traffic, no McDonald's litter and best of all no Californian-like yuppie dreamers. One grocery store, a solitary gas bar, no bank or newspaper; finally I was positively 100 percent high-rise free. A place that was at its best at the turn of the century and slowly headed in an undefined direction ever since. The gaps between the few businesses left on Main Street were testimony to the past. Unused buildings here quickly became empty lots that nobody wanted.

In the mornings, Dundurn was in a near pristine state of emptiness. It was so unusual for a car to travel our street that it became impossible not to move to the window and look out. I adapted adequately, in less than a month, to being a small-town man who shunned the bustle of city life but who couldn't resist staring at anything that moved. Each day I walked to the post office and put my key into the lock that opened the tiny window to my past. It was always vacant of news but full of junk mail. I read the ads about used farm machinery and various pamphlets on weed killers and super fertilizers. I studied the posted town bylaws and I went to the café and sat among the locals drinking coffee, listening to their repetitive comments about the weather. It was always the same; too much of this or too little of that.

At dusk, I walked miles from the edge of town, sometimes wandering far out into the fields of durum, once I urinated my name on a flat sandy farm road. I watched the police-car making its rounds, it never stopped for anything. I was invisible as an idea and free of anxiety. Time became my friend because it had a sameness, a texture of familiar pattern. The stately old mansions were surrounded by classic verandas. It occurred to me as the weeks went by, that I never saw anyone sitting on their porch or encountered another walker. What did they do at night? Many of the houses were dark every evening. I imagined these might be the ones where old people, who went to bed early, lived. Dogs were on chains in yards that were, for the most part, immaculate. Maybe they got up at dawn, did their yard work, sat on their porches and took their walks while I was sleeping. Perhaps they were invisible like I was, even to each other. One night feeling tired, as I had for days, I decided to take the extended hike before retiring. The Northern Lights were rocking the sky, the Big Dipper was sitting above the biggest tree in town. Walking slowly along the tree-darkened streets it came to me. Every few houses along the way would reveal a glimpse of eerie indefinite light. They were emotionally addicted to their television sets.

Dropping by the store for a package of cigarettes I found myself standing next to a wizened old man wearing a green army beret. "Lovely evening," I remarked. He looked at me through moist red hound-dog eyes. The mouth in his strangely elongated chapped face answered, "It's a good night for a murder." I heard his name mentioned by the grocery man. It was something like Oldie Clark or Oddie Quark, I didn't hear it clearly or much care to get it right. At the time I thought his comment odd, but later that night around ten o'clock when the moon was partially eclipsed, I knew exactly what he meant.

This forgotten prairie town took on the same aura that affected White Rock when the full moon basked in the waves. Of course, there were differences. The long, noisy White Rock night consisted of partying, arrests, reckless driving and otherwise frenetic activity. This prairie town had a more subtle but equally disturbed sense of itself. All night long, dogs howled from every direction, answering the coyotes from the farm fields that encircled the town. Teenagers were whooping it up at the railroad crossing. A single black 1960s vintage Mustang, with a tilted front end and a pair of gigantic dice in the windshield, cruised the dusty streets. Bats slashed the night air, whipping along the hedge tops. The shunting of the boxcars by the Pioneer elevator was louder than thunder. In the lane behind the house a couple were having a heated argument.

"I know you screwed him. I'd like to kill you with my bare hands."

She screamed back, "You're a liar, and you know it, you loser."

I began to believe I was somewhere I didn't want to be. Soon I evaporated into sleep only to be awakened by a strange buzzing sensation. I assumed, at first, that one of my fillings was bringing in the Voice of America or a radio signal from the nearby army base. Turning on the light and listening carefully I discovered a large angry fly trapped in my pillow case.

DEAR MR. GREYHOUND

Twenty-six hours, Regina to Vancouver: the bus was hell. The woman sitting across from me had a better time. Putting a mini Mae West around her neck, she blew up her head and bobbed effortlessly through the night on a bumper of air. My neck is permanently fixed to the south-east.

It wasn't all bad. I read day and night.

There was an awful crowd of people, some with pillows, sleeping bags, baskets of health food and mineral water: campers on wheels. Others were loaded with reading material: romances, crime fiction, and books on growing your own. (On planes, travellers read fashion and golf magazines; on the Greyhound, it's motorcycle mags and movie-star-baiting tabloids.) There was a couple making out all the way. I couldn't understand how their lips could take it. The old people, who started out sitting ramrod straight, wilted under the relentless hours of swaying. Bingo would have helped. You should think about introducing the game on your coaches — it would keep the old ones fresher. I scrambled from the bus with the clack of smokers who sprinted at every five-minute stop. (There are a number of these; you seem to have a good business dropping off packages in prairie towns.) We stood on the lee side of the bus, trying to get adequately seduced by our addiction.

I know it's not your fault that the middle of Canada is flat and straight and forever; still, the passengers who had ridden for days from the far east appeared to be suffering from tropical diseases. I saw faces loaded with droopy heaviness, distended bodies trapped in paroxysms of fartless discomfort. I hoped there would be somebody at the final destination with a hat pin to puncture their guts and relieve them of their misery.

I made notes. A young man, about 19, from London, Ontario, with a headband and long hair proclaimed himself a hippie in a loud voice. He started up a conversation with a more reticent teenager who had a similar appearance. He intoned, "What do you think about the rockers and the punks and the preppies in Toronto. I'm a hippie myself, non-violent but modern, not like the hippies of old." It got louder through the afternoon. "Smoke a lot of pot and hash. Got some mushrooms that I'm taking to sell in Vancouver." By evening his mood had turned to other things. "Would you jump your best friend's girl if she was begging you? I'm not bragging but I'm way above average in size." It was so bad I couldn't concentrate on my book on the Zulu wars; every paragraph, I heard his disjointed nasal monologue. "Did you get a look at that one in the back in the black spandex? Classy, eh!"

At Medicine Hat, when we stopped for lunch, he sat at the adjoining table. I took the opportunity to tell him he knew dick about hippies and that he ought to shut up for a while. He reminded me he was non-violent and bummed a cigarette. I took one of the sciatica pills I had in my pocket and told him to drop it before getting back on the bus; his seat mate, devouring a cheeseburger, was amused. (He had taken me into his confidence by rolling his eyes whenever the "hippie" made another ridiculous leap of logic.) "What is it?" the hippie asked now, reflectively rolling the pill around in the palm of his hand. "A horse tranquillizer," I answered. "See you in about a week. You won't feel a thing and don't worry if your urine turns green." He looked me in the eye and swallowed the pill with a swig of coffee.

I'd hoped the pill might have some psychological impact: maybe the hippie's mind would shut down, thinking it should, for instance — the power of belief over physiology. It had the opposite effect. He got louder and more intense, stupidly announcing he had drugs in his suitcase. I doubted it. Magic mushrooms are scarce and expensive in Toronto. They're indigenous to the west coast and they travel east — any druggie knows that. Still, I congratulate you for having the hippie detained in Calgary and for the thorough searching of his bags. I suppose the driver phoned ahead, but I prefer to think it was one of the blue-haired bingo-loving grannies who turned him in. He was just a talker, looking for attention. You gave him some.

When you let him back on the bus he didn't say much. At the smoke breaks he attempted to find a sympathetic face to share his burden of false accusation. By then, though, everybody thought he was a jerk and even though you probably violated his rights, and nobody enjoys seeing the police, his comeuppance made the rest of our journey more pleasant. (When he finally make his move, the spandex girl, who had big earrings and big glasses, told him to try his hand.)

The bus hurtled through the Rockies at the edge of darkness. I shivered, drinking more of your wretched coffee at Golden and Revelstoke. I am one of those never-come-prepared types who are at the mercy of drink machines and despicable restaurants. The beef sandwich tasted of freezer. The butter tarts were brutal. And what do you do with all the leftover grease?

A liberal friend once told me you see interesting people in bus stations but it's dangerous to talk to them. I think she's both right and wrong. I understand her meaning. You might risk having someone sitting next to you who is outrageous and interesting for awhile. Twelve hours later, when your ears volunteer to close, outrageous becomes annoying and interesting evaporates into boring. Both are hard to turn aside. Retreating into a book won't work because you have already granted entry into your private space. It's easier to look dangerous or vacant or perfectly invisible, a trick that half the people in the world have mastered. What ever you do, don't cluck any baby you meet on a bus or you will live to regret every cute little story about teeth and toilet training that comes at you. The mother is often on her way to the father, worrying that he isn't going to be at the other end. "Lady, I wouldn't bet on it," I nastily think, while making some inane comment about the weather.

One last thing. Your bus schedule is incomprehensible to intelligent people. Nobody I asked on the street could understand it. My dentist spent an hour confusing himself. Jack, the bar man of the Monarch Room in the Hotel Saskatchewan, has been on the job for 37 years and he couldn't fathom it. The manager of the Thai restaurant near the Hydro building took it next door to a psychic book shop and they offered to ask the crystals for an interpretation. They called it the Greyhound Book of the Dead. It has a confusion of blue numbers and symbols with an incomplete key and mysterious departure times. I got the picture when my friend the brain surgeon said, "It's obvious that bus drivers can read it because they already know it." That made sense. I've decided that once before I die I'm going to attempt your long bus journey again. But I'm going to get one of those Mae Wests. I'll blow my head up in the air bag and read effortlessly, leaving the driving to you know who.

DROUGHT

ACROSS THE VAST FLATLANDS of the central prairie the sun is breathing through its eyelids.

Nothing moves fast in the vast clutch of heat softening the highway's asphalt. Heat sticks to the gas station truckstop like a time bomb attached to the concept of patience. A ticking sound of frustration in the heatscape — sandflies in the stubbly ditch come home to feast on bare ankles. Black crickets are scattered like random dice on the cracked hardpan. It was once a planted grain field but nothing much came up and what did manage to poke through the earth stands broom-straw-still under the sun.

Life in the middle of drought goes on. The party of six ask the waitress at the Ranch House Restaurant to bring glasses of water all around. On his deathbed, Alfred Jary the brilliant French dramatist, while dying of malnutrition, in his last words requested a toothpick. It was a trick of fate that made Jary go out on such a clever note just as it was a trick of fate last night when falling rain evaporated before it hit the ground.

That's why the paint dries quickly around here. The Hutterites were frustrated — one of the boys said there was "no use breedin' the cattle this year because the bull semen will evaporate before it hits the cows."

It has not rained in appreciable amounts for nearly three years. Just the odd thunderstorm here and there from thunderheads that came on with promise but passed to the north or fizzled out and left without dropping much or any precipitation. Sometimes a local shower fell or even a local downpour but only too briefly and not enough to make a difference. Once it rained for an hour a few miles down the road. In the morning, by 9:00 am, the sun had sucked it all back like a greedy kid with a straw. On the northern prairie in summer the sun comes up at 4:30 am — by 7:00 am it is already stoking the inferno.

Potholes in the surrounding countryside are dry and cracked like ancient eccentric pottery with thick muddy bottoms, illustrated by deep cow tracks and if one looks closer, by bird tracks going in every direction. Mud has turned harder than concrete. Once grassy pastures are reduced to dirt fields with patches of dead or half-dead weeds. On the back road dust rises from the back of a vehicle whipping up a great shroud that comes down like confectioner's sugar on the scrubby trees and clumps of red willow.

In this season of West Nile disease there are virtually no mosquitoes because there is no standing water to speak of anywhere for hundreds of square miles. Even a curse like drought has its benefits — fewer mosquitoes, less chance of people getting West Nile disease. Scientists have developed a vaccination for horses, but people are not as well-researched as the equine world. What horse would want to run on a day like this across the sun's anvil. Once bright yellow canola blooming in a field now burnt a brown shade, announces its demise officially from lack of moisture.

Water at the right time makes a big difference in the final outcome for the dryland farmer. If the rain doesn't come the land is no use for man or beast. Burnt is burnt. There is no other scapegoat definition. That is how the fields appear except in places with irrigation. They stand out in the distance like emerald mirages or the yellow hair on a beautiful girl.

Summer storms passed by without the massive peals of thunder and the usual jagged lightning bolts that turn the night briefly into day like a enormous light bulb in a flash unit. The biggest banger of the season, a bolt of lightning as loud as God can yell, knocked the cornucopia off the top of the town hall and set it on fire in the schoolyard next door. But not a spitball's worth of rain.

For 50 days and nights the sky stayed motionless without a single cloud passing on the dome of it. Prairie blue and bright sun reflected in every direction from chrome trim, bumpers, panes of glass and broken bottles — the vision as unreal as the realist's painting of anything he thinks he can portray. The prairie landscape lets one down in spectacular fashion because it is so prone to be depicted in cliché. Grain elevators, which are disappearing at a frightening rate, appear in thousands of images that go click-click-ga-ga in the mind. Ditto stock farm images in cute frames coming over the transom on ugly calendars. Bad horse painters are endless in the gulches of the art emporiums where badly painted cows are herded for all they're worth. Look how real the chuck wagon looks with its dangling pots and pans and the fat cook eating a big plate of beans.

I saw death this afternoon, a nondescript piece of road kill on the side of the highway near no place, if that makes sense. Between somewhere and somewhere but not anywhere in particular. The road runs long like a river. A lot of it seems nearly the same but it's not, each place is as individual as the next. The problem is to know when to stop and risk having a definition about place. How far is it from where? The highway presents the same dilemma as the river because they both travel so quickly across the land. Heat mirages dance on the highway. Sun pierces water images, light explodes into fragments.

Something dead is only dead once and then quickly disappears or slowly devolves into something less than it was in every one of its dimensions. Like a piece of leather around a fat gut or the soft shoe pampering a cramped foot. A product made from the essential animal being reduced by degrees into being functional wear for sedentary bank managers or ironically turned into a leash or a halter for the controlling of another species of animal or perhaps its own. Never mind thinking about the concept of being consumed by a creature that not only resembles a carnivore but loves mashed potatoes and gravy as well. Finally, expelled into excrement the ultimate recycling act. Deader than dead, if you know what I'm getting at? Finis. Microbes do the rest.

In uninterrupted nature sun-cured remains dry up and blow away into the grassless sea of emptiness that haunts the coulees. The desiccated fade away and disappear into the void without witness.

Some act like totems of magic when they are accidentally disturbed or found. The butterfly on the hat in the photo of Sitting Bull, the Hunkpapa medicine man, taken at Fort Randall in 1882, after he returned to the US from his self-imposed exile in Canada (1877) showing the whimsical sense of humour in his personality that went largely unrecognized by his principal enemy, who thought him to be a humourless, stoic man. A particular Monarch butterfly lives on, isolated from the multitude of its previous generations by an arbitrary act of history.

The fact he spent so much time at his cabin at Grand River with the widowed white woman, Catherine Weldon, a gentle Victorian woman of many talents, including portrait painting, and who served as his secretary and advisor, tells the reader much more. Weldon, an early anti-war crusader who taught the "domestic arts," wrote, "I honour and respect S. Bull as if he were my own father." The newspapers had a field day, calling her, "Sitting Bull's White Squaw."

The man with the butterfly on his hat, public enemy number one in his own time, a historical twin to the modern Osama Bin Ladin, in a nation that viewed George Armstrong Custer (aka Long Hair) the Indian hunter's "massacre" as they called it, on June 17, 1876, at the Little Bighorn, to be as heinous a crime against America as Pearl Harbour or 9/11.

The man with the butterfly on his hat — prophet of his people, patron saint of the downtrodden and the underdog? Or the bloodthirsty killer portrayed in newspapers and in the popular fiction of the era? A man whose name terrified decent woman and little children.

Sometimes these images are created, or taken over and adapted by man to define his mythos: a northern Plains Cree shaman's dried-up woodpecker skin hat; a Crow wearing his tutelary spirit, the eagle on his head; the slightly bemused Hunkpapa man in the picture with the whimsical butterfly on his hat. At other times they are bent to the will of nature: the hawk crucified on barbed wire turned into a salt encrusted paper-like-state, its bones torn apart by the sun.

The sun's magic power gives us light and the ability to see far out over the land and the energy to preserve food or provide heat. It warms the seed and nourishes the plant. It dries up the dead. It causes a terrible beauty when there is an absence of water. It is our salvation or our destruction depending on the situation. We worship it in every way including baking our skins on purpose. We are fascinated by how quickly it can scar nature and redefine the land form. We have been known to pray for rain as well as creating countless images of the sun to mark our time under its beneficent exposure. We celebrate it in myth and in song in every ethnicity that exists in our human lexicon.

The coulee bottom where beavers once made dams and flooded the landscape with the overflow from their ponds now full of cracked and spent dwarfish trees and scrubby, wind-tossed sun-abused-bushes where water once sat, now thirsty as only the dried out sandy soil can get. After all these years finding the remains of that long-lost tom cat in the bottom of the dried-up well. Something must live so something can die.

The finest wild mint is always found growing on top of the beaver's lodge. In this period of drought the beaver has gone from the coulee, having travelled overland to a more reliable source of water

to build his dams. Nature is always advancing or receding, deciding what will live and what will die. How long into the future is
the answer. Countryside shrivelling by degree from lack of moisture, defining living resources in finite detail. What is gone and
what will come back from hidden roots or dormant seeds? I stand
in the shadows. The bruised clouds brood in the southwestern sky
with a light show and uncomfortable disdain for everything under
the sun.

TRANSFORMATIONAL THOUGHT

AN ACCIDENT THAT TRANSPIRED on the number 11 highway near Dundurn, Saskatchewan, has given me a great deal of insight into exactly how the transfer of information occurs in human circles, especially in rural areas.

It was reported to me at the rink while I was watching my son's hockey team practice that a local couple and their two children were involved in a serious accident. They collided with a caribou while driving in their small green Japanese-made-car on the highway near the northern Saskatchewan community of La Ronge. By the miraculous intervention of the gods none of the family members was seriously injured, although the vehicle itself was a total write-off. This story quickly circulated through coffee row and travelled by telephone around the RM.

The next day, when I went to the store to buy a gallon of milk, I heard about the corpse of a moose that was left on the edge of the highway a few miles from town. The existence of a large number of roadkilled animals between Dundurn and Saskatoon on the number 11 highway is a sad fact that seems to manifest itself in the fall and winter months. A large percentage of the dead are made up of animals from the local deer population — both whitetail deer and their dumber cousins the ubiquitous mule deer. They inhabit the coulees and bush lands that abound in the grain-growing and grazing lands that surround the town.

Early one day in the month of November I counted 15 deer carcasses on the 35 km drive between Dundurn and Saskatoon. There is no doubt that November being the rutting season probably contributes to the numbers of the dead. The deer seem to grow careless and become emboldened by their hormonally driven activities. At least until the hunting season opens later in that month. Perhaps the fact the highway is more austere in winter, with ditches and medians cut and baled means there is less cover to hide the bodies, which are run down mainly by freight trucks and unfortunate passenger vehicles that ply the main route, the number 11 divided highway that links Saskatoon to Regina.

When the light of dawn arrives on a fall or winter morning on the prairie, the pristine snowfall in the night is material for the illustrator's hand. Shattered, torn, obliterated carcasses are smeared across the white landscape in a vivid pattern of carnage that is less visible in the spring and summer when the median and ditches are filled with two-foot-high waves of grass. Occasionally a wide, long ribbon of blood and meat on the pavement leaves a stain that tells the story of deer that have been pulverized into a smear of colour by a semi pulling a b-train. Deer and headlights are a bad combination.

Recently, moose, which have always inhabited the area in small numbers, seem to be on the increase in this region. Several friends and neighbours have reported seeing a large bull on the back road and others have reported cows with calves foraging in various nearby locations. So I was not particularly surprised when I heard about the moose carcass on the side of the highway about five minutes north of town. Since there had been no report in the newspaper or on the local media about anyone injured from driving into a moose it was safe to assume the animal probably was involved in a collision with one of what seems like an endless train of freight trucks that ply that route between the two main population centres in Saskatchewan.

Another day passed before I ran into my friends who had been in the accident. They were tender and sore from the experience, having suffered minor scrapes and bruises as well as whiplash. However, they seemed free of any permanent injuries. I asked them what had happened and they explained that in the middle of the afternoon on the return ride home from Gemini hockey rinks near Saskatoon where they had gone to watch a relative from La Ronge playing in a hockey tournament they had driven into the broadside of a 1200-pound bull elk that was crossing the highway. They were travelling at the listed speed limit of 110 kph when the collision occurred. The elk came up from the ditch and material-ized in front of them, they said, as if it were a cloud or a wisp of smoke. The result was a horrible impact that left them in a total wreck when air bags deployed and they found themselves upside down in the ditch beside the highway. The elk had flown straight-up in the air and somehow landed on the back of the car putting its ample rack right through the metal into the trunk. Within what seemed to them like only a few minutes an RCMP highway patrol officer arrived and rescued them from the wreck before he mercifully put 2 slugs into the head of the elk that was still alive, albeit in pretty desperate shape.

My friends' accident occurred hundreds of miles south of the northern community of La Ronge and the animal they collided with in no way resembled a caribou. It was a bull elk from the sel-dom-seen herd that resides in this local region. They were hang-ing out on the 90 sections of bush land and sand hills that make up the Dundurn army base about 10 km northwest of town. The big bull had left the herd and decided to set out for new territory when he met up with his fate while carelessly crossing the divided highway.

The fact my friends' relative was playing hockey in the area and the very nature of the accident spawned the story about the inci-dent occurring near La Ronge. A far more likely region to spot a caribou, than in this area which is way too far south for caribou. In addition, the report of dead moose on the margins of the highway on the way to Saskatoon was also a bogus one. What was lying dead beside the highway was the bull elk with its enormous rack. It's hard to understand how any resident of this region or anywhere in Canada, for that matter, would have a problem identifying the remains of an elk by confusing it with a moose.

Within in a few hours my friends' unfortunate incident had taken on mythical proportions. The event was suppose to have happened hundreds of miles from the real scene of the accident. The caribou in the first report metamorphosed into an elk, which it was in the real story, before becoming a mythical dead moose on the highway. The question this incident provokes is: How can we believe anything anybody tells us? The facts in this story show how distortions and inaccuracies haunt the human condition promoting unreliable rumours. An accident that happened a few minutes from town was reported to have taken place in a totally different region. A caribou that was really an elk was purported to be a moose. Who knows how much of what I have created here in this interpretation of events will live on to fuel the gossip mill and contribute to the exactitude or inexactitude of observation?

NOTES FROM THE OUTSIDE

THE CHANCE TO SING

EVER WONDER WHY A MAN OR A WOMAN might spend all their working hours scratching poems onto pieces of paper? Sometimes I think only people who have written poetry for a long time could ever really understand the poet's urge to communicate in such an odd manner. Not only do you have to write the songs but you have to find the right voice to sing with. A poem can be as complete as whole story or be as brief as a one-sided piece of conversation. It can be short or long, thin or fat, it can be deadly serious, or totally absurd; it can rhyme or not rhyme. It can be any of the above things and more in any mixture you could care to think up: love and death, dogs and cats, rainbows and rubber boots, hummingbirds and wars, visions and hysterias, hyenas and paranoias, politicians and poodles, wine and sulfur, bridges and linguistics, mothers and fathers, sex and sunsets, snow and blacktop, mountains and anthills, moleskins and herring fins, butterflies and blood cells, cancer and cancer rising — these are all good subjects for poems.

A poet has no latitudes: he is a lonely fencer and fixer of words. How do they work together? Do they ever quite make it? If so, why? If not, why not? There are singular poets and there are schools of poets just as there are schools of fish in the oceans. Nearly every poet is swimming in some opposite direction from the next, scattering in the current like seeds sprouting fins or wings. Some stay inside and gather themselves in the geography of the mind and body. Others climb over mountains and soar into space transmitting sound back to earth like radio waves. Still others find their situations and expressions in the faces and habits of their neighbours and fellow riders on the job or on the street. Poets are noisy. Poets are notorious liars — because poems can be true or not. And when all is said and done, who cares if the poem is precisely faithful to the feeling and the actual emotion? If it communicates some joy or horror or some kind of understanding then the poem made a mark like a fingerprint and the poet left a little of himself with you. Why does a person write? If you have to ask you probably don't need an answer. But here goes: why does a frog croak, a dancer dance, a bird fly, a baby cry or a girl get kissed in the dark?

All the billions of textures and phenomena in the natural and unnatural worlds are the overlapping subjects for poetry. The poet works with a plain blank sheet of paper. Add some imagination and sweat, mix well and stand back. Of course it's not quite that easy. Luck and skill thrown in will probably make the difference between boom or poof. When the full moon rises the poets come out on the landscape like mushrooms. Where do you find poets? Wherever you look — in offices, beer parlours, driving trucks, at universities, in prisons, down the street, up town, out of town, chicken plucking, driving nails, biting nails and you are absolutely guaranteed to meet one if you spend time in a library — any library. Chances are that person you noticed on the bus reading a book was a poet. You see reading and writing are together as are eating and living. A poet is nourished by the work of other writers, and that doesn't hold just for poets — you are what you read. There are so many millions of things to read, from the yellow pages to the bibles of the peoples of the world from all the ancestors in the dizzy past that if you can't find what interests you in a book you are just plain lazy.

Poets often read other poets and imitate them. This is a form of poetic licence — a corny phrase used mostly by nervous professors at faculty cocktail parties or for the benefit of first year students. The truth be out: poets steal ideas and constructions. They would be at an insurmountable disadvantage if they didn't. Usually the better the poet is, the better the poets he has chosen to plunder. Writing good poetry is sometimes a matter of taste, knowing who to steal from and how to disguise it. A poet has to experiment just like a painter and therefore learn from other poets as painters learn from other painters. This is not stealing, it is more akin to borrowing a spring board for takeoff. All true poets eventually find their own style from the processes of imitation or deconstruction or some other variant on the human poetic condition.

Poets seldom get rich, the ones that do are usually slightly more proficient than the people who write greeting card verse. Along the meandering path called history poets have been put in jail and persecuted for writing, of all things, poetry. Garcia Lorca, the great Spanish poet, was murdered and thrown in an unmarked grave lest he be the rallying point, the symbol, the martyr for the dignity and spirit of the people. Garcia Lorca ceased being merely a man; he was a giant who inspired fear in his political enemies because his voice was so strong. He was important in the culture of the common man. Killing a Garcia Lorca or burning books can never erase the song of the poet. While there is one person left on earth with that song in their head the poem lives in the minds of all men. Not in the hearts, but in the minds. The heart pumps blood and works hard to keep the body alive and jumping, but the mind, the mind is the capital of the spirit.

I am interested in writing poetry about the fragments and bits of people, places, and scenarios that survive in the crevices of the imagination as if it were a sluice box that traps the tiny molecules of our transcendency and captures the essence of water, blood, earth, flesh, light and bone. I want to take beautiful flowers and plants in a gorgeous pottery vase and smash the whole works to pieces on a white marble floor. Then with the glue pot of the psyche close at hand, painstakingly reconstruct the objects into something else, something that was unseen before but that makes perfect illogical sense. Something new and slightly twisted that gives greater understanding and meaning than the objects had before they underwent the trial of human interference.

Poetry is the essential life force that allows the mind the freedom of escaping its round bone walls by proposing that anything is possible within the confines of the universe. Here the hesitations in time, the lost hours, the deaths of loved ones, the memories of childhood, the temptations and travesties of the flesh, the circus of scary clowns are all played out like the hands in an endless game of chance. I want to write poetry everyday without stopping so that I can deal with the issues of the human condition that play out over and over again in the daydream land of creation. Even taking out the garbage at 20 below zero is an act of poetry if I am writing about why I am writing after the lid comes crashing down. Freedom to smash beautiful predictable images of the peeled and deveined soulless society that wants every kid in the world to read the same book, Harry Potter, and makes business a thousand times more important than pleasure.

I have been writing poetry for 40 years, since I was addled by it as a teenager. The result is a dozen books. During my adult life I have worked at an inordinate number of ridiculous jobs in order to keep the flames stoked in the furnace that has consumed me like endless cords of punky wood. What I crave is the luxury of several consecutive months to do nothing but argue with myself about this mysterious process that has kept me in its grasp like a poor insignificant bug trapped in a phone booth or in a spider's web or in the sludgy bottom of your coffee cup. Poems piling up from the industry of my human interference as the beautiful glass vase full of trembling blooms goes smashing into the numbing marble of justice and faith. There I am in the background, in the foreground, everywhere in the picture with my one good eye staring into the problem while my tongue travels over the words. A book that I might call *The Fat Man Dreams a Thin Shadow* or *Dogs and Other*

Reliable Witnesses.

Poets as well as other artists are the mirrors of the people. They describe and illuminate in depth the passage of a people in their time and at their place on earth. Art is a part of the mystery that makes man the most complex compelling creature. The artists of the primitive people have provided a legacy for understanding the little we know of the past, just as the artists of today leave an impression for the future world. A culture that ignores its artists is fighting against permanence.

A poem, a few simply constructed words, may be the sabre tongue of the prophet railing against injustices, a joyous celebration of the people and the living, a subtle twist into the human psyche, a so precise charting of the landscape or the empty chattering of magpies. Poetry can be a powerful weapon to ward off evil spirits or to bring them on. Poetry can survive the generations with the everlasting constitution of stone or pop in the air instantly like a bubble. Poetry has all the beautiful intangibles in creation and existence. It is the poets who take up the chance to sing!

NOTES FROM THE OUTSIDE

SMALL TOWNS AND WHISTLE STOPS abound on the miles of highway that cross the great Canadian plains. The casual traveller sees the signs advertising cold beer, cafés, and gas stations. He seldom leaves the comfort of highway stops to detour into the small towns that are almost always built a short distance back from the divided highway.

Dundurn, Saskatchewan (pop 496), southeast of Saskatoon on the highway to Regina, is as good a place to start as any. A red sign with white lettering offers off sales at the local hotel. G&D's café, named after the owners' initials, is the "home of the trapper burger." The bright yellow signs with the representation of a jolly chef holding up a huge layered burger are strategically placed at the ends of the town. They compete with the Lazy J Motel sign and the orange and white Mountain View Gas Bar advertisement that proclaims the price of gas and offers sundries and a welcome rest stop.

If you should decide to leave the highway and travel the quarter mile into town you will find a quiet place lost in its own receding history. Dundurn was bigger than Saskatoon at the turn of the 20th century. The stately mansions and the few remaining historically interesting buildings; the Northern Crown Bank, the United Church and the original school are testimony to a sense of permanence. But what is missing is the troubling part of searching a small prairie town. One of two original hotels, the solid train station with veranda, the hardware stores, the pool hall, the barber shop, the lumberyards, the bowling alley, the dance hall, and the solid turn of the century storefronts have been removed as if they were bad teeth yanked out of a mouth.

Abandoned buildings do not fare well in a dry prairie climate. The wood shrivels into dry tinder and the threat of fire long ago convinced the townspeople to remove vacant buildings. A town that once boasted 900 people is now home to barely 500. The Mayor, Alvin Lamabe, who has been in the job for nearly 25 years, has an agenda. If the town grows much larger the cost to the local taxpayer for increased Royal Canadian Mounted Police vigilance becomes untenable. However, should the tax base lessen, then the cost of municipal services will increase. In the early '90s the mayor and his council determined that the population was at a dangerously low level. So local serviced building lots that cost $3000 were lowered to $10 providing the purchasers built at least a foundation during the first year. The lots went fast and Dundurn got its five minutes in the big city press. Besides the above mentioned businesses there is a grocery store, a car wash, a building supply outlet, a concrete company, and a bakery on 2nd Street.

If you are passing by Dundurn early in the morning it is worth stopping in at G&D's café for breakfast. George Stanley, a large man in a white chef's outfit, will be on duty. Conversation is his speciality. He has strong opinions about everything, especially politicians and the state of the nation. If you're still hungry after he serves you breakfast he'll feed you a second time, no extra charge. If you wait long enough the locals will gradually fill up his living-room-like restaurant that has a log exterior. Coffee row, they call it; a place to visit with your fellow citizens over coffee while discussions about farming, hockey, politics and social events abound. There are no newspapers in Dundurn, events are chronicled by word of mouth. Strangers are not entirely unwelcome. If you sit like a slug chances are the locals will ignore you but not George, he has a way of making people talk. If he's in a foul mood you'll know about it. If not you're likely to go away feeling better than when you arrived.

If you desire a tour of the local museum, give Maxine Wilson a call. She'll come down and open it for you if she thinks you're serious. The guy riding on the grader or hauling garbage is likely to be His Worship the Mayor. Before you leave town drop by the Busy Bee bakery, you can't miss the fuzzy bee sign. Best cinnamon buns in this part of the world.

The small prairie town that looks like a sleepy burg to a stranger contains a surprising array of services. In Dundurn there are only a half dozen visible businesses, but the community is extremely resourceful. If you ask around you can find most services that are available in a larger centre. Josh will rototill your garden, trim your trees and cut your lawn with his ride around mower. Mary-Anne, the seamstress, remodels suits, alters clothing, or will build you an outfit from scratch. Jamie, trained in acupressure, treats bad backs and other physical problems. Leanne, Shawna, and Debbie cut hair in their home styling shops for half the price in the city. Shelley sells second-hand kids' clothing. Dwayne fixes cars. Art repairs and sells lawn mowers. Chuck understands heavy mechanics. Larry does plumbing in a pinch. Bill will tell you dirty jokes and fix your furnace in his own good time. Linda makes and sells several varieties of good Ukrainian perogies. Jackie reads Tarot cards and tells fortunes. Laverne raises succulent six-pound chickens that put Safeway to shame. Claude delivers fresh large brown eggs for $1 a dozen. Dwayne and Vern fix eavestroughs and reshingle roofs. Garfield, who has a face that you'll never forgot, will build you a fence, a picnic table or construct an array of wooden lawn furniture. Sheila and Gary supply healthy bedding plants from their backyard greenhouses. Granny has a photo copy service. Faxes can be received and sent anywhere in the world from the town office for $1 per page. If you're desperate Edie, the school secretary, will type your business letters. Randy custom cuts meat. If you want something local to read go over to the book rack at Mountain View Food & Fuel and pick up one of Harvey Mawson's books. He is the dean of Canadian cowboy writers. He'll also build you a saddle tree or sell you one of his beautiful wood carvings.

If you drive on by without taking a look or prefer the role of sophisticated cynic you might easily think that small towns are filled with rubes. It ain't necessarily so. These people don't have many secrets, their lives are interconnected by family and long standing friendships based on mutual aid and neighbourly considerations. Unlike the city where hardly anybody knows their neighbours, the country is a place where people work at being accepted. When the unexpected or a tragedy occurs they come together. The feuds, the petty arguments, the political differences are put away. They understand the importance of community and hang onto it through desperate times. The inhabitants of tiny towns and sleepy hamlets are the backbone of the country. They are stubborn people who are humble and proud at the same time. If you visit you'll find out things about Canada that most people have forgotten or never bothered to find out.

The spring of 1992 has been the hardest in recent memory for the people of this small but resilient town, perhaps the toughest year in the decades since the Second World War when the town registered the tragic loss of men killed on the battlefield. Seven teenagers, in a car on their way to Watrous to cheer on the Dundurn Wheat Kings in the hockey playoffs, ran off the gravel shoulder. The car flipped end-over-end into a field killing three and badly injuring the others. There is no way to comprehend the workings of the universe to find a rational explanation. Three teenage lives from a high school class of fourteen were extinguished in a freak accident on a desolate back road on a bad night in March.

The big city media in Saskatoon and Regina jumped on the accident like a dog on a bone. Lurid stories about teenage drinking and wild behaviour circulated in the press and on the late night

TV news. Reporters rushed into the town and began asking questions of the bereaved. For three months, hardly a day went by without some mention of the Dundurn tragedy, usually after a feature on the evils of young people drinking. The facts are not so hard to find out if you really want to learn them. The citizens of Dundurn already in shock retreated further into themselves after hearing and reading so many inaccurate sensational reports. The funerals of these young people were attended by more than a thousand people, many who came from surrounding towns including a large contingent from the local Hutterite colony. This was not an appropriate example to provide propaganda for middle class values. It was a horror and a devastation that affected the lives of every citizen in Dundurn's history. A time for grieving and burying the dead was turned into a media circus to sell newspapers and satisfy the advertisers. The feelings of family, friends and fellow citizens were discarded in the fires of sensationalism. These were the brightest, the most level headed, and the best of a whole generation from a town of 496 people. They may as well have been faceless statistics to satisfy the moral prerogative.

These kids were not drunk, although they had an unopened case of beer in the car. The most accurate report suggests that two of them may have had one beer before starting out. The media's lurid reports were never substantiated by evidence stronger than rumour. Blood test results released months later by the RCMP proved that alcohol was not a factor. By this time the media was no longer interested in correcting the record. These kids had spent their day at school, three of them started out after putting in additional hours at their part time jobs. These were not yahoos who had been partying up a storm and then drove off into the night like demons. These were farm and town kids who had good academic records, athletic accomplishments and reputations for good behaviour in their community.

In the country kids grow up differently than in the city. They learn to drive sooner and they acquire adult skills at an early age.

They are expected to put in a hard working day on the farm or in the family business. They are brought up knowing almost innately that helping their parents by learning the ropes and becoming useful will only help themselves in the future. They drove down an empty country road on their way to cheer on their friends playing in a game of hockey. The passion of their country. They died because of unusual circumstances that were exacerbated by the treachery of the spring thaw. They and their families did not deserve to be pilloried by a kangaroo court or buried under an avalanche of half-baked media hogwash. Candace, Kyle, and Ira will be remembered dearly by the citizens of Dundurn long into the future until the town ceases to exist. They were kids to be proud of and they will be remembered because they were too important to be forgotten. No matter what the years will bring Dundurn will endure but never really recover. There is too much sadness and pain that has touched consenting lives. The unit of human living here is so small the loss is monumental for all the reasons nobody can understand.

I have driven many back roads to small Saskatchewan towns. The landscape, always changing in subtle ways offers a variety of experience that is hard to explain. Fields of wheat, barley, oats, canola, sunflowers, alfalfa and other crops are textured like enormous quilts. The car passes farmers moving strange-looking pieces of machinery or Hutterites standing in fields in their formal black attire. Sometimes arriving in the middle of a cattle drive, moving slowly down the road surrounded by fat steers and weather beaten cowboys on lathered horses. Chances are a passing vehicle will be a pickup truck, an enormous 15-year-old American luxury car, or an antiquated yellow school bus.

The British Columbia licence plate on my old black bug splattered Oldsmobile announces I am from the outside world. It permits them to give me a second look. I think it makes them wonder what I'm doing back here so far from the main hustle of Trans-Canada passage. "Looking at the country," I always answer.

"Just looking at the country and finding new roads to travel." In Saskatchewan there is a way of easing oneself into the rural psyche. It is called the wave. Every passing vehicle, machine working a field or person encountered in the landscape whether walking, riding a horse, a three wheeler or peering from a farm house window is looking for the wave. If you offer it they wave back and relax knowing that you are someone who understands the customs. Drivers sometimes offer a single digit from the steering wheel in a kind of cursory acknowledgement. It is almost unheard of for a rural resident not to wave back and offer that subtle human exchange. Sometimes men or women working in the fields will shoot the over the shoulder greeting without looking while they wrestle a hay bale into a loader.

The wave is the universal signal offered by every citizen in small Saskatchewan towns. It is more demonstrative here in the confines of tiny, nearly deserted streets. You might be the only vehicle driving down this street today. The sound of your motor brings eyes to windows, turns heads that have a vested interest in appraising your passage. The first time I drove through Dundurn I received my education about the essential nature of the wave. A half-paralysed older woman riding slowly down the shoulder in her electric wheel chair with her shopping bags loaded around her struggled to give me her wave of approval. I noticed she couldn't move her torso. She lifted her hand with a great deal of effort to say hello. I looked and saw the gesture and the smile on her face. I have been waving back at everyone since then. If you want to travel comfortably through these parts, even if you have green hair or are wearing a pink tutu remember the wave. They won't pass judgement about you unless you fail to notice their existence. They'll know you're a suspicious stranger who refuses to acknowledge your species and they'll rightly wonder what the hell is wrong with you.

I am almost always amazed by the city dweller's attitude to the great plains. "It's so flat and boring! You drive for hour after hour with hardly any variation. What's there to see?" Truthfully, the prairie is only flat in the most obvious sense. There are no mountains or hills of any size to mar the vista of vast horizon. The dome of the sky dominates the land. Vast cloud formations build in the distance like ethereal ranges of mountains in the sky. Wind rushes directly across the earth with no obstacles. The heat of the day creates mirages of mirrors and water where there is nothing but fallow fields. It is a landscape that permits the casual viewer only an overview of the whole. The huge fields are tables slanted in every direction. The land is a myriad of dips and coulees between the levels of the optical illusion. The fields are divided by hedgerows of caragana, willows, Manitoba maples, Saskatoon bushes, elm trees, and other varieties of scrub.

Grid roads built up from the land on gravel beds tell the story of farm culture. If you veer from the main highway and find your way across the land leaving your ribbon of dust you might see the true land form. Skunks and porcupines waddle the edges of the road with impunity. They always seem to be investigating things no further than two feet in front of their faces. Mourning Doves fly up from the gravel. Black and white Magpies making harsh pronouncements flit across the road. A startled coyote disappears quicker than a blink. You can stop and walk around for hours and never see him again. It was only by a fluke of the moment or distortion of the wind that you saw him in the first place. Hawks soar on air currents or sit in solitude on fence posts. A jack rabbit bounds down the gravel road faster than the car. In the far distance a herd of white-rumped antelope move in single file to the extremity of the horizon. A great horned owl perches like a big house cat on the top of a telephone pole. In the evening white tail deer hiding in the dense scrub cross over into the fields. Mule deer bouncing as if equipped with springs for legs bound into the coulees. At first the does and fawns gingerly work their way along the tree line nervously trying out the fields before walking out into the open. When the sun is down and edges of it wither in the bush tops the bucks follow warily. If you wait long enough in a quiet place near the does and fawns and look back at the trees with your eyes tilted slightly at the little light left in the sky you might see the rack of a big buck sneaking out from the bush. A farmer working the field with a big machine is hidden by a landscape that swallows up everything including the human eye.

People in Saskatchewan pay particular attention to the weather. Not a day passes without some comment about the length of the year. Nine months of winter and three of summer is how one old man put it. Overstated? Of course, but not so far out of order. Spring is hardly a full fledged season here. When the weather gets warm things change quickly. Trees fill out with leaves in a few days. The top of the soil gets a dry granular look about it. Farmers are seeding for a new crop. At coffee row they're moaning about the low level of the water table. If it rains steadily for more than a few days they are moping about whether or not they will be able to get machinery into the fields. The ideal year brings a winter of big snow followed by a few weeks of gentle but persistent rain. And please, no frost after the middle of May.

The dryland farmer hopes for rain again after planting and then bring on the heat. If the gods of thunder work their magic and bring the chains of summer storms the wheat will grow without irrigation. If the heavens fail the crops wither and the yield per acre becomes academic. So much depends on the weather. People here have their senses tuned to it. They talk about it in most conversations. They make up for it by adjusting their work schedule to take advantage of it. Tractors stay out long into the night to finish the work. When things go well farmers linger in the coffee shop looking smug and feeling at ease. But their faces tell the story and they talk about the worst scenarios in the best of times as if speaking of it will not let it happen.

Being a creature from the coast I had no consciousness or personal experience with the essential elements of the plains. The long hard winter was over. It all seemed to happen in a day. The snow got dirtier as the months passed and suddenly the streets had turned into mud. Nights were still brisk but the days came forth with a glow of warmth. Dead looking fields and the brown flatness were filling in with lush green grass. The great pattern of migratory birds had descended from the jet stream. The marshes were alive with pintails, mallards, blue-winged teal, lesser scaups, American avocets, swans, curlews, pelicans, sandhill cranes, and red-winged and yellow-headed blackbirds. A great flock of Canada geese settled into the marsh on the edge of Dundurn. They came back each night from feeding on tender grass shoots in the still desolate wheat fields. A long black wave of squawking birds passed low over the town followed by small groups and the plaintive honking of stragglers. Songs of the meadowlark pierced the din. A Swainson's hawk hovered over the marsh effortlessly adjusting the tilt of its wings for a stroll in the air. Eurasian coots putted around the edge of a pothole, bobbing as if on the verge of some kind of neurological breakdown. Somewhere in the distance a strange bout of coughing turned into the full-throated call of the coyote. For an instant things were quiet and still. The moon was growing larger in the cobalt sky. The red ball of the sun dropped like a stone beyond the horizon.

SMITH

SMITH ATIMOYOO, distinguished elder and teacher in the northern plains Aboriginal community, was born of Cree-Saulteaux origins on February 12, 1915, at Little Pine Reserve. The name Atimoyoo, a Cree word, translates as Dog Tail. It was earned by Smith's great grandfather, an honoured warrior, who had the ability to turn himself into a weasel and enter an enemy's camp surreptitiously, wherein he promptly dispatched the early warning system by killing the dogs. When the war party returned to their people and warriors danced with the scalps they had taken Atimoyoo danced with the tails of the dogs he killed tied to a stick.

Smith attended the day school at Little Pine before attending King George Public School and completing high school at St. George's Boys College in Prince Albert. While in high school Smith participated in all sports. He was a member of the St. George's Boys College basketball team that won the city championship.

In 1943, Smith became a student at Emmanuel College (Anglican) at the University of Saskatchewan. He studied arts, sciences, and theology while participating in a variety of clubs and sports activities. In 1947, Smith graduated from the University of Saskatchewan and was ordained Minister of the Anglican Church of Canada. During those years Smith continued to ride broncos at various rodeos throughout the province and he played soccer, hockey, baseball, curled and ran long distance races.

Smith made a personal decision to become a teacher. He taught for three years at Pelican Narrows, five years at Shoal Lake, five years at Big River Reserve, five years at Sturgeon Lake and two years at Fort-a-la-Come (James Smith) and Thunderchild. At all these postings Smith taught beginners to high school. In addition to regular curriculum he also taught Cree and other languages and at every location, organized both boys, girls and adult sports teams and arranged cultural and social activities such as dancing — the two step, waltz, Fox Trot, and square dancing.

In the early 1960s Smith attended Teachers' College at the University of Saskatchewan and completed his teaching degree. "I did this because I had taught for a long time and I wanted to improve my skills to help teach about my own culture." Smith Atimoyoo was the first Director of the Friendship Centre in North Battleford. He stayed in that job for two years, long enough to organize an annual powwow and help start the P.A. Aboriginal Hockey tournament (the first all Indian hockey tournament).

In the mid-1960s Smith returned to Saskatoon and worked at Saskatchewan Indian Languages Institute. During this period he worked to establish the Saskatchewan Indian Cultural Centre (1970) and the Saskatchewan Indian Cultural College. He was Director of the Saskatchewan Indian Cultural Centre for five years. In the 1980s, Atimoyoo and a group of elders founded Wanuskewin Heritage Park.

Smith is a Storyteller, teacher, linguist, and cultural ambassador. In 1949 he married Rose Morin. They had three children and seven grandchildren. At the age of 81, although handicapped by strokes, Smith Atimoyoo is a great man in a state of grace. He speaks many First Nations languages, including Cree, Saulteaux, Blackfoot and he understands syllabics, as well as other languages, including a smattering of Ukrainian.

Smith has the ability to communicate with human beings in

remarkable ways. He travels to Wanuskewin nearly every day of the year to conduct sweet grass ceremonies and he is the central figure in articulating on matters of traditional teaching and culture. Smith is a spiritual man with astonishing dignity and respect for every man. He is a simple, unpretentious man who has never stopped learning things and is reticent to take credit for his achievements in life. He simply calls himself a teacher.

The following interview took place on a sunny afternoon in May, 1995, outside at Wanuskewin Heritage Park. News about an oral history project at Manito Lake had recently travelled south. Manito Lake and the sand hills near Neilburg and Marsden are sacred places well-known in the oral tradition and in non-First Nations history as an important spiritual place for northern plains people. In the mid-1900s, the Provincial government lifted the moratorium on gas and oil exploration in the Manito Lake region. The sand hills, which are rich in archaeological and cultural sites, became the focal point of a controversial debate about the appropriateness of allowing resource exploration at a sacred place.

For the better part of this century, two communities, Saulteaux and Cree, co-existed in the region. Some of these people were the relatives and follower of Big Bear who never took treaty. The history of Manito Lake as a community had a tragic conclusion for several reasons. The worst being influenza epidemics. I mentioned to Smith that I had been hearing about a project at Manito Lake. He said, "I don't know very much about Manito Lake and the people who lived there, but my mother came from there. She lived there nearly all her life with her brothers and her mother."

What was her name?
Osakechik.

What does that word mean?
Curly hair, curly locks. She didn't like her curly hair 'cause it always got tangled, tangled-up. She lived with her mother and her

grandmother at Manito Lake. I don't know what her mother's name was because she never told us. That was the old custom. You don't name the old people because they're gone. And just out of respect.

Is it the same for the brothers?
Especially the brothers who were very close to her. She had a lot of respect for them. And it was the traditional way to keep respect for your elders, your brothers, your sisters, your fathers, your mothers. That's why a lot of names are lost.

Do you know what year your mother was born?
No.

Did she live to be old?
She lived to be 96.

When did she die?
About 1963.

She would have been born around 1867.
Yes, she lived a long time. She had a lot of horses she had gotten from her brothers who had a herd of horses, mostly all wild. When her brothers died she looked after the horses. She broke them herself. She was a good rider and she did all the chores like hauling wood for her mother. Her mother was old. All I can remember is I didn't even know my uncles. They died at the time of the flu. Many people died in the time of the flu. Then families began to leave one by one. I think it's because they couldn't get groceries. They didn't have any support from the government. They didn't have treaty. That was the excuse the government gave. It was another way of getting rid of them. They more or less just disappeared.

My mother married dad. Dad had a lot of horses at Little Pine. They joined their herds and had about 100 head. They lived at Little Pine with all those horses. My mother taught me about riding. We lived off those horses. We sold some for a measly price. Twenty bucks is the most they paid. White people bought them for farming. Horses were widely used for farming at that time.

Those horses were the private property of my parents. They had no ID on them. The Indian Affairs people wanted to get them too, like they had the cattle. You had to brand your cattle with an ID brand and they belonged to the Indian Affairs Department. But not the horses. Later my dad had his own registered brand GA for George Atimoyoo.

Were there ceremonies about horses?
We had horse dances. It was a ceremony that involved horses. It was one of the old customs. They had prayers, and so on. A regular routine. My dad did the ceremonies along with the elders. There were special songs.

Do you know those songs?
Well, I have an idea.

What time of year did they have those ceremonies?
The ceremonies were done in the summer time. Not all the horses were blessed. Because they were wild. Only the ones that were used for saddle horses and that were blessed in the ceremony. It was quite a time for us young folk. We were drawn in a circle with all the horses. All the young fellows joined in. They joined in because they wanted to get their horses blessed too. They had their own customs when they rode the horse in the circle. The parents, or owner gave a gift of a blanket or something to the elders. It was a very important ceremony because they wanted to give the horse credit for being good support. They were used to make a living. Without the horse there wouldn't be too much of a living.

We were very poor. We sold the horses whenever the farmers came, especially in the fall. We'd round up our horses and the farmers picked out the ones they wanted. Broken horses and wild horses. I still have a few horses. They're hard to keep. You have to make hay for them. It was a good time in the summer when people gathered together to help each other make hay. They mowed the hay, bunched it up, and stacked it. All done by free labour. My father had to go help others when they branded their horses.

Did everybody break their own horses?
That's how we all became good riders.

Did you race horses in those days?
Oh yes!

How far did they run?
Oh, half mile. We had half mile tracks. Every reserve had their own tracks.

Was there much gambling to do with horses?
Well, a little bit. Whatever they could give they threw in a pile and the winner takes all.

Must be something to have the fastest horse on the reserve?
Yes. Sometimes people didn't have fast horses, so they couldn't really race with the others. We always had some fast horses that we kept. We conditioned them. At five o'clock in the morning I'd get up and gallop horses. And we went to all the little fairs around the country. Little race meets.

How old were you then?
Oh, 10 or 12 when I raced our horses. Later on when the market was a little stronger the farmers from the south used to come up and buy our horses. They bought them because our horses seemed to be a better strain. Every family had their own horses. They raised their own horses.

There was a story about a horse at Manito Lake that used to come up out of the water to mingle with our horses. A dappled grey, beautiful horse. They tried to break that horse. But it ran wild with the herd. There are a lot of stories about that horse. Once there were many good horsemen from Manito Lake and from my reserve, Little Pine. That was a fun time.

What changed that?
School. We were kept in school.

What happened to that dappled grey horse?
When people left Manito Lake that horse never appeared again.

So those Manito Lake horses were highly prized?
They were sacred. They were considered sacred. It was considered a good omen to have a horse. That's why the people respected the horse and they improved the breeding carefully because they wanted to keep on improving the herd. Taking on horses from different reserves, including the States. My father went to the States, and got a stallion in Montana and rode it back to Little Pine. He paid quite a bit for it. A good race horse.

Did you give them all names?
No, well, we gave them names but that wasn't important to us.

THE TRADITIONAL AND SACRED
ON THE NORTHERN PLAINS

During a two-year interval in the mid-90s (1994-1996) I had the opportunity to work as Consultant of Intellectual Property at Wanuskewin Heritage Park, on a variety of important cultural projects under the supervision of First Nations elder Smith Atimoyoo. Wanuskewin had assembled a unique group of traditional teachers, artisans, artists and storytellers who interpreted North Plains Culture for a diverse audience that came from every corner of the world. These resource people included: Joyce Whitebear Reed, Theresa Hohn, Virginia Lowen, Wes Fine Day, Carol Raintree, Lamar Swindler, Lorne Carrier, Gerald Gaddie, Joseph Naytowhow, Maurice Royale, Linden Tootoosis, and Mary Lee, among many other important contributors. Unfortunately because of financial problems and an increasingly dysfunctional hierarchy Wanuskewin was greatly reduced in scope and manpower and in recent times has become a pale vestige of its former self.

The exciting years of Wanuskewin's Aboriginal renaissance coincided with a terrible period in Aboriginal/non-Aboriginal relations in the nearby city of Saskatoon and indeed in various parts of Saskatchewan. First Nations people were being harshly treated by the Saskatoon Police Department which manifest itself years later when several shocking race related incidents revealed deaths that were covered up by a corrupt police department. These incidents which grew in number and gravity under a blanket of denial further eroded the community and gave the city of Saskatoon a serious black eye to the outer world.

Wanuskewin Heritage Park represented a rebirth of traditional First Nations history that celebrated First Nations culture back 10,000 years. Many of the people who found a calling as interpreters of First Nations traditional knowledge had lived hard lives that saw them experience residential schools, extreme poverty, abuse, dislocation and in some cases prison. Wanuskewin was as much an idea in people's hearts as it was a heritage park because it was also a sacred place with a medicine wheel and the valley provided sanctuary for those who aspired to learn about traditional teachings. This essay, written with input provided by Lorne Carrier, Gerald Gaddie, Wes Fine Day and the late Smith Atimoyoo, was written with the intention of providing basic information while respecting the sanctity of the ceremonial, on how to go about accessing traditional First Nations teachings on the northern plains. The quotes in the storytelling section are by Wes Fine Day.

THE RETURN TO THE TRADITIONAL has been a profound influence in the modern cultural and social revolution in nation building that is redressing decades of First Nations oppression on the northern plains.

Destruction of an ancient culture based on buffalo, loss of traditional land and freedom of movement, failure of government to live up to treaties, the banning of ceremonial practices, residential schools, loss of language, the shameful treatment of war veterans, and the denial of simple rights such as freedom of assembly, voting, and legal representation that other Canadians took for granted were common to the First Nations world.

Lack of opportunity and dislocation from community values caused enormous social problems, including the separation of individuals from their relations. The cycle of poverty and the stress of social pressures have created great turmoil in the lives of the people, in families and in communities. These problems continue today in diverse regions of the country including the cities. The movement to self-government is gradually seeing changes in the administration of education, health care, justice, penal administration and policing practices and attitudes. Self-government is an evolving process that may manifest itself in several different forms depending on circumstances and conditions that prevail in regions and according to the will of the people.

Throughout the 20th century people have suffered poverty and social indignities; many of them turned to alcohol, drugs and violence, and abuse. The result is families were torn apart and many children were taken away or grew up on the streets. The spiritual and social reaffirmation of traditional values has inspired many people to find inner strength. Today many people are turning to these practices and values in finding their identities and reclaiming their lives.

Northern plains people — Cree, Saulteaux, Nakota, and Dakota — developed an efficient life style that allowed them to travel great distances in their yearly cycles. The people lived in tipis made from buffalo hides stretched over suitably cured poles. The tipi of the plains was a portable conical structure. It was covered with buffalo hides sewn together with sinew. The conical shaped dwelling was held up by peeled lodge poles. The tipi was practical for buffalo hunters on the prairies who moved from place to place. The tipi was easy to dismantle and the poles became part of the travois. When the horse was introduced the tipi became larger and more elaborate, and the number of foundation poles were more consistently patterned. The tipi represented the foundation of family and culture.

Each of the 15 poles symbolizes values: (1) obedience, (2) respect, (3) humility, (4) happiness, (5) love, (6) faith, (7) kinship, (8) cleanliness, (9) thankfulness, (10) sharing, (11) strength, (12) good childrearing, (13) hope, (14) ultimate protection, (15) harmony. These reminders built in to the understanding of dwelling, or living space, establish an ordered social code of behaviour designed to aid in human cooperation. An unwritten but well-known philosophy providing a strong framework of ritualized meaning to the sanctity of the dwelling. The relationships symbolized by each pole, the cover, the pins, the pegs, the flaps, represent moral principles. These principles must be respected and followed if the family, and ultimately society, are to hold together and function in harmony.

Northern plains customs to do with tipi culture are shared by other First Nations peoples who lived primarily from hunting buffalo. Often three generations lived in a tipi. The extended family was a common practice. A person did not have to be related by blood to be adopted into a family. Sometimes an adopted person resembled a relative who had been lost through death. Orphaned children were usually adopted by aunts and uncles. Family members lived by the traditional system of respecting privacy by formalizing relationships. Fathers-in-law did not speak to daughters-in-law and mothers-in-law did not speak to sons-in-law. Customs were adopted to allow people to live harmonious lives in relative comfort by establishing invisible walls between relationships to respect the integrity of social congress. Kinship was essential to the beliefs and values of the ancestors. Teachings from the elders ensured that the concept of kinship was understood. The ancestors believed that a person's name was sacred. Therefore, people did not call each other by name but by relationships. This was their way of showing respect for each other.

Centuries-old practices of social order based on the sacred and ceremonial with family in a formal but cooperative community with many specialized societies (including warrior and medicine societies) and a strict code of accommodating the laws of access in a sacred manner are fundamental to the northern plains. Ceremonies are important as the means by which an individual can pray to the Creator. The individual, the family, the people, the Creator, the cycles of the seasons, and the spiritual world are all in the Circle of Life. The circle is a powerful symbol of unity and renewal in many aspects of the cycles of life. The teachings of culture, language, morals, and values are a life long lesson. Elders teach that a person learns everyday but still can never know everything. It is only the Creator that has this knowledge. Ceremonies are sacred and complex. They are best understood within the context of all other aspects of the culture.

Aboriginal people throughout the world use herbs in "smudging ceremonies." On the northern plains, four sacred plants were given to the people to give as offerings: tobacco, sweet grass, sage, and cedar. On the plains, sweet grass is usually braided together in bunches as a person's hair is braided. Burning sweet grass while praying sends prayers up to the Creator by the wisps of fragrant smoke.

There are protocols for accessing the ceremonial. The sweat lodge is a place of prayer and holistic healing. It is a place where body, mind, and spirit are cleansed, renewed, and made stronger. Sweat lodges are not to be photographed or disturbed, neither should places be disturbed where people put out cloth. It is necessary to consult elders when one wishes to learn about these practices. In the past people illustrated their tipis with their own particular symbols and stories. These sacred pictures made by people who lived traditional lives in the sacred manner must not be displayed or depicted in any meaningless way.

The use of pipes is widespread throughout the northern plains and elsewhere. The smoking of the pipe is a sacred experience for Indian people and is an integral part of their spirituality. High Hollow Horn says in *The Sacred Pipe*, "Its fragrance will be known by the wingeds, the four leggeds, and the two leggeds for we understand that we are all relatives; may our brothers be tame and not fear us!" Sharing a pipe is a way of giving thanks to, and asking guidance from the Creator.

Pipes, pipe bags, medicine bundles and other objects have individual, spiritual, cultural, and ceremonial reasons to be respected as sacred objects that must not be disturbed. They should be returned to the owner or family or brought to the attention of elders so they can be properly dealt with in the sacred manner. These spiritually infused objects are on the move, they should be quickly and efficiently turned over to the community for ceremonial and cultural reasons. When any of these sacred objects appears elders, should be consulted, just as they must be consulted for guidance and instruction when human remains or artefacts are found under any circumstance at any time.

Elders are the grandmothers and grandfathers of all the people. Each generation of elders passes down the teachings of the people to the next generation. Elders teach people how to do things, provide details of history that are passed down in the oral tradition and teach many things about animals, plants, and the natural world. Elders have knowledge about the ceremonies and the spiritual world. Many of these things are told in stories.

Winter is the season of storytelling. First Nations people depend on oral history passed from generation to generation. The oral tradition tells the story of the people and often challenges the "official history" that has been documented by a dominant culture. This powerful oral tradition that is manifest in storytelling continues to this day. Traditionally, stories provided entertainment on long cold winter days and nights when outdoor activities were curtailed and people were living in close quarters. "If these stories were told out of season the plants might stop to listen and forget to grow. The animals might stop to listen and forget to feed their young. The resulting chaos would create a terrible imbalance in nature."

The philosophy inherent in storytelling — accommodating the laws of access, approaching in the sacred manner — are the steps on the road to earned knowledge. Stories explore the complicated relationships between sound and the telling. Singing and dancing complement the story. Stories teach people about the traditional and the ceremonial. The teachings of the lodge represent the family. Plains longhouses, sweat lodges, Sun Dance structures (Sun Dance is a term that has come into common usage to describe the ceremony known as the Thirst Dance) renew community and spiritual relationships. Land must be left in the condition it was found, therefore these temporary structures were designed to return quickly back to the earth.

Healing stories help people by provoking different emotional responses and to provide healing for the psyche. "Laughter with abandon massages the internal organs in a way that cannot be done from the outside." Stories as therapy enable human beings to deal with the various realities they encounter on the journey through life.

Tales of power delve into the mysterious and unbelievable where spiritual prophecy and aspects of the supernatural are found. These are stories about power songs and the journey to the spiritual world.

Sacred stories tell about the origins of the world; the origin of mankind. "These are tales about our relatives in the physical world and our relationships with spiritual matters including the little people and other spiritual figures."

Stories of animals tell about the relationship between people and the animal kingdom. They are about the use of feathers and fur and the traditions that allow man access in the sacred manner to animals for sustenance and for the ceremonial.

"Plant and medicine stories tell about the time of the meeting in the dream of plants and animals and the reason plants gave their spiritual names and other secrets to human beings."

Stories as history are passed on by generations through a culturally reliable oral tradition. Ownership of stories, the telling of stories, the selling of stories are based on a system of oral traditional First Nations copyright that is determined by cultural and ceremonial guidelines and the laws of access.

Storytelling includes traditions and customs that are uniquely the domain of women in the storytelling circle.

Story Circles — Earth, Fire, Water, Air; Infancy, Childhood, Adult, Old Age — these are the stories about the role of elder and the relationship of each person to every other person in the community.

The ceremonial role of storytelling follows the ancient traditions about courtship, marriage, divorce, the naming of children and adults and of death. The traditions of tribal law in maintaining social order have been orally passed down for centuries.

The concept and practice of copyright is an ancient one that has deep roots in the foundations of Aboriginal cultures and communities. Everything in the traditional world is governed by approaching in the sacred manner. On the northern plains, songs and stories and artwork such as those displayed on tipi covers were personal in nature, belonging to individuals. That is why traditional Aboriginals objected to people taking pictures of a painted tipi. These powerful personal images were the property of the owner who was usually, but not always, the artist. When painted tipi covers wore out or needed to be discarded they were usually buried in the ground.

In his seminal work, *The Plains Cree: An Ethnographic, Historical and Comparative Study*, first published in 1940 and reissued in 1978 by the Canadian Plains Research Centre in Regina (undertaken under the wise council of the great man Kamiolisihkwew, Fine Day), David Mandelbaum wrote:

An indispensable element of every ceremonial activity was the singing of revealed songs. While ritual smoking beckoned the spirit powers and offerings gratified them, songs placed a stamp of authenticity upon ceremonial procedure as emanating from genuine vision experience. To be accepted as a true vision innovation, a song had only to vary in minor details from one already known, such as the substitution of one word for another. Every grant of power from the supernaturals was accompanied by the imparting of a new song which was to be sung when the power was being exorcised. These songs were owned by the visionary and could not be sung by others unless the right had been transferred. Certain secular songs, those used in gambling, in secular dances, in distributing gifts, could be sung by anyone.

The artistic portrayal of images from visionary experiences (or singing songs or telling stories) is traditionally protected by a system of Aboriginal copyright. The process of transfer of songs and stories from the owner to another involved a formal social procedure that also included payment for the right of use. This payment might have been made in horses, trade goods, blankets, furs, suits of clothing, or decorative objects. The system was almost similar in every respect to the concept of copyright that governs modern day use of intellectual property. The owner of the story or song taught the work to the buyer who promised to render it faithfully after providing payment. Usually these transactions took place at the places where people gathered and they were held with much honour and ceremony.

After payment was made it was customary for the seller to return a part of the payment to show good will about the sale of this important cultural material. Occasionally these transfers were inter-tribal and involved one group acquiring the right to tell the story or sing the song of an admired member of the other group. This has been documented on the northern plains in scholarly work and in sources from the oral tradition. The deeds and honours and knowledge about the natural and spiritual worlds that individuals acquired in their respective lifetimes were inexorably entwined in the fabric of the community and its relationship with others. Stories and songs were essential personal and community cultural properties that were not only highly spiritual in content but were deep affirmations of social and cultural life as well as documenting the historical record. In addition, they had considerable intrinsic value.

The elders are the link to the past that connects First Nations people to the roots of their traditions. The veneration of the role of elder has endured through decades of hardships and cultural oppression. Traditions have survived because the elders have nourished and passed on stories, songs, dances; protected the integrity of the medicine and spiritual world by treating nature with reverence; and respected and honoured the birds, animals, plants, by returning a part of them to the earth.

The wealth of information and knowledge available from First Nations people is diverse, powerful, and traditional. In-depth knowledge of spiritual matters, ceremonies such as the Thirst Dance and cultural traditions involving medicines and plants, involves gaining knowledge that must be earned. The same policy of approaching in the sacred manner applies when people are seeking knowledge of the traditions about singing. All aspects of First Nations cultures involve complex personal, social, cultural, and sacred ceremonies that have powerful spiritual connections passed down through time for thousands of years through the oral tradition. The journey to the healing lodge is also one that needs the guidance of elders and ceremonialists.

Tobacco is offered to elders when asking for help to solve problems or for advice about spiritual matters. This can be done by placing a package of cigarettes, a packet of tobacco, or one cigarette discreetly before the elder. If the offering is accepted, then the visitor can be assured that he or she will be given consideration and help if possible. Storytellers are also honoured with an offering of tobacco which is presented before the storyteller begins telling stories.

Knowledge of the basic tenets of accommodation and the role of elders in First Nations societies are major first steps in helping non-First Nations people learn about customs. Perhaps the most basic and profound custom is the greeting in the form of the handshake. It is a formal recognition of respect and affection to offer one's hand when greeting other people. It is especially appropriate when elders are present to shake hands on meeting and on parting. It is a gesture of openness and goodwill. It is commonly accepted in the First Nations community that non-First Nations people are often so anxious to learn that they affront the culture by asking too many questions without listening. It is especially important to be a good listener when seeking the guidance of elders.

People sometimes make jokes and commentary about "Indian time." This is the cliché that purports to explain that First Nations people have a concept of time that makes them chronically late for appointments. The storyteller Wes Fine Day comments on "White man's time," claiming that preoccupation with watches, clocks and marking time in a European manner is completely foreign to the traditional functioning of Cree society. Wes Fine Day, talking of his days at residential school, remembers the shock of being thrown into an environment that was controlled by loud bells going off to signal the beginning or the end of daily activities. Measuring time in tiny increments by seconds, minutes, and hours; dividing days into units of work and free time; tracking history by precise notations of time combined with the dominate culture's obsession for paperwork and official documents imposed a tyranny of cultural imposition that impacted enormously on northern plains people after the treaties were signed. The resistance to the concept of being ruled by a system of marking time that is foreign to the culture has remained to this day. In its worst manifestation the reference to "Indian time" can be seen as a rude stereotype. The reality is that First Nations people often regard this reference with a kind of amused tolerance. Because of ceremonial, cultural, and social reasons First Nations events usually happen as the participants move into place, not by some precise punctuation set down by a timekeeper. Often, First Nations people see public events as a chance to socialize and visit before the proceedings begin.

In traditional northern plains life, children were only punished under rare circumstances. In addition, they had liberty during the most sacred rites. Many of the customs associated with child rearing have remained till this day. At powwows, storytelling festivals, and other events First Nations children are allowed freedom to circulate as they wish. Allowing children this kind of liberty is quite opposite to the traditions of many non-First Nations cultures. It is no accident that whenever singers begin the children move to the vicinity of the drum and stand as close as they can get to the singers. The explanation is simply that northern plains people believe that when the children run around and play they are playing with the spirit children while all the ancestors look on. The people feel good when they see children laughing, playing and being drawn to the drum.

CHARLES AUGUSTUS PARMER:

THE MAN WHO DIDN'T REALLY EXIST

AT THE PICTURESQUE WILSON MUSEUM in Dundurn, Saskatchewan, there is a plaque installed on a boulder that reads:

CHARLES AUGUSTUS PARMER
LOCAL LEGEND
1839-1935

PARMER CAME TO DUNDURN, SASKATCHEWAN IN 1905
HE HOMESTEADED AT NW 4-34-4 W3, ENGAGING IN
LIVESTOCK PRODUCTION, HIS FINE HORSES WERE A
BOON TO EARLY FARMING AND TRANSPORTATION.

IT IS THOUGHT THAT PARMER WAS A CONFEDERATE
GUERRILLA, A MEMBER OF THE INFAMOUS QUANTRILL
RAIDERS. IN THIS WAY HE WOULD HAVE MET JESSE &
FRANK JAMES. LATER TO MAINTAIN AN ASSOCIATION
WITH THE JAMES GANG, PARMER ADMITTED TO
SHOOTING TWO RUSTLERS WHILE WORKING FOR
BUFFALO BILL CODY AS A FENCE RIDER. FACTS ABOUT
PARMER'S LIFE BEFORE HE EMIGRATED ARE SCANT,
RECLUSIVENESS MADE PARMER BOTH FEARED AND
RESPECTED LOCALLY.

AT THE AGE OF 96, HE DIED AND WAS BURIED ON
CHRISTMAS DAY IN AN UNMARKED GRAVE IN
HILLCREST CEMETERY, DUNDURN.

Erected 1999 by the Dundurn Historical Society

The legend of Charles Augustus Parmer, the 19th-century gunman who lived to the ripe old age of 96, has been avidly promoted by The Dundurn Historical Society. This group sponsored and published a monograph in 1998 by local cowboy poet Harvey Mawson entitled, *Fast Gun: The Life And Times Of Charles Augustus Parmer, Dundurn's Legendary Gunman.* At the back of the monograph is the following statement: "The fondest wishes of the Dundurn Historical Society would come true should the contents of this booklet be deemed to provide sufficient information of historical value to meet the criteria of the Saskatchewan History and Folklore Society's Local History Marker Program."

The details about the Saskatchewan History and Folklore Society's "marker" program are listed at the back of Mr. Mawson's monograph. The gist of it is that, on presentation of enough information and documentation, the Saskatchewan Historical and Folklore Society, a nonprofit organization with partial funding from Saskatchewan Lotteries, will provide a grant to a community organization so that a "metal historical plaque" may be struck and exhibited in order to acknowledge and preserve "an area's historical significance." The plaque situated at the Wilson Museum is evidence that the Dundurn Historical Society's "fondest wishes" were granted.

Fast Gun, an 82 page, letter-size, coil-bound edition with clear plastic covers, contains a series of newspaper and magazine articles as well as reminiscences by various authors including Harvey Mawson who is listed as editor. In his Foreword, Mr. Mawson calls his monograph "a biography with missing chapters." This is an extremely generous interpretation of the contents of this volume. Biography it ain't. The "missing chapters" must contain the proof that is necessary to prove the premises that are supposedly revealed in this publication. Namely that a local man by the name of Charles Augustus Parmer was a member of Quantrill Raiders, and later, a gunman who rode with Jesse James and worked for Buffalo Bill Cody. As it stands, the poorly written chapters that are included in this book go a long way in totally debunking the legend of Charles Augustus Parmer.

With all due respect, *Fast Gun* is the repetition and perpetuation of a number of accounts without much substance that recur in nearly every author's pieces, including those of Mr. Mawson. These airy speculations about Charles Augustus Parmer seem almost totally based on local gossip and unsubstantiated rumours. They have been pulled together by Mr. Mawson in a romantic manner that hearkens back into echoes of wilder times in the 19th century in the American heartland. Why, the mere association with Jesse James sets hearts pounding and invokes the era of the famous James Gang, a story that has captured mass attention throughout the decades and spawned hundreds of books on the subject. James has remained a character in American history whose charisma has never waned. Every aspect of his life has undergone examination. Impostors galore have come forth claiming every kind of relationship with the legendary outlaw. Authors of books on the times and life of Jesse James lament the number of false trails that have been left by people with bogus claims of association by family, friend, or deeds. Genealogical claims, facts and dates that were made 50 or 100 years ago that might have been false were almost impossible to disprove. Today the massive amount of shared research in the writing of so many volumes of history combined with modern technology and researching tools such as the Internet have revolutionized genealogical research and for the most part, have made records far easier to access.

Fast Gun is filled with pictures and maps that locate Charlie Parmer and his son, Earl, on their land not far from the town of Dundurn. In addition, there are numerous pictures of the notorious Jesse James and his brother Frank, as well as pictures of their family and associates and maps that document their lawless pursuits across the American Midwest. The cleverly arranged pastiche of maps and pictures from various eras (from Saskatchewan in the early 1900s back into the America of Jesse James) all mixed together certainly seem to provide a casual reader with enough evidence to believe that Charles Augustus Parmer probably rode with the James Gang.

However, there isn't a scrap of evidence in this rustic monograph that proves that Charles Augustus Parmer was in any way associated with Jesse James — or for that matter, with Buffalo Bill Cody as the plaque prominently displayed at the Wilson Museum suggests.

During their time with Quantrill's Raiders, Frank James and Cole Younger became friends with a man named Allen Parmer. Parmer was suspected of being a member of the James Gang who participated in the Liberty bank robbery on February 13, 1866, but it was never proven. A few years later, on November 24, 1870, Allen Parmer married Frank and Jesse James's sister Susan. Later Parmer moved to Texas with his wife and became a respected landowner, farmer, businessman and politician. Much of the link between Charles Parmer and Jesse James in *Fast Gun* is based on the constant premise that, since Charles's brother Allen was married to Jesse James's sister, Susan, Charles must have had a relationship with Jesse. In her chapter, "Part 2, Gunfighters," Theresa Heuchert asserts that Charles Parmer's brother Allan [sic] was married to James's sister, Susan. This bit of speculation is once again reiterated by Barb Glen in her chapter, "Part 5, Find The Man History Forgot," originally published in 1992 in the *Saskatoon Sun* and in turn by Vera Falk in "Part 6, Parmer Story Relived," first published on June 17, 1997 in the *Davidson Leader*. Later, in another chapter called, "Part 7, Dundurn's Outlaw Farmer," originally published in *Western People*, Theresa Heuchert once again repeats the statement that Charles Parmer's brother Allan [sic] was married to Jesse James's sister. In "Part 8, Second Hand Recollections of Charles Parmer," in an account of his own, Harvey Mawson recollects a conversation he had with Charlie's son, Earl Parmer, where Earl is quoted as stating that his father's brother was married to Jesse James's sister:

"His father never rode with the James' gang. 'He was too young, but he did keep remounts for the boys when they were raiding. Father's brother was one of them. Married Jesse's sister, he did. Moved with her to Texas.' "

In his chapter entitled, "Part 12, What's In A Name," Harvey Mawson writes the most astonishing sentence, part of which he underlines for extra emphasis. "Despite Jesse's objections Allen Parmer courted his only sister and on November 24, 1870, Susan and Parmer were married. (This would make Charles A. Parmer, Jesse's brother-in-law)."

To provide an answer to this constant claim that Charles Augustus Parmer was Allen Parmer's brother I consulted with the researcher Linda Snyder who is an expert on the James family and who has produced *The James-Younger Gang and Their Kinfolk*. Here is her answer to my query about the possibility Charles Parmer was Allen Parmer's brother:

Isaac Parmer [Allen Parmer's father] was listed in the 1850 census as follows:

— 1850 MO Clay County, Platt twp
655/655 24 Sep
Palmer* Isaac 35 m farmer 1200 OH
Barbara 28 f OH
Louisa 7 f MO at school
William 5 m MO at school
Allen 3 m MO
Manery 1 f MO
Bull James 12 m KY at school
McGoffin John 55 m farmer KY

*In the original handwritten document, it is written "Palmer" instead of "Parmer," a frequent occurrence.

Ms. Snyder further went on to write: "If Charles was a son of Isaac and brother of Allen he would be listed as 11 years old here. He would not be the first person to claim relations to the James-Younger bunch. I hope you find him."

To double check Ms. Snyder's proof that Allen Parmer had no sibling named Charles, never mind one born in 1839, I consulted other available reference works on Allen Parmer and found her information to be reliable. I researched Isaac Parmer's numerous siblings to give Charles Augustus the benefit of the doubt that he might have been a cousin who was stretching things to make himself sound more important. I found no male child born in the Parmer family named Charles Augustus Parmer.

Allen Parmer's genealogy is proof that Charles Augustus Parmer was not Allen Parmer's brother and completely refutes any argument contrary to that fact. Further it displays the weak research skills that are possessed by the writers in *Fast Gun* since Allen Parmer's genealogical details are easily discovered in available sources. Harvey Mawson's statement that Charles Augustus Parmer was Jesse James's "brother-in-law" is a strange one, considering the facts.

Another myth that is constantly mentioned in the chapters of *Fast Gun* by its various authors is that Charles Augustus Parmer was a member of Quantrill's Raiders, and that that is how he met the James boys. There is huge interest in the history of the Civil War in the United States which leads to re-enactments and in endless compilations of information about various details of every aspect of the war. On the Kansas Heritage List Server on the Internet, I came into possession of Richard A. Ensminger's work: *Members of Quantrill's Guerrillas in the Civil War*. This remarkable piece of work not only documents every known member of Quantrill's Guerrillas (over 300) but follows up their lives and provides a brief biography of each member. The listing for Allen Parmer is as follows:

Parmer Allen H. survived war
Went to Kentucky with Quantrill, and was surrendered there
by Capt. Henry Parker to Capt Young, US Army, at Samuel's
Depot, Nelson County, Ky on 26 July 1865, paroled.
Died in Wichita Falls, Texas, in 1927. He was a brother-in-law
of Jesse James (married Susan, Jesse's sister).

In this exhaustive research document there is no mention of anyone by the name of Charles Augustus Parmer or any name similar.

The same list of authors who produced the slim chapters in *Fast
Guns* have also perpetuated the notion, without proof, that Parmer
was associated with Buffalo Bill Cody. The most graphic instance
of this fact is displayed in a chapter entitled, "Part 4, Associate of
Notorious Jesse James, Man who Boasted Two Notches on Gun,
Charles A. Parmer Dies Near Dundurn," subtitled "Plainsman, 96,
who Rode For 'Buffalo Bill' Laid to Rest." This account first appeared on December 28, 1935, in the *Saskatoon StarPhoenix* newspaper. The unidentified author of this obituary article produced a
question and answer session with Charles Augustus Parmer based
on an interview Parmer gave to visitors who came out to see him
at his homestead in 1932.

Did you join Jesse James' gang? was the obvious question.
Then Parmer would tell how the famed outlaw asked him
what he could do. "I told him I could shake any big man." But
James had told him he wasn't bad enough. "You haven't killed
anyone," he told Parmer.

"So he sent me to Bill Cody [Buffalo Bill] and I worked
with Bill for nearly two years as a fence rider." On that job
Parmer would speak of his famous chestnut mare, to which he
attributed saving his life on one occasion.

The old range rider told of riding into a pair of toughs who
were branding cattle for rustling. "One pulled his colt .45 on

me and so did I, but I jumped the mare at him and knocked him off his horse. He began shooting as he fell, but I settled him," Parmer often related.

"Just then, I felt a streak of fire through my hip. I was wounded by the other fellow, but I whipped around and got him, as he ran. Then the old man would tell how he rode 14 miles to a doctor, who lifted him from his horse. His boot was full of blood. But they found two dead men there," he gloated.

William F. Cody, known widely as "Buffalo Bill," was a famous figure in the old west. Many historians have claimed that by 1900 Cody was the most recognizable public figure on earth. Buffalo hunter, Pony Express Rider, wrangler, Civil War veteran, stagecoach driver, scout for the US Cavalry in the Indian wars, Bill Cody was a showman and entrepreneur. Buffalo Bill Wild West Show, a circus-like production with 1200 performers, travelled in North America for 20 years and toured widely in Europe. Cody built and founded cattle ranches, railways, newspapers and towns in his beloved state of Wyoming. Friend of Presidents, Kings, Emperors, music hall stars, famous writers and celebrities of every ilk, Buffalo Bill left behind a substantial record of his personal life and business affairs.

If anybody can make a legitimate link between Jesse James and Buffalo Bill Cody I would certainly be eager to see the proof. Hollywood has taken the liberty to portray them together inaccurately in a number of movies, including Walter Hills's *The Long Riders*. An endless stream of western schlock in badly written pamphlets, articles and books over the decades have corrupted history by making bogus claims about associations and relationships between historical figures from the "Wild West." While they were contemporaries, Cody (b. 1846) and James (b. 1847) lived very different lives. Buffalo Bill was a flamboyant self-promoter and pop star of the times who has been accused of inventing many of the details about his life that have been turned into historical gospel.

Jesse James, constantly on the run and wary of every turn in the road, lived under aliases and maintained a low profile. Cody lived a long life. In the end, he endured the ignominy of watching poor investments and rising debts greatly reduce his once impressive holdings. He expired of natural causes on January 10, 1917, at his sister's home in Denver, Colorado. James, living under the alias Mr. Howard in St. Joseph, Missouri, was shot down while in his mid-thirties on April 3, 1882, in his own home by an associate.

The famous St. James Hotel in Cimmeron, New Mexico claims to have numbered among its patrons both Buffalo Bill Cody and Jesse James in a guest register that reads like a catalogue of names from the "Old West." Cody stayed there along with Annie Oakley when he was mounting his wild west shows. James patronized the hotel on several occasions always staying in room 14, signing the register with the alias R.H. Howard. However, there is no claim or proof that Cody and James actually stayed at the hotel on the same dates.

My research indicates that it is unlikely James and Buffalo Bill Cody ever met one another. There is no source to corroborate the fact that they did. William F. Cody was a well-to-do business-man and empire builder. Jesse James was a low-life gunman who robbed banks and murdered people along the way. It seems pretty obvious they moved in different circles.

It defies the known record to speculate that Buffalo Bill Cody ever encountered Jesse James, never mind knew him well enough that Jesse could send his friends to him to get them employment. This outrageous claim quoted from the lips of Charles Augustus Parmer certainly gives the reader a great deal of insight into Mr. Parmer's character. He seems be a man somewhat concerned with building himself a mythology based on rubbing shoulders with major figures of his times.

I contacted the Buffalo Bill Historical Centre in Cody, Wyoming, an institution that is devoted to the legacy left behind by the great man, and requested they search Cody's papers and public record to see if there were any references to Charles Augustus Parmer. The researchers at this institution were cooperative in dealing with my requests. The fact that it was alleged that Charles Augustus Parmer had killed two rustlers and been shot up himself while working for Buffalo Bill made him of interest to the museum staff. After a few weeks time they reported back that they could find no evidence anyone by that name was ever employed by Mr. Cody, nor could they find reference to the above mentioned dramatic incident. They also provided information that Jesse James was not a known associate of Buffalo Bill. William Cody lived a spectacular life and left a well-documented popular legacy that is not easily broken into.

One of the maddening defects inherent in this monograph is the lack of attention put into editorial details. Thus, as well as being a volume without indices, names and places are sometimes muddled. For example, the name Allen Parmer appears in some of the articles as "Allan Parmer" and the supposed birth place of Charles Augustus Parmer on May 13, 1839, in Ohio is listed as Brookville, Brooksville, and in one instance Brookfield.

In the chapter designated as, "Part 12, What's In A Name," Harvey Mawson has documented the car trip that two local Dundurn area couples, Harry and Anne Friesen and Glen and Verna Peters, made on behalf of the Dundurn Historical Society. The four individuals went to a great deal of trouble and expense to travel the vast distance to Brookville, Ohio, the reported birthplace of Charles Augustus Parmer. However, their journey of discovery turned out to be futile. After visiting the local Brookville Community Museum and Genealogy Research Library, they were not able to locate any information about the birth or the early life of Charles Augustus Parmer.

During the past six years, Dolores Reimer, an experienced genealogical researcher, and I have spent a good number of hours searching for information about Charles Augustus Parmer. We have investigated the records in the Montgomery, Drake, Miami and Preble Counties that are represented by the Genealogical Research Library at Brookville, Ohio, without any luck. There are definitely Parmer (Palmer) families in these locations, but we have yet to find a match.

We found a Charles A. Parmer born in 1839 in Ohio, but he turned out to be a prominent attorney who died in 1914 in Indianapolis, Indiana. His official given names turned out to be Charles Anthony. We thought we had struck pay dirt when we found a Charles Augustus Parmer who was born within two years of the 1839 birth date of our Charles Augustus Parmer. However, it turned out this Parmer was a black man and, as well, we were able to locate his death date. We are aware that the name Parmer and Palmer have often been alternated in the same families and that because early records (birth, deaths, census) were written by hand that it is possible for "Parmer" to be easily transposed as "Palmer" and vice versa. Keeping that in mind in all our research attempts we have consistently searched for both "Parmer" and "Palmer." In addition to searching for a birth reference for Charles Augustus Parmer we have also investigated various Parmer/Palmer family histories and talked with Parmer family historians. We spent an inordinate amount of time investigating US census information during the mid to end of the 19ᵗʰ century in Ohio (stated birthplace of Charles Augustus Parmer) and in Pennsylvania (where Parmer claims to have gone with his family) as well as in Missouri (birthplace of the James boys) and in Kansas (the state in which it is reported that Parmer and his son Earl lived before they emigrated to Canada in 1905). After several years of looking and coming up empty of finding a trace of Mr. Parmer we suspended our beliefs somewhat and began look for him in New York State, New England and other American regions including California. We found a few males born with the name Charles Augustus Parmer but after investigation none proved to be a match. Then we changed our strategy and began looking for records on Earl Parmer, the son who emigrated to Canada with Charles Parmer, hoping to pick up a thread to follow through his vital statistics. Earl Parmer, buried in an unmarked grave next to Charles Augustus, was born 1870, according to references in *Fast Gun*, and died in 1950 at the age of 80. Again, after pursuing a number of possibilities, we ultimately came up empty handed.

In six years we have not been able to find a birth record or any proof of the existence of a man named Charles Augustus Parmer or for that matter of his son Earl in any of the US locales we have attempted to search. Dolores Reimer points out that it was possible for an adult in the late 1800s in the United States to avoid the census taker and to live in the underground without leaving much of a trail but it was impossible for an infant or a child to accomplish the same feat. Birth and death records are pretty hard for any man to avoid. Local folks who champion the notion of old Charlie Parmer the bank robber riding with Jesse James will tell you that nobody kept or cared about records in the era that Charlie was born; genealogists will wisely tell you otherwise.

The complete absence of any reference to Charles Augustus Parmer (and his son) in the arenas it is purported he operated in would lead one to believe that he used another name when he resided in the United States. He is reported in the *Saskatoon Star-Phoenix* by his own words to have been somewhat of a "faker." It is possible he lived under a number of aliases.

Before his arrival in Canada in 1905 at the age of 66 (rather old for a homesteader) there is absolutely no trace of Mr. Parmer at any of the access points that his supporters claim are reference points in his much acclaimed adventurous life. Not only can we not prove that Mr. Parmer was an American but we cannot prove that his son Earl, at age 35, who emigrated to Canada with him was really his son. Earl is as elusive as his father was in avoiding detection by birth, census and other records while living in the United States. Once entering Canada, listing himself as a farmer from Kansas, Charles Parmer, and son, becomes totally transparent, completely opposite to the pattern of his 66 years living in the

United States. In various homestead renewals that are filed in subsequent years Parmer lists himself as born in Ohio and a widower with two children. Charles Augustus Parmer's records exist in the Saskatchewan Archives for anyone to access. My partner and fellow researcher Dolores Reimer and I have copies of Mr. Parmer's homestead papers which were filed in Hanley District on May 16, 1905, and papers from subsequent filings for renewals.

We have copies of the pages of the 1906 census that locate Charles and Earl on their homestead near Dundurn. Coincidentally the local census record taker was Harvey Mawson's great grandfather, John Mawson, a remarkable pioneer in his own right who has left his own indelible legacy on the region. While in Canada the various newspaper accounts of Parmer's life before he crossed the border gradually begin to take shape in the series of newspaper accounts that appear throughout the decades, primarily in the Saskatoon press. How is it that a man with a notorious past, who leaves absolutely no trace of his existence in the United States can over a period of time become a well-known character in Canada? Somebody had to be talking to somebody for these larger than life accounts of Mr. Parmer's life to become a matter of public record in his newly adopted country.

(To be fair and accurate, there are a number of older members of the Dundurn and area communities who are of the conviction that nearly everything about Charles Parmer's reputation was made up by others and that the old man and his son were completely tight-lipped about the past. Nearly everybody in Dundurn, young or old, has an opinion about the legend of Charles Augustus Parmer. Some are openly hostile at any deviance from the story they have heard no matter what the public record reveals. Another faction of old timers seems to believe that history is a sacred trust that must not be disturbed too much lest it become something different than what they have been entrusted with. It's as if they are the keepers of a secret story that nobody is supposed to talk about. Two of the prime sources who are quoted and mentioned in the various chapters of *Fast Gun*, Johnny Bethune and Alex Sawchuck, who were Parmer's neighbours, are always praised as being honourable men who told the truth as they knew it. A simple conversation about the validity of the Parmer legend sets coffee row buzzing with grousing and speculation. It was delicately explained to me in the following terms by one of my neighbours: "Why, what in thunder possessed you to open that can of worms?")

The most startling realization that comes out of this mysterious lack of information is that Charles Augustus Parmer probably wasn't Charles Augustus Parmer at all but a man who created an identity for himself (probably using a false name) for some unknown reason. Perhaps he took on the name Parmer because it allowed him to feed off the conjecture that his brother was married to the infamous outlaw Jesse James's sister and thus elevated him into a kind of companionship with the immortal gunman. If that was his rationale, it certainly was a solid strategy because it accomplished that fact aided by the good citizens of The Dundurn Historical Society.

The famous Canadian spy master William Stephenson once said: "Nothing deceives like a document." In the case of Charles Augustus Parmer, that premise might be altered to read: Nothing deceives like a lack of documents. That's not to say Parmer wasn't an interesting guy who probably lived a life fairly close to the one he hankered for. He walked around armed to the teeth, gave everybody the willies with the two notches on his handgun's handle and the limp that suggested that he had been badly shot up. He handled weapons with a dexterity that enhanced his reputation as a gunman. His formal manner put off some of his neighbours and gained him a local reputation as a man not to be trifled with. Yet others found him to be a lovable curmudgeon who cared deeply for his son and his friend's daughter. He was a noted horseman and an honest businessman who had the respect of his community.

Why would a crotchety old guy want to project such a dastardly image as that of the western desperado in hiding or in retirement?

Fast Gun points out that rumours abounded that Parmer might have had half a million dollars in American gold coins stashed somewhere on his property. Was he afraid some local thugs might blow his brains out just for the thrill of saying that he killed the man who rode with Jesse? Obviously he was, or he wouldn't have bothered to booby trap his porch and the door and window frames in his shack. On his trips to town he wouldn't have put on his shoulder holster with its .38 calibre pistol or carried his loaded .44 calibre revolver under his coat. He was living in Canada in the relatively peaceful countryside, not in the lawless American west. He had the locals convinced that he was once a bad dude and nobody dared step too far out of line in his presence lest they gain some ventilation from one of his many weapons for he was a man in love with his guns. They were an extension of his personality.

Fast Gun contains some entertaining stories about Parmer's acumen with his arsenal of weapons as well as stories about the details of his life homesteading near Dundurn and his interactions with the local community. In almost every case the reminiscences of various folks who personally knew the Parmers end up speculating about Charlie Parmer's possessions which people avidly collected after Earl Parmer's death. A saddle that bears the initials of Jesse James, said to be given by James to Parmer has found its way into the hands of a local Dundurn farmer. From time to time individuals have contacted the Dundurn Historical Society with offers to sell them weapons that are purported to have belonged to the long dead gunman. In the chapter, "Part II, Cold Steel And Hard Ground," Mawson admitting there is no documentation to support his argument, spins off into fantasy with the question, "Was this trusty .44 [Parmer's revolver] given to Charlie Parmer by Jesse James?" His foundation for his premise that Parmer's Belgian-made Smith and Wesson replica might have been a gift from James to Parmer is based on some fuzzy notion about Jesse James's "widely known generosity," and he concludes this is a "definite possibility," without presenting any evidence.

By his own admission, Charles Augustus Parmer had lived his life as a "farmer" and "faker." In the Part 4 obituary chapter from the December 28th, 1935, edition of the *StarPhoenix* that I quoted from earlier in this article, Parmer was asked a number of questions in 1932:

> Parmer would snort when asked if he fought in the Civil War. "Naw," he would answer. "I came to Canady and got myself a substitute. I got substitutes for a lot of my neighbours that were drafted," he would explain.
>
> The old faker would tell how he built a "petrified man" out of cement. He used a living man for the cast. "The people bit like fleas," he would chuckle afterwards explaining the reason he got rid of the petrified man was because other showmen copied the idea. "I traded him in for a farm."

In "Part 5, Finding The Man History Forgot," Barb Glen of the *Saskatoon Sun* reports: "In 1933 the *Saskatoon StarPhoenix* asked Parmer point blank if he was a member of the legendary bank robber's [Jesse James] gang. Typically a man of few words, all he would say about James is, 'I knew him.'"

Despite the notions of high idealism and honour that Harvey Mawson attributes to Charles Augustus Parmer and to his son Earl, we can only retreat to Parmer's own words in an attempt to understand his personality. Two separate reports that appeared in the *Saskatoon StarPhoenix* in 1932 and 1933 quoted Charles Augustus Parmer as claiming a personal relationship with Jesse James. These are not just statements of hearsay but are quotes attributed directly to Parmer from a reputable source. So much for the theory that Charles Augustus was a close-mouthed man who avoided speaking of his past. In these two documented cases he has no difficulty in making his claims publicly in a newspaper of record.

In his chapter near the end of the booklet, "Part 12, What's In a Name," in summing up Harvey Mawson wrote:

Who was Charles Augustus Parmer? We know, of a certainty that no one ever came forward to verify his stories of high adventure. All of his statements concerning his life before he came to homestead at Dundurn must stand on their own merit. As it has never been reported that anyone called the old man a prevaricator while he lived there seems to be no earthly reason to call him a liar now.

I beg to differ. The scholarship in *Fast Gun* is substandard, the lack of documentation in the form of footnotes, references, editorial direction, credit for pictures, photographs and maps means that the quest to identify and document Charles Augustus Parmer has failed in the most lamentable manner. The fact is, "no one ever came forward to verify his [Parmer's] stories of high adventure," because they were probably nothing but a collection of invalidated malarkey. The premise that Parmer's own statements about his life before he came to Canada must be taken on their own merit is preposterous considering how poorly his statements stand up under the light of even cursory investigation.

In his own words, Charles Augustus Parmer admitted to being a "faker" and a carnival man who travelled around with a phoney petrified man fleecing the suckers. Now, 70 years after his death, the old gunman has become a household name in these parts, has an honoured place in the local museum, and a legacy on the Dundurn Elementary School website, and he continues to con the suckers into promoting his dubious reputation.

The sad facts are, there are many worthier local heroes who should be honoured in the Dundurn area, including the founder of Dundurn and important Saskatchewan agricultural pioneer, Emil J. Milieke, author of a seminal prairie book, *Leaves From the Life of a Pioneer*, the scientist Henry Thode, and John Mawson the patriarch of the Mawson family and the first rancher to come to this region. These three men and others are far worthier candidates for a "metal historical plaque" than the might-have-been gunman of

Dundurn. They are all far better role models for our young people and for future generations.

What exactly was Charles Augustus Parmer's claim to fame? Parmer was certainly not a humanitarian or a man who inspired his fellow citizens to reach out to others or do good works. No, he was associated with the darker side of life. His supporters fantasized that he rode with Quantrill's murderous guerrillas and participated in Jesse James's reign of terror, robbing banks and shooting innocent townies in the process. Parmer's mystique was rooted in the fact that he handled his guns like a professional and he lived for nearly 100 years. Most gunman in the old west with notches on their Colts went to their maker not long into their twenties. By all appearances the man who called himself Charles Augustus Parmer was an eccentric man who got the most out of his God given talent. There is no record to support the contention that Charles Augustus Parmer was ever born. Most likely the man who wore Parmer's boots was somebody else. In the case of Charles Augustus Parmer, it is likely the Saskatchewan Historical and Folklore Society and the Dundurn Historical Society honour a man who didn't really exist.

EAGLESMITH

I was born on a Greyhound bus
My momma was a diesel engine
Fred Eaglesmith
"I Like Trains"

ON A WINDY HIGHWAY IN NORTH AMERICA any time of day or
night you're liable to come upon a 1958 Wing touring bus headed
to the next gig down the highway. More than likely its driver is
the ubiquitous Fred J. Eaglesmith, song writer and performer who
travels with his band and tours 290 nights a year playing in beer
joints and dance halls across Canada and the United States with
jaunts across the water to European destinations.

Eaglesmith, who frequently tours the UK, is popular in the
Netherlands, the country of his ancestors (the Elgermas family
from Friesland), and on the other side of the world in Australia,
another country that has warmed up to the wandering troubadour
spirit that haunts Eaglesmith's every performance. One can hardly
assume that the old bus makes its way across the water. Fred and
his band of travelling musicians do. I can see them clearly, rocking through a cloud of smoke in beautiful downtown Rotterdam
or playing in dusty saloons in the Australian outback where thirst
is slaked with small cold beers.

Eaglesmith is a modern phenomenon, a country singer/song writer/bluegrass picker/rock star/roots singer, who eschews fame and the life that goes with it to be a good ol' boy fronting a band and driving the bus between engagements. Eaglesmith also keeps the bus running, not a hard job for a preacher's son farm boy, one of nine children, who grew up poor on a marginal family farm and has stayed a farmer/handyman with firm ideas about where and how he wants to live.

For years he was anchored on a farm near Port Dover, Ontario, where he employed wind and solar power and remained firmly embedded in his rural lifestyle. Now his son lives there while Fred mostly inhabits Port Dover. Sadly, his home, a studio on a dock on Lake Erie, burned down in the spring of 2006. When he's home, Eaglesmith paints. His pictures have been exhibited at the Lighthouse Theatre Art Gallery in Port Dover and at the Rockingham Arts & Museum Project in Bellow Falls, Vermont. Fred owns his own music company called A Major Label, and is completely oblivious to the siren call from the contemporary music industry. In an interview with Jedd Ferris on February 3, 2006, in the *Asheville Citizen-Times* in North Carolina, Eaglesmith offers his own succinct comment on his own situation: "I'm trying to get away from making just another American record. I'm burned out on that. It's 2006 and our music needs to move forward or it's going to become another ghetto. That's what country music became for years. Somebody has got to say, 'I'm not going to do it safe.'"

Fred Eaglesmith is a rebel with a cause, an outsider who has built a career in the entertainment business from trial and error. He has evolved into an underground star who is not particularly in search of publicity, fame, or fortune. Although in 1997 Eaglesmith won a Juno Award for *Drive-In Movie* and his work constantly appears in the top ten CDs of the year by music publications, he remains an independent commercial entity. In interviews with newspaper music critics, Eaglesmith often comments that he is famous enough already and his financial needs are being met.

He travels endlessly, playing dates in every corner of the continent with a need to write songs and play music as much as he can. Appearing at a sold out concert at the German Concordia Club in Saskatoon, Saskatchewan, in April of 2006 Eaglesmith remarked, "This is as good as it gets for me."

Eaglesmith has an immense profile on the Internet, where a lot of his CDs are sold. The Fred Eaglesmith Daily Digest and The Eaglesmith Port Putley Digest have lively postings from the fan base that follows his ever evolving career. Eaglesmith is a surprising man. He seldom stands pat for long. The only constant thing about Fred Eaglesmith's band is his long collaborative relationship with the legendary Willie P. Bennett (Juno Award for *Heartstrings*, Best Roots & Traditional Solo Album, 1999), which has been going on for 21 years. Eaglesmith has always played with a group of stellar musicians that have included, among others, Ralph Shipper, Washboard Hank, Kim Deschamps, Craig Bignell, Peter Von Althen, Roger Marin, Darcy Yates, Dan Walsh, Kori Heppner, and Luke Stackhouse. In addition, Eaglesmith's songs have been covered by the Cowboy Junkies, Chris Knight, Mary Gauthier, Dar Williams, James King, Kasey Chambers, Blackie and the Rodeo Kings and are heard on the soundtracks of Martin Scorsese and James Caan films.

An energetic group of fans, supporters, or devotees, estimated to number somewhere around 10,000 by Fred's own estimate, call themselves Fredheads. These fans are predictable. They are willing to go to great lengths to get to his live shows. In January, 2006, in one of the Digests, someone wondered how it would have worked out if Eaglesmith's first name was "Dick."

Fredheads socialize long before the band hits the stage. There is a buzz of electricity in the air when they set eyes on the '58 Wing parked on the street or in the parking lot. If you look closely the guy with his head in the works is probably Fred. This is a man who communicates well with his own species and has absolutely no pretentiousness about him. Fred Eaglesmith is a down-to-earth, common man, a decent man who writes songs about his times. He performs them with a rollicking band between deadpan discourses on his reason for being here at this place in time. The result is a series of Fred Eaglesmith weekends, including the "Northern Picnic" at Cobalt and the annual "Charity Picnic" at Aylmer, both in Ontario, as well as at Bellows Falls, Vermont, and at historic Gruene Hall in New Braunfels near San Antonio, Texas. These events attract the hard core devotees who come from afar, camp out and participate by playing music and jamming as well as enjoying the entertainment provided by Fred and his friends. The "Rocket through the Rockies" is an annual train trip that Fred and his musician friends and fans take across the Canadian mountain wilderness to the west coast. Eaglesmith has written a number of railway songs, including "Freight Train," "I Like Trains," and "49 Tons" that rival the best in that tradition, as exemplified by Roy Acuff who wrote "The Wabash Cannonball," "Freight Train Blues," and "Midnight Train to Memphis." Eaglesmith is a throwback to earlier decades in country music when performers like Acuff travelled across the country by bus or train and played every night in honkytonks, roadhouses or in ornate theatres.

By his own estimate, Eaglesmith has written 1,000 or more songs. He is constantly writing and recording in what can only be regarded as his spare time between tours. Eaglesmith is a modern troubadour with an incredible catalogue of songs. He performs, solo or with Willie or with bands named The Fred Eaglesmith Trio, The Flying Squirrels, The Smokin' Losers, or The Flathead Noodlers, depending on the circumstances and the personnel, in an annual series of tours that criss-cross Canada and the United States. Wherever Eaglesmith plays fans send the Internet sites reports about the performances, often with complete playlists and commentary about Fred's remarks and the nature of the crowd. Fred's already hours long gone down the highway, headed a few hundred miles to the next theatre or hall, passing by the small-town and whistle-stop exits that define every highway. This is living life to the max: a bus with eight bunks and owner-driver Fred Eaglesmith, by choice a small business in an industry dominated by sharks. Imagine Mariah Carey or Puff Daddy trying to figure out Fred Eaglesmith.

What sets Eaglesmith apart from many of his countrymen is his affection for what has been called the "average American." Fred Eaglesmith first achieved recognition in the United States and his fan base in that country has been increasing as his reputation has grown legendary. Both Digests have plenty to say about a wide range of contemporary roots and country music. The musicians that have left Fred to go off on their own or join up with other bands are not abandoned. Their gigs also get advertised. It is true there is a subtext by a small group of insider fans but it's generally not offensive. The information that gets passed along speaks volumes about the community of Eaglesmith. From time to time there is plenty of controversy brewing. It might be about the fact Eaglesmith has been spotted arriving at a gig in an SUV or is being pilloried by critics for speaking or singing with an American accent. Months of brouhaha fulminated on the Digests about Fred's recording and release of a CD called *Dusty*. This solo album backed by strings and keyboards went too far awry for many Eaglesmith devotees. There is no doubt Eaglesmith is appreciative of his fans but it is obvious he pays no attention to the day-to-day gossip that follows him around on the Internet. In an interview with Fish Griwkowsky in the *Edmonton Sun*, Eaglesmith was quoted as saying: "They got very culty, is how I saw it. It's not like I'm a Christ figure, it's more like, 'he's a normal guy like us thing.' It's very weird, except I like them because they didn't have to do it."

The most interesting aspect of the two Digests is the cultural and political exchanges that take place between Canadian and American fans. Cultural differences are apparent and political realities are manifest in endless reams of material. However, there is little acrimony or rage and the politics is often handled with a joke or a satirical reply. Fredheads on both sides of the border are approximately the same. Their differences are perhaps best explained by the demands of their cultures. Eaglesmith talks about Canada on his US tours and while in Canada urges Canadians to separate ordinary working class Americans from the policies of their political masters. The Eaglesmith philosophy goes something like this, "Don't sweat the small things." That and the subject matter of his songs, which document the general demise of rural life, the loss of the family farm, the romance of the open road, the mystique of the railway, and the often-told story of love gone wrong, are all important components in defining the Eaglesmith personae. His music somehow imposes a kind of truce on his fans when they get going on one another in political arguments. The cross-cultural effect has made Fred Eaglesmith a lightning rod for a broader discussion about contemporary country, roots, blues, rock and alternative music. Eaglesmith appeals to fans around the world who for the most part have abandoned popular culture because it is too infused with plastic at all levels.

I first noticed Fred Eaglesmith about 10 years ago in a picture in a newspaper article. He was leaning against a car talking about the show he was about to play at the Broadway Theatre in Saskatoon. A few weeks before, I had heard a cut from one of his CDs on CBC Radio in Regina. The 500-seat theatre was filled when Fred and his band, the Flying Squirrels, hit the stage. Willie P. Bennett on mandolin and harmonica and the ultimate percussion guy, a man named Washboard Hank, were pretty vivid characters. The Eaglesmith band lit up the classic old building. Fred Eaglesmith talked, told jokes, played his songs and the audience danced in the aisles. They had come from near and far and they were primed for what they received. Running Fred Eaglesmith's name on the Internet will bring up about 140,000 hits. One quickly finds out his 16 CDs are for the most part unavailable except through Eaglesmith's website. I have come across the odd one in a main stream outlet, they are more often found second-hand in an alternative music store, head shop or bookstore. Hmmmh, it seems there is an underground economy, especially in funkier parts of the country. Imagine my surprise in the summer of 2004 when I entered the hallway of Friends Café in Dundurn, Saskatchewan, and I discovered a poster advertising Fred Eaglesmith appearing at Darrin Qualman's big red barn on the back road about five miles from town. The event was billed as a fundraiser for child hunger and the ticket price included dinner.

On the evening of July 3, 2004, a crowd began to gather on the Qualman farm where a 1958 Wing tour bus was already parked beside the barn. Glorious summer weather embraced the big old barn in the midst of a vast hay field that was filled with round bales for as far as the eye could see. A Saskatoon band named the Spiffs opened the show playing Bob Marley tunes as well as an eclectic mix of blues and rock covers. Later in the show Fred referred to them as the "Spliffs." The venue, a stately red barn, a hundred feet long by sixty feet wide, built by three carpenters during the summer of 1918, is a classic structure in great condition. Qualman has done a great job in adding a bar and rewiring the place and as a result he is in possession of a first class dance hall in the finest prairie tradition. Two hundred and fifty people paid $25 a head to hear and see Fred play two sets on a stunning warm summer night with a million stars overhead in a completely isolated rural area about 35 km from Saskatoon. Tickets sold out quickly by a few notices being put up in public places in neighbouring towns and by word of mouth. The organizers said as soon as notice of the event hit the Internet they received inquiries from all over North America. There are always people travelling vast distances from diverse locales in search of their Eaglesmith fix.

The event was a fund raiser for a local child hunger and education program (CHEP). Fred and the band started cooking right off the bat. The crowd danced from the beginning to the end of both sets. Fred stated that there was a rule concerning musicians who played in classic barns. He said they got the right to acquire all vehicles and motors that have been in the barn for more than

20 years. Fred was interested in acquiring a motor that was stored in the lower section of the building. Darrin Qualman was heard to state, "That might be a good place to start negotiations to get Fred back for next year." Fred cracked a few jokes about the band, notably about crossing the border with Darcy Yates. The band thundered through the ancient building like a train coming down the tracks in a barn with better acoustics than most concert halls. Willie P. Bennett's solos, vibrant and haunting, were worth the price of admission on their own. Fred Eaglesmith, master song writer, consummate performer with the legendary Willie P. and a tight energized band on a summer night, surrounded by hayfields on the northern plains. What could be better? Nothing. Near the end of the second set Fred announced that the band was leaving right after the show down the highway to Dauphin, Manitoba. The band came back for an encore that drove the audience into a dancing frenzy as everyone realized the show was coming to an end. Eaglesmith and his band members packed their own equipment onto the bus and visited with fans while the rest of the audience sat down for a farm-style midnight dinner of roast beef and all the trimmings. Darrin Qualman's 85-year-old barn had been blessed by the music of Fred Eaglesmith.

In 2005 I was invited to perform my poetry on the spoken word stage at The South Country Fair that has been going on in southern Alberta for two decades beside the Oldman River, on the outskirts of Fort MacLeod, Alberta, in the foothills of the Rockies. When the organizers sent me a package I was pleasantly surprised to see that I was going to be on stage on Saturday night just before Fred Eaglesmith. The South Country Fair, a gathering of the tribes interested in various artistic disciplines, includes a spoken word venue and a main stage for musical acts. The weekend attracts an audience of several thousand who camp out and party enthusiastically for three days in one of the most scenic regions of the country. The promoter, Maureen Chambers, always promises an interesting lineup of amazing performers and delivered big time that year. The list of artists included McQuaig, Cousin Harley and the Piglets, Captain Tractor, The Bills, Gary Comeau and the Voodoo All Stars, as well as Fred Eaglesmith and his pal Willie P. Bennett (who was also appearing at the fair as a soloist).

The fair got off to an auspicious start on Friday night with some remarkable performers tearing up the night while fires crackled and a mellow audience settled into a long night of celebration. By early Saturday morning the skies had darkened and thunder rumbling in the distance soon closed in. A hard relentless rain came down on the venues turning the walkways and roads into muddy paths. At least a temporary respite from the hordes of blood thirsty mosquitoes that had occupied the evening with their insatiable appetites. Despite the weather the performers went on while the audience found relief under tarps and tents. By late afternoon, the trails and pathways were drying out and the affable Fred Eaglesmith was spotted in his weathered Stetson in the cook house. At 8:00 pm the skies were clear and the sun was shining in the willows when Fred Eaglesmith with Dan Walsh and Willie P. Bennett took to the main stage.

Fred said it had been seven years since he last played the South Country Fair, a venue he broke into when he was recommended to the organizers by Willie P. Bennett. Willie, a musical legend in his own right, has been called "The Jimi Hendrix of the Mandolin" by an enthusiastic critic. He and Fred exchanged some banter about Willie taking to wearing bad hats everywhere and Fred navigated his way through a wide selection of his classic and new favourite songs. He played "White Rose," "Lipstick Lies & Gasoline," "I Shot Your Dog," "49 Tons," as well as "Crowds" from his *Dusty* CD and the John Deere tractor song and a song about a woman named Evelyn. Fred took some pot-shots about the nature of Albertans and on Canadian politics as well as commenting on why he thought he should never write another song about a dog. After a loud mechanical noise in the distance got Fred's attention he asked the audience what it was. Voices yelled out that it was the "shit truck" come to empty the port-a-cans. Fred thought they were saying "chip truck." He muttered on about waiting for the "chip truck" to leave while the enormous hulking "shit truck" did its business and then bumped its way over the muddy road and out of the fair grounds. Dan Walsh on dobro and Willie on harmonica and mandolin played up a storm with an animated Fred who seemed to have also taken up doing monologues and stand-up comedy. The crowd at the South Country Fair grooved on the show while the sun spread over the bush tops.

At the end of his set, Fred came back out on the stage alone and played a strange song about a place in southern Ontario called "Bobs, Dogs and Burgs," really as much a monologue as a song.

"See you again," he yells to the crowd, or, "Catch you next time."

Fred makes himself available at the merchandise stand to meet his fans and sign CDs before he vanishes under the star map of a prairie night. He is a song writer and artist who depends almost exclusively on live performances and word of mouth to sustain his musical career. Fred Eaglesmith is only as good as he was playing his last job. He is not mastered by a corporate image-making machine and mustered like a resource in commercial campaigns that maximize the artist's exposure to the main stream. You won't find him on television very often, occasionally on CMT and the CBC but seldom on commercial radio and you'll never find him on Letterman. His music is not available in the music market-place, but it's easy to get on the Internet. You can get it from Fred live, and with it you might consider buying a CD, a Fredhead button, an Eaglesmith tire gauge or a "Fredhead with bedhead" door hanger, for your next stay in a hotel, if you're so inclined. If you're like me, you'll be happy you caught Fred Eaglesmith in a classic old theatre, in a vintage red barn on a farm or on an outdoor stage beside the Oldman River. It's the kind of place you have to go to find him. Eaglesmith is an old-fashioned artist in an new-fangled world that is being vastly altered by changing technology. He is a song writer and a performer who owns his own music and he has successful fans. Without being hyped by any of the conventional apparatus that surrounds a musical star, Eaglesmith is sustained by a computer literate fan base that is geared to attending his live performances in character venues, buys his CDs and is knowledgeable about his music. They have spread the news by word of mouth and by word in cyberspace. The result is that Fred, along with Alanis Morissette and Bono, has become a spokesperson for Oxfam's Make Trade Fair and Make Poverty History campaigns.

In his February 3, 2006, interview in the *Asheville Citizen-Times*, Eaglesmith talked about his supporters:

> "Fredheads are great fans," Eaglesmith said. "I talked to a guy last night that came to see me here in Florida from Holland. But I'm not sure it's as much about me as it is the association with other people. Soon I think they'll be like Deadheads and just stay out in the parking lot. I wouldn't blame them, I see some people at eight shows in a row and think, 'You've got to be tired of this. I am just not that interesting'."

If you're inclined to check Eaglesmith out, your best chance is to get on the Internet and take a look at his yearly schedule which will be posted on his website. Chances are, if you live in North America, Eaglesmith will be appearing somewhere not far from where you reside. Nearly every night of the week for months at a time, in any recent year in memory, Fred Eaglesmith has been on the road in his succession of touring buses to meet his fans face to face. The venue will be funky and tickets affordable. There is no accounting for popular success or taste. Just about every manifestation of human behaviour is celebrated in theatre on the screen or in song. In the age of supercharged image making machinery and ultra mass conformity Fred Eaglesmith is an outsider who has built a reputation on being an alternative to the commercially driven market that dispenses fame and fortune from the dominant culture's Pez dispenser.

SOLITUDE

I ARRIVED AT ST. PETER'S ABBEY (est. 1903) in Muenster, Saskatchewan, a Benedictine monastery with a working mixed farm, market garden, a printing plant, a college, a Press and a fine newspaper, *The Prairie Messenger*, during the harvest of 1999. I was grateful for the opportunity to occupy a room in the guest wing, Severin Hall, for part of each week for one year during my term as writer-in-residence in the nearby town of Humboldt. By this fortunate appointment, I managed to witness the yearly cycle of the seasons in the life of a Benedictine monastery between intense bouts of pondering the works of local writers, finding the time to balance the energy drain from community involvement and writing my own text. It is the practice of my life to always be working on another book, and usually nothing can interrupt the transmission of the signal. My vision has been described as "that of a very artistic Martian." While it is disappointing to admit I am not a Martian, I admit to being a full-time poet, who on occasion writes prose, not a position I would encourage anyone to advertise. It is a habit that has been fed continuously for 30 years, like a fire glimmering from out of the well of darkness.

Many beautiful images of St. Peter's Abbey remain a vivid legacy in the visual catalogue of the mind. The splendidly treed lanes and grounds of the Abbey made walking out each day a marvellous experience. In the hush at the end of August the newly harvested gardens glowed in the warm sunlight of the late afternoon. In September, flocks of mallards toiled about the itinerant cornfield. Early one morning a flock of more than a thousand geese flew in under the cover of the red ball of the sun and gabbled in the grain field nearest the hermitage until noon. In October, a scarecrow in the paper cornfield awaited the first killing frost. Someone left him a plain brown wooden chair. A dozen broken pumpkins littered a corner of the garden. Decapitated greenery from the harvest was scattered about like lost clothing. Homely, discarded root vegetables that resemble punched-in heads, peered out from the composting piles. The coming of winter plays out on the prairies like nature's passion play. The most beautiful pleasures of summer are KO'd by the short fall season. One mysterious day, by thunder, all the trees have dropped their leaves.

Snow arrives on Hallowe'en and then the freeze-up. In this climate nothing gets a second chance.

In winter the Abbey, torn by the bitter wind, sent streaming steam and smoke into the frozen eyes of the stars. An imposing wall to the bitter cold. On winter nights I wandered many frozen miles under the icy glittering carpet. A whitetail buck startled me, jumping out from a row of blue spruce trees and bounding over the road into the field beside the soccer pitch. I followed the fresh tracks in the new snow, plunging across the field until the icy wind called me back. Returning along the road toward the lights — the bell tower and abbey walls stood in stoic brick permanence; sanctuary for the spirit against the bitterly cold night. An open door that is always open for mankind, no matter the season.

The legacy of St. Benedict has endured for 1500 years. At St. Peter's, in the tradition of all Benedictine abbeys, the life of community and contemplation dedicated to the worship of God go on in a transparent world that encourages and welcomes guests. In this highly structured society under *The Rule of St. Benedict*, the monks and other members of their community live pious lives devoted to serving Jesus Christ.

How ironic that such a community has provided so much solace for writers who pursue the most selfish agenda imaginable: trying to put form and emotion in the shape of language written in symbols on a blank white page. St. Peter's has developed a reputation for being an important place for writers because of its retreats, its writing colonies and the college. It has become a special place for writers and writing because it provides the ambience and the locus for the contemplative life that the writer, in a similar way, shares with the inhabitants of the abbey. Usually writers do well when they are well fed and well looked after. They desire peace and quiet and the convenience of being anti-social or not, depending on the options either position might supply. In the St. Peter's environment writers are free to be as visible as they choose, and the place is rich in the tradition of hosting writers and integrating them into the greater or lesser community, depending on the writer's inclinations or desires. St. Pete's is a thinking place, a place to start new projects, or a place to pull something together.

During the long string of winter months I shared the basement wing of Severin Hall with another writer. A woman, it was rumoured, who had come by bus from New Jersey and was holed up at the end of the hall writing a television script. I heard her shuffle something from time to time, and caught her once or twice in my peripheral vision when she put the key in her door lock.

She was wired to a process. I never had the occasion to come across her walking outside or glimpsed her in the kitchen hall. She had ridden a long way on the Greyhound for her solitude. It resonated on the ultra-shiny linoleum floors. One day somebody mentioned they thought she had gone. It was true, I assumed, on "the dog" back to the big show.

I felt the enormous weight of contemplation, prayer, devotion, and thought that permeates the monastic environment. The presence of it falls around one's shoulders. In time, I began listening to the voice of God speaking through men as fragments of the liturgy reached out the cathedral doors to the rest of mankind. This is a holy place. Sensibility toward the human condition and the love of God abound here while a community functions around the simple labouring tasks necessary to sustain the spiritual life. The light in the cathedral windows inspired me to start reading about the history of the world. Many nights I travelled back through the Middle Ages until finally, after several months, I arrived in the 6th century in the Sinai via the lively text of St. John Climacus, a fine writer who wrote, "Let the remembrance of Jesus be present with each breath, and then you will know the value of solitude." I found an abundance of solitude in the ambience of the outdoors at St. Peter's and in the serene atmosphere of Severin Hall. I spent most of my waking hours there, reading or writing. What writer could ask for anything more?

On contemplative summer evenings, when the blue sky stayed out until late, the warm brick and metal roof seemed fused to the green light of summer that reflected from the ornamental trees and the flower beds. A bright yellow canola field could be glimpsed from between the gaps in a hedge row of evenly spaced evergreens that seemed as innocuous as pawns on a nearly empty board. Further along the path, under the taller trees that seem like an army marching when the wind is in their tops, a strange carpet of detritus dries on the bottom of the forest. Maturing trees that must have all been planted nearly at the same time. An impractical but functional adult forest that only the will of mankind could impose upon the landscape. Much like the aged "forest of tree-men" who have given of so much of themselves to serve their Lord and find themselves growing ancient together. Only a few younger trees come up to replenish the tired forest. The generations pass like waves through the decades of history. I laugh at the humid summer night. Mosquitoes dance around the edge of the window sill.

No matter how loud the laughing of student voices outside my window, or how squeaky the shoes passing my door in the middle of the night, or how intense the coughing fit through the wall, I hardly paid heed to other influences. This is God's house, his spirit lives here and his agents, and those most in need of his services naturally dwell here or come and stay when they are in need or feel it is necessary to make his acquaintance again in this most intimate way. Breaking bread with and near those who serve him and finding solace and security in being in his presence. The stories of men and women guests who stayed many nights in the isolated darkened basement wing of Severin Hall unravelling in the evenings resonated like a kind of theatre of the absurd. Characters from real life, more vivid than the fictional kind: Nature Boy, Rubber Woman, Chicken Man, Kaptain Anger, Salveena Morgue. I gave them all pretend names.

Nature Boy was my favourite. In his late 30s, wearing cutoffs and a tee-shirt with a tiny backpack, the tanned picture of health with long, curly hair and a flowing beard. He claimed to have walked overland from Vancouver via the Okanagan and the Kootenays and across southern Alberta. He stayed and worked for a week, driving the farm dump truck, until he was spotted joyriding in it a little past the town of Bruno. Gone, they said, bought him a bus ticket, put him on the bus in Humboldt, sent him, with a few hotel vouchers, on his way to Winnipeg. A week later, a little after 2:30 am, I was awakened by a repeated tapping on my door. I thought carefully for a moment before I opened it, wondering who it could possibly be and why? It was Nature Boy standing before me wrapped in a blanket.

"Have you got a match?" he asked, holding an unlit cigarette in his hand.

"Where are your clothes?" I inquired while giving him a book of matches.

"They're in the washer down the hall," he answered.

"Where are you staying?" I asked in the confusion of the moment.

"Think I'll continue sleeping around," he offered with a chuckle.

Nature Boy, obviously not on his way to Winnipeg, was moving from empty room to empty room one jump ahead of the nervous housekeeping staff. At first I figured he must have stolen a pass key. Then I decided he wouldn't need one, he possessed the knack of how to play invisible. I could see him folding himself into the linen closet and lying there in comparative comfort amongst the clean towels. He stayed another few days, revealing himself again late at night, before he departed for the empty road. A resident Father at St. Peter's, driving to his parish, spotted him walking at the crossroads 80 miles down the highway.

Sometimes in the morning one of these characters, in the fashion of Nature Boy, was suddenly and obviously gone for good, as if their time was up. The mood changed. Mortals and angels stopped by on their way to somewhere else. They rested, refuelled their bodies and their psyches. Some worked for a while or helped out in some miraculous way for a few brief hours and then they were gone to the bus or the highway. Others waited for a propitious moment to pull their con and some, I have no doubt, fell in love with the Lord or were reclaimed and stayed forever, doing the most menial jobs with pleasure for their life's work. Most travelled light. Some were encouraged to move on for various reasons. I could never really tell the difference between the chosen and the desperate. They all had a certain kind of edge. I formed a theory that some of them were truly angels who had been sent to accomplish certain deeds or who needed temporary sanctuary.

Thank God I am not a monk or a priest but merely a fisherman without a hook or a net. The only soul I was hoping to pull from the deep was my own. In the dialogue with God, for lack of a better way of describing it, I found my own voice was beginning to speak of emotions and feelings about love and spirituality inspired by the atmosphere of peace and tranquillity required by the laws of holy men. The simpler the life the more convenient it is to approach God without the baggage of mankind's accumulative, possessive nature. I tasted the sweetness of serenity.

In the blackened dullness of the most miserable winter nights, I scribbled poems on yellow pads with lead pencils. I made popcorn and real coffee with fresh ground beans. The yellow cinder blocks seemed mellow like softened bamboo or rattan while I sat mesmerized by the pile of great books I had accumulated for such an occasion as this, the pursuit of happiness without the encumbrances of duty. I followed the First Crusade to Antioch and I returned back through Turkey on the way to some land that felt like home but wasn't, even to my ancestral blood that survived through the generations in Eastern Europe. I dreamed of angels dancing beside dying French soldiers at the frozen Bersina River in Russia while Napoleon hightailed it back to Paris. I wrote poems about history, including one about a shark shadowing a galleon in the 18th century and others about the righteousness of human beings, the sieges of cities, the murder of innocents, the injustices of tyrants, the general pestilence of man — the beautiful survivor because of his belief in God.

The God who forgives those who believe in him, even if it is at the last possible second of a despicable life. There must always be the chance or there would be no choice. Without the converse there's nothing to believe in but the confusion of time and place and the curiosity of the mind. How is it these poems strike off the end of my pen and land on paper surfaces? I didn't plan them or require them to attend — but they came to visit me at Muenster, as is their habit with many other writers. Many of us have a perilous relationship with our muse. We have cultivated and developed different ways to cope with our impossible relationship. At St. Peter's, we can ignore it or indulge it. After a while, the peace and solitude and the harmony of the relationship between reading and thinking become an entrancing lure to attract the written word. Here we are permitted to like writing and act like writers. The clarity of ambience tells us we are safe and sheltered behind these walls of this Christendom, free to reveal our eccentricities and expose our vulnerabilities. This is a bit of a shock compared to the normal obscurity of the real world.

We are the keepers of word order, we anticipate that at some point in time, we'll be talking to God on a direct line, especially on our last day on earth. Is it a futile gesture? Whenever more than one poet is in attendance anything can and will transpire. We are the green aphid gossips of the universe and when whole groups of us gather we are referred to as "a plague of poets." I have taken to avoiding the rest of them for the sake of my own salvation.

I wrote pages and pages of memoirs about the people in us so long ago before we became today. I remembered the old woman in the old neighbourhood we thought was a witch because she covered her black and white TV screen with blue plastic creating a scary eerie glow in her living room window, and the grinder man who pushed his wheeled apparatus and never changed his clothes or bathed from one year to the next — crying in the street and sharpening our mothers' scissor and knives. I woke up in a cold sweat, thinking I had just witnessed an execution in a pea field in Bosnia. For a moment I thought it was about my own boots. How I got them on in the middle of the night is hard to figure. Later, when I couldn't sleep, I went walking while it rained and rained in sheets and torrents that rushed into the fields like the wind does at sea. I saw Salvador Dali peeking at me in the round mirror when I came out from the shower in the steamed-up bathroom. I wrote a note to him with my finger on the steamy glass. You see, there was nothing to stop me from thinking about everything — like the process of my art that attacks me in a nonlinear fashion in three different disciplines. I could get confused, the stuff could hardly pile up into a sensible form. The writer is only as good as his last book. The writer might never write another book. The writer is right behind you thinking you might be right.

Near the end of August, I wandered the gravel roads and trudged across the fields, sat in the bowers reading or on the edge of the vegetable patch, or beside the double hedge that enclosed the cemetery. I proofread all the monuments and headstones and walked for miles down the long straight railway tracks until after dark when the blinding headlight pushed me back into the shadowy trees until the earth-shaking sound faded far into the distance. I made notes in my green portable writing tablet that I packed in my black shoulder bag with my ultra deluxe pen that writes under water. Abbey still as a postcard. I wandered back into the picture, below the great stone lintels that rise above every window space in the building, each a fine detail among the exacting bricks. I watched the birds roosting in the chimneys. Evening songs on the rooftop or in the treetops seemed like messages being transmitted to another dimension.

Early the next morning, before morning prayer, I pack up my possessions in a couple of cardboard boxes, almost exclusively books and papers. It's the end of summer again, where I began one year before, the cycle repeats itself. I take one last look around, walking over familiar ground that I know I will never be able to keep straight when time begins its erosion at the centre of my thought production. I am forever caught up in a web about time in the broader context of why and how it is appropriated for what purpose. How my writing life is on a delay. I am already on the way in my imagination to the next place on the journey without resolving what I will make from this experience. The words have begun to come out but I am busy trying to finish dealing with the recent past — a manuscript that has been piling up for five years. Almost like raising another child without knowing it. I wrote it to sleep every night. Now I am sunk in a momentary sense of loss before leaving. The luxury of solitude is not easily abandoned. I wondered how I could be somewhere else while the solitude in this place is still going on. There's nothing crazy about my duplicity; it's a human condition. I left early in the morning. I still think back about the scraps of sun in the poplar trees and the thick taste of dust on the winding wash board road. The car door rattling like a reminder about faith. Watching my eyes in the rear view-mirror, I took a last glance, the picture remains fixed in my mind's album.

MEMOIRS OF A SMALL PRESS JUNKIE

HAVE POEM WILL TRAVEL

MOST OF MY LIFE I have been interested in writing poems. It started as a teenage preoccupation when I discovered, in myself, a contemplative side that could be tuned in to provide relief from dealing with the chaos of the real world and the repetitious cycles that dominate our daily habits. The dwelling of self contained a private room that soon became a sanctuary for the meditative pursuit of writing poetry.

My teachers thought I was taking notes when I was perfectly disguised working on something else. That something else grew steadily through the years, until an avocation turned into an obsession and finally became a half-assed occupation. It is common for poets to be visited by a presence, a voice, a visitor, a spiritual advisor, angel or experience other manifestations, such as automatic writing. Poems are essentially gifts inspired by a mysterious process between the writer, and what is appropriately called the muse.

I saw an angel standing behind the choir in a church in North Burnaby when I was nine years old. The voices of dead people I have known talk to me at times. Often I answer back, but I am more interested in the living than the dead. My church is the bus station, truckstop on a long stretch of highway, a back road in the middle of July, or a small-town hockey rink on a Friday night in February. I wander on odd Saturday afternoons in the bookstores on Queen Street in Toronto or Pender Street in Vancouver. I'm there in a corner of the photograph of the Blue House on the hill above the beach in White Rock, in a field of oats in the middle of summer near Dundurn, at an auction in a barn at Lonesome (bidding on Grandpa Clampett's last painting), stopping at Little Pine, passing through Big River, broken down at 42 below zero near Findlater, or reading a magazine in the library at Humboldt.

Life is a river. Time takes the place of water. Images and fragments of people and places flow by. Poetry is spiritual language, usually with an "ism" attached to it. The doctrine of construction. I think the only "ism" worth its salt is humanism. Writing poetry is an essential habit that has taken over my life. Making poems of free moments that have expired on buses, in motels, airports, cafés, and endless nights of bingeing. These are the pulses of DNA leaping out from the end of my doodling pen into note books and eventually finding their way into various editions of my work. In this poet's mind, the poems written over so many years have blurred in a pattern not unlike a quilt: words, ideas, and images rehearsed and arranged like colours and textures in the fabric of the landscape or the social world. Pieces have been left here and there in my small pantheon of poetry books. Sometimes I think the river of life is a stream of dreams and visions in time, travelling through space. Like memories and nostalgia, liquid in human brain cells, flooding the mind with torrents of clarity. Poems are like children; sooner or later they come home and take a walk around the old neighbourhood. Alas, time can also be a powerful eraser, softening the shadow of the emotional life or rubbing it off the page.

Poems are neither artefacts nor photographs, but in a way they are similar. Each artefact, photo, or poem is an individual entity. When they are joined with their ilk they are altered by the process and become part of something else. The artefact is a cultural indicator, the photo a virtual witness, the poem a voice in the text. In the case of poetry, the individual poem is often a fragment in an evolving process that is not linear or best defined in any chronological framework.

Writing poetry began for me as a interesting way to fill in time, recreation for the psyche; somewhat in the same manner games such as baseball and hockey or chess and billiards exercise various human needs. This "time filling" recreation evolved through my teen years that by the time I was in my early 20s I had resolved to do it for my life's work. A rather pathetic prospect for the future — becoming a poet in 20th-century Canada. Most people thought it a recipe for a steady diet of wieners and beans. They weren't far wrong. However, my brain had been bitten by the bug, and despite my best efforts to straighten up and get respectable I fell into the wasteland of poetry. To be completely honest, it has been a mixed bag, never boring, often fraught with peril. It is a discipline with tricky political shoals and unusual conditions because of its marginal commercial appeal. One poetry wag that I know has likened it to getting a job riding a roller coaster 24 hours a day for minimum wage.

Now a long way down the back road of a lifetime, I am still "filling in the time" by writing it all down in many drafts that have piled up around me like a block-house made of paper. These drafts, through a mysterious process that has kept me entranced in a compulsive grip for over 30 years, have evolved into a series of small press books that were published and are still being published in various locales across the country by the most devoted hardcore cranks in modern history — the small press publishers. In my case, the whole underground world of the book arts that encompasses a wide spectrum but principally they are: Blackfish Press, Porcupine's Quill, Oolichan Books, Black Moss, Polestar Press, Exile Editions, Thistledown Press, and Hagios Press. Thank God for them or I probably would have ended up writing obituaries or proof reading recipe books — not to say that there is anything wrong with the above tasks especially if one can get paid. Along the way I have worked in a variety of jobs that have been closely associated with writing or editing.

I am proudest to have picked up the label of "utility writer" from the late Verne Clemence, book columnist in the *Saskatoon Star-*

Phoenix, who, after reading my work, established me in that niche. I told him I took up writing prose to prove I could write. Something writing poetry doesn't always do. Eventually, I began to prefer being called a "utility writer." It beat trying to explain what a poet was to a hog producer or someone in chicken feed. For me, it meant being a writer who was willing to take on any writing job and took pride in getting it right, even if the client had no idea how good it really was. You see, I had a secret, one that I managed to harbour in myself for most of my adult years. I was the best "utility writer" around because it gave me the beard I needed to disguise the fact that I have always been totally absorbed in writing poetry, no matter what writing and editing or administrative jobs I had to tackle to keep on doing it. I became adept at accomplishing in five days what was expected to take ten. That gave me several days in a row to work on my poetry. I feel like a sinner confessing all to the local parish priest. Forgive me for forcing the reader to participate in my catharsis.

Being a poet is a complicated problem with many variations. Conditions change for practitioners as the avocation develops into vocation. Some fall by the wayside, others thrive on a sudden surge of publicity and success. For a few, this means good book sales. However, success and book sales are not mandatory. Others are judged to be brilliant after being discovered by the *literati*. Obscure critical factors that are measured by awards, pecking order, and appearances in the popular press or invitations to appear in the "beautiful people's" poetry events in English Canada — which has enclaves across the country but for the most part is centred in Toronto — can make or break reputations. A few gain immediate success, conquer the field and go on to unimagined levels of fame and good fortune. A handful in every generation survive the test of time and become semi-iconic in the most esoteric practice in all the literary arts by sheer persistence and longevity, producing an astonishing number of titles over the long haul. Some are nourished by the academic/establishment environment which has created a kind of national salon of university professor/beautiful-people-approved poets. This claque of the chosen which has roots from coast to coast, has a great deal of influence, not only in literary publishing but in deciding who wins the major poetry awards, such as The Governor General's Award, various provincial book awards and the Griffin Prize. The latter $50,000 award, sponsored by a businessman with ties to the "language poets" and the power elite in Canadian writing, is generally given out in a process that rewards a poet whose book exemplifies a certain party line.

In general, poetry attracts a small but loyal discerning audience. There is no money in it. Reputations are largely made by the winning of awards and the recognition that comes with it. There are a lot of back-room under-the-table deals, mutual back-scratching, and coming-to-the-aid-of in the selection of books for various short lists. A few chosen experts tell the media in various ways what they envision to be the best writing, and the media passes the message along. Hardly anybody but insiders and a small audience read the books, so there is no popular public opinion about what is particularly good in poetry. The stories that abound about the shenanigans in many of the past Governor General's Awards juries for poetry are by now a legendary part of our literary history. Probably poetry politics is the most sophisticated (I have avoided saying Machiavellian) and lethal of all the artistic disciplines. Fortunately, poetry always lives on the streets and finds nourishment in a thousand other places in every corner of the country.

By definition, I am in another category all together. I am the insider's outsider, the professional journeyman who has largely stopped playing the game unless it lands in my lap. I have no address or phone number, just a box number and an email address. Frankly, I can't kiss ass, lie through my teeth, stop saying it like it is, or escape an erroneous reputation as a shit-disturber for supporting too many lost causes. I have long been a reclusive who has remained out-of-touch for more than a decade in rural Saskatchewan. I am a dropout who in midlife retreated into the small to find solitude of a kind that is unobtainable in a large city. I write poetry because of a compulsive habitual desire that haunts me like a man with a sweet tooth in a candy store. I am an addict who found a way to help explain the unexplainable or to delve into the mysterious world of self-discovery and amateur scholarship to satisfy the spiritual appetite. I am a refugee from the literary rat race. I needed to escape to satisfy the inner voice that kept yakking at my conscious self, saying, "Find a quiet place to write and don't look too hard over your shoulder."

Poetry fulfills one of the most universal of human needs: the desire to be creative and make something from nothing. Writing for me is a compulsive act that perpetuates itself. I took it up because playing with ideas and words seemed a natural way to think. The process of writing poetry over a long period of time opens doors into mysterious corners of the universe as the dialogue in thought stimulates the imagination.

Born in Vancouver, raised in a fishing family in North Burnaby, afflicted by nostalgia and a longing for the ocean, the west coast will always be in my blood. I have no doubt that is where I will end up when I am doddering over my keyboard. For nearly two decades I lived on the hill above the pier in White Rock. Sooner or later I passed through most of the writing scenes from coast to coast in Canada like a loose turd passing through a goose. I have read poems in night clubs, libraries, halls, classrooms, bookstores, art galleries, literary festivals, bistros, colleges, legions, museums, churches, parks, drug stores, delis, golf courses and cemeteries in nearly every province and region of the country. I have had the good fortune to have had short term writer-in-residencies in Chilliwack and Kamloops, and two year-long-residencies in Humboldt and Estevan. In 2003 I was honoured to appear at the prestigious Cathedral Arts Festival in the Cathedral neighbourhood in Regina. In 2004 I was the "Poet Laureate" at the Peter Gzowski Invitational Golf Tournament for Literacy at Michael Cowpland's The Marshes Golf Club in Kanata, Ontario. In 2005 I appeared at Lotus Land, the spoken word stage, at the South Country Fair on the Oldman River at Fort MacLeod, Alberta. And so it goes. In my poetry travels I have visited Emily Carr's house in Victoria, Robert Service's cabin in the Yukon, Max Braithwaite's childhood home in Nokomis, Saskatchewan, Margaret Laurence's house in Neepawa, Gabriel Roy's house in St. Boniface, and Lucy Maud Montgomery's house in Prince Edward Island. Perhaps I will end up a writing gnome in a vaguely well-known somebody's garden in some forsaken burg in the middle of nowhere in particular. It could happen. Instead of a fishing rod I'll be holding a pen. Mine is a career that was forged in the urban cauldron. It now exists on the margins of the urban landscape and in the heartland of a vast country that I have never grown tired of exploring.

Canada is networked with an alternative culture that exists in some form in almost every small town and urban neighbourhood in the vast regions we call the true north. A small, vital audience, that reads poetry and often writes poetry as well, turns up to keep the tradition alive. It may be in a deli in Swift Current, a bookstore in St. Johns, a club in Vancouver, on a college campus in downtown Montreal, the Great George Street Gallery in Charlottetown or at one of the various writers festivals across the country such as Eden Mills, Harbourfront, or the legendary Living Skies Festival of Words that takes place near the end of every July in Moose Jaw or at the cherry festival in Bruno.

One day I woke up and decided to move to a relatively isolated place without taking it to the extreme. I was crazy from an inability to communicate and the final realization that nearly two decades had turned into the spectre of a nightmare. I was time's dupe living in the past in an out-of-style suit. It occurred to me after a hideous affliction manifesting itself by a ringing in my ears — like the voice of metal on metal — that I was no longer relevant. I was a wild card in the game of life. I needed to find a place where I could rest, far away from the urban rush, and attain a more tranquil lifestyle that would allow an itinerant poet time to think and write without interruption. I needed a new horizon to help heal my aching psyche. Most of all, I craved the calming cloak of isolation to give me the opportunity to regroup and rebuild. I became a kind of "reborn writer" who decided to try and restart the creative "motor" and keep it running for one good shot at becoming the writing life. Out here, in the middle of nowhere, beauty and harshness merge; the brilliant summer and seven months of winter. This is the country that Anne Marriott portrayed so vividly in *The Wind Our Enemy*. Nowhere to hide under the dome of the prairie sky. People here take time to give thanks for what they have carved out of this inhospitable, bittersweet, glorious landscape of extremes. I give thanks by writing every day.

For those reasons and others I have spent the best part of the last dozen years living in Dundurn, a small prairie town of 500 people about 35 km south of Saskatoon on the number 11 highway. It is a tiny dot on very few maps of Canada. I am happy to see it stay that way. If you wonder why I am here, spend a few hours in the summer wandering in the garden or an evening on the back road watching deer just outside the town limits. You will pass miles of sullen, fruit-laden chokecherry bushes that are painted in dust and the wind-shaken orange flames of western prairie lilies growing in the grassy ditches. Watch the unpolluted night sky without the glaring lights of the cityscape. Accept the absolute silence of the darkness, bereft of ambulances and fire engines whining in the forever distance. Let the kids out in the backyard without having to guard them. Listen to the distant sound of cattle in the distance bawling on the wind, the faint noise of jumbo Canada geese calling in the fields and the lamentable coyotes yapping and howling nearly all night from the edge of town. Leave the doors unlocked and pray there are no mosquitoes in the bedroom. Hunker down in the winter close to a fireplace and listen to the wind howling across the flatlands or walk to the rink in the 40- below weather being careful not to freeze one's face or other extremities. Watch the Northern Lights careening overhead in the middle of the night. Listen to the sounds and sight of 10,000 white geese over-head, remember the vision of sandhill cranes dancing on a hillside in a stubble field. When there's nothing to do, but nothing to do, and nowhere to go, it's easy to make a bonfire and have a picnic in the snow. If you're thinking about taking up writing it's not a bad place to be.

LITERARY GRANDMOTHERS

IN THE FALL OF 1968, after a spell of travelling around in various locations in Europe, I came home to find out that I had been accepted as a student at Simon Fraser University. This was a bit of a revelation to me, since I had been a somewhat indifferent high school student and I had only applied half-heartedly, imagining that I would be turned down for having a mediocre record. When I turned up to register, I was aghast at the lineup that encircled the gymnasium like a giant human snake. The relatively new university was burgeoning with new students. It was the peak of the counterculture that was sweeping through populations of young people everywhere in the western world. The hippie culture was in full swing and the "freak" generation was well represented by both students and faculty at the half built university on the top of Burnaby Mountain.

About a week into the first term, my high school pal, Malcom Ramsay, who was really hip with tie-dyed clothing and Afro hairstyle, and I decided to go and hear Allen Ginsberg who was giving a reading in the gym. (Malcom later became a renowned polar bear scientist and was subsequently killed in a tragic helicopter accident in May of 2000 while conducting research in the high Arctic). We stood in line for about 15 minutes. When we reached the doors we discovered that we did not have enough money between us to pay the entry fee. As we turned away an older woman behind us offered to pay our way in. Malcom and I both wrote poetry and we were reading one another's work while killing time in the slow moving line. The woman said that she would buy us tickets to get into the Ginsberg show if we would sell her a couple of our poems. We agreed, each giving her a handful of poems and she paid the man at the door. When we thanked her she asked us what we were studying. Malcom was already a scientist type and I was a nominal arts student. I blurted out that I was an English student. The woman told me that she was an English professor and she gave me her card and told me to drop by her office sometime if I wanted criticism about the poems I was writing.

This fortuitous meeting with a remarkable teacher, Philippa Polson, undoubtedly changed my life. Philippa had came late in life to the academic world, having begun her university teaching career in her 60s. English-born, she was possessed of a cheerful personality and a precocious mind. During the war she had supervised a factory of women who put airplanes together. For years she worked in Vancouver for a concert promoter before she decided, in her late 50s, to go to university. She earned a BA from UBC and an MA from Simon Fraser in 1968 — her master's thesis, submitted in December 1967, was entitled *Language Structure and Verse Structure* — and she soon got a job teaching at SFU. She taught linguistics, had a passion for classical music and Dante, and was a going concern on the campus. Within a short time Philippa was critiquing my poems and lending me books from her extensive library, encouraging me to write more and expand my horizons by thinking about things that had never occurred to me. She was an eclectic reader who could operate in several languages. Her bookshelves were filled with arts books and she had a large collection of poetry that included editions of T. S. Eliot, Edith Sitwell, D. H. Lawrence, Dylan Thomas, W. B Yeats, Kathleen Raine, and Elizabeth Jennings as well as a good number of poetry in translation from various languages. I still have her copy of the first edition of Edith Sitwell's *Canticle of the Rose*, which I borrowed just before she made her last trip to Sechelt. Her office walls were lined with English novelists. She loved Virginia Woolf, Evelyn Waugh, Joyce Carey, Joseph Conrad and Ford Maddox Ford. She had volumes of Herbert Reid, George Orwell, and V. S. Naipaul, as well as a good deal of anarchist and political literature. For enjoyment, she read Joyce or Swift or Thomas Hardy. She also had a staggering collection of American and Canadian literature, and of old British literary magazines including *Horizon* and *New Writing*. She gave me a key to her office and told me to use it whenever she wasn't around.

In a nutshell, she opened my eyes to various periods in art and literature — she was in love with all things Pre-Raphaelite — and encouraged me and other students who were interested in writing to get on with it. From her I learned the habits of spending part of each day in the reading room at the university library listening to classical music on a headset while perusing the paintings of great artists from the university's collection of art books. She was a remarkable teacher with an infectious enthusiasm for knowledge. At noon hours she presided over an informal group of students and faculty who read Dante aloud, in the Italian, and discussed his work. She corresponded with Noam Chomsky and Linus Pauling and wrote articles in her discipline, including work she did with preschool children. She had accumulated a large number of tapes over the years, and sometimes played them for her students. My favourite was her recording of Aretha Franklin's father preaching in his church in Detroit. I howled when I first heard Ezra Pound's voice; he sounded almost identical to a recording of Edith Sitwell pretending to be her brother Osbert.

One of Philippa's other students, Christine Hearn, who came from the small Kootenay outpost of Salmo, was also writing poetry, and soon I met another poet by the name of Tom Wheeler, a friend of Malcom's, who worked in the university library. He introduced me to another young poet by the name of Brian

Brett who was a part-time student and library worker at the time. Philippa was adamant that the way to improve as a writer was to get involved in a scene by starting a magazine or a press in order to find other people with similar interests. She preached that the give-and-take between writing, editing and publishing new work was a process of immense value to new writers. Brian Brett and I hit it off, and soon we were talking about starting a little magazine. In 1971, we brought out the first issue of a new little magazine that we decided to call *Blackfish*.

Unfortunately, my relationship with Philippa was far too short; three and a half years after I first met her while standing in line waiting to hear Allen Ginsberg play his harmonium and a year after the inaugural issue of *Blackfish* magazine, she suffered a massive stroke and died (on November 15th in 1972) at her seaside home in Sechelt. I was absolutely stunned and bereft. However, as time went on I began to realize that for some reason Philippa had been tutoring me and by the time she was gone I was already fully immersed in the writing life. Brian Brett and I were well on our way to establishing not only a magazine but also a press. Thirty-four years later on I can still vividly remember the sound of Philippa's shrill voice and the laughter in her eyes. She was a brilliant woman who had a natural ability to inspire others. I had become one of her projects for enlightenment. I had a long way to go but she got me on the road and I never looked back. When I met her I was relatively unknown to myself; by the time she was gone I had a much better idea who I was. I had no choice but to continue on in the same fashion. She took it for granted that I was already in it for the long hard ride.

Philippa was good friends with the already reclusive wheel chair-bound Ethel Wilson, whom she visited in her art deco apartment building that was on the beach at English Bay. Early on in the life of our new publishing venture, Philippa had told me that she had many other friends in the writing world but one in particular she wanted to introduce me to. That writer turned out to be the prolific poet and well-known literary figure Dorothy Livesay.

Born in 1909, Dorothy Livesay spanned the decades with a prodigious output since her first book, *The Green Pitcher*, had come out in 1928. A member of a patrician literary family, her father J. F. B. Livesay was a founder and the general manager of Canadian Press. Her mother was the poet and translator Florence Randal, whose work appeared beside Ezra Pound's in *Poetry Chicago*. Dorothy grew up in Winnipeg and Toronto, attended the best private schools, and earned degrees from the University of Toronto (1931) and the Sorbonne (1932). She later studied at the U of T School of Social Work (1932-1933). For a couple of years she worked for the Communist Party organizing textile workers in New Jersey. Later she served on the editorial board of *New Frontiers* (1935-1937). In addition, she produced over 20 volumes of poetry — receiving Governor General's Awards for poetry in 1944 and 1947, and the Lorne Pierce Medal in 1947 — as well as half a dozen collections of memoirs and literary non-fiction. In the 1960s she did a stint working for UNESCO in Paris. She taught English in Africa (three years in Northern Rhodesia) and received an MEd from UBC in 1966. Throughout her life, Dorothy remained a committed left-wing politico and a Canadian nationalist. She was also a staunch feminist who was regarded as an icon in the women's movement in Canada.

Dorothy, known as "Dee" to her legion of friends and acquaintances, travelled the breadth of the country, networking with young and old. In her youth, she had been a fervent communist, organizing workers and devoting herself to the revolution. Later in life, she stayed in touch with her cronies and remained a repository of historical information about various movements and publications while devoting herself to a more academic and literary life. Although she had had a cancerous lung removed and had suffered a broken leg when she fell on the ice during a nasty winter in Edmonton, she was an energy source with a constitution that would put most people to shame. The Dorothy Livesay collection at the

University of Manitoba library lists over 1,800 correspondents.

Dorothy was always on the way to somewhere else and she visited with close friends as she travelled through the various regions of the country. She once wrote, "Those of us who are travellers become so from sheer greed. We are greedy for life."

By the time I met her, there was scarcely a writer, academic, university, publisher, small press, little magazine, or literary association or movement in Canada that had not experienced an involvement with Dorothy. She was connected in the writing scene in every major centre of the country. Her books were published by important presses in central Canada, such as Macmillan, Ryerson, McGraw-Hill Ryerson. She was an important influence on the literary/cultural renaissance in Vancouver in the 60s. She had a working association with Seymour Mayne which resulted in Ingluvin Press in Montreal bringing out *Forty Woman Poets of Canada* in 1972 — the first major anthology of Canadian women poets. She also found time to organize the literary scenes in Victoria, Edmonton and Winnipeg.

When I first met Dorothy she was 62, dyeing her hair a chestnut brown colour, looking quite dowdy in her old lady outfits and flower pot hats. She was knowledgeable about classical music, theatre, dance, and visual and other performing arts. She was fluent in French and pursued a full cultural agenda. Dorothy promoted her country's artistic culture by recognizing a great many of its practitioners and by attending countless performances and openings. At the same time, she was surprisingly straight about various elements in the counterculture world. She remained virtually oblivious to rock and roll, and she had no real comprehension about the drug culture which she often inhabited or passed through without comment. Dorothy was open-minded, progressive, theoretical, impractical, opinionated, persuasive, and an indefatigable dynamo who was almost totally self-absorbed while pursuing her agendas.

She was a bulldozer of a woman with a remarkable constitution. She also had a drinking problem, which sometimes brought out the worst in her, as if she were in possession of twin personalities. The sober, deeply committed writer and political activist who was interested in everybody and constantly stirred the pot encouraging literary activity turned into a bully when she got into the brandy. When she was imbibing she often passed out and woke up hours later in a sheepish mood, wondering what damage she had done. In Victoria, she was occasionally found by the police sleeping it off in her car parked in Beacon Hill Park. Sometimes her drunken encounters with friends and other writers were accompanied by physical action — while in her cups Dorothy is alleged to have punched Patrick Lane, breaking his glasses. After one of these episodes she would be contrite and kittenish as she attempted to repair the damage that she had wrought the night before.

She was often catty about poets of her own generation behind their backs, but she maintained a huge repertoire of writer friends who understood her nature. Most of them chose to overlook her excesses and stayed friendly with her for a variety of reasons. Dorothy basically had a good heart and she networked at such a pace that she often was at the centre of the writing action, whether it be putting together an anthology or starting a new literary venture. Dorothy's friends and associates got action from every direction. She acted as a conduit to facilitate relationships with people from disparate locations and perspectives across the nation in the arenas of literature and politics. She had connections at every level in the establishment, from her birthright, educational opportunities, and her ability to network. She remained a high profile figure with a major reputation in academic and literary circles.

Dorothy was every kind of contradiction. She was a fun-loving, straightlaced woman who had a bit of a bawdy side, especially when she drank. In many ways she was extremely naïve about what went on around her. She had relationships with nearly every important writer in the country as well as with most of the emerging writers in every decade for more than 60 years. Most of the poets of her own generation — especially the woman poets such as

PK Page, Anne Marriott, Elizabeth Brewster, and Miriam Waddington — managed to navigate the controversies that Dorothy brought onto the literary scene like mini-bouts of plague.

Dorothy had a capricious side that afflicted her life with numerous misunderstandings and fallings-out. She was a self-appointed talent scout who discovered and helped many new writers get published. She was a "leftist" all of her long life and wrote for the working class while extolling a vision for humanity. The roster of writers and artists she helped would take up pages of print. Dorothy had no trouble in promoting her discoveries or in quickly denouncing them for what she perceived as a lack of political content. Wherever she went controversy was never far behind. Writers chose to react to her in a number of ways. Dorothy was a symbol for the literary political left that inspired the feminist movement. Who could forget the press conferences that Dorothy held in whatever city she happened to be in to highlight an injustice or promote a cause? Who could forget the sight of youngish woman writers in Toronto dressed in khaki military fatigues marching about the edges of sanity in Daytons while their hero in coiffed hair and woollen suit with sensible shoes attacked the ruling class for being oblivious to social justice? It is fair to say a number of writers probably avoided Dorothy altogether, for a smorgasbord of reasons. Joe Rosenblatt and John Newlove prided themselves on their ability to virtually disappear into thin air whenever Dorothy came into earshot. The poet and raconteur *extraordinaire* Robin Skelton and Dorothy were natural opponents, as if their DNA were made inflammatory by the presence of the other.

In her old age, Dorothy came out with collections of memoirs that began with *Right Hand Left Hand*, published by Press Porcepic in 1977. She intimated that she had had sexual relationships with women while in her youth. In one of the collections there was a picture of Dorothy and a friend sunbathing topless. This kind of confession from a figure like Dorothy titillated the cultural world and feminist circles for a while and Dorothy became hotter than ever. Dorothy was a tease always intimating this or that to enhance her already over the top reputation. She knew how to keep her career chugging along. She intimated coyly that she had had an affair with Stanley Ryerson when they were both students in Paris in the early '30s. I chided her with some moronic remark about that being the reason she was published for so many years at Ryerson Press. She guffawed with laughter and said it made no difference, as tears of laughter ran down her cheeks.

Dorothy had an uncanny ability for losing friendships and developing feuds that lasted for decades. The most famous incident being her unwise accusation in an essay which Eli Mandel included in *Context of Canadian Criticism* (1971) that tried to make the case that "David," Earle Birney's famous poem, was an autobiographical experience. Her accusation that Birney himself had pushed an injured friend over a cliff while mountain climbing drove Birney into a rage. He felt that Dorothy was essentially labelling him as a murderer. Birney claimed the incident in the poem was nothing more than invention. He denounced Dorothy and sought legal recourse and was successful in having this reference expunged in further printings. Earle was an extremely sensitive man and the incident insured that he and Dorothy, who had a relationship going back to the early '30s, remained alienated for the rest of their lives.

In her 60s Dorothy took on a number of teaching positions at various universities across the country, including the University of Alberta, University of Victoria and at St. John's College at the University of Manitoba. In her teaching life, Dorothy was deeply involved in organizing students and faculty, as well as the street poets and other writers and artists who happened to be in the vicinity. Though she seemed to be slightly out of sync at times she had a uncanny ability at reaching out to young people. She was always looking for somebody new and fresh to discover. Occasionally she got carried away pushing some unfortunate piece of writing or championing somebody who had little talent but had the cachet Dorothy craved for the moment. On the whole she had sound instincts and she helped a huge number of would-be-writers find their way in the dog-eat-dog literary world of Canadian writing.

By 1974, Brian Brett and I had carved out our niche with Blackfish, which evolved from being a literary magazine into a small press that produced a number of limited edition broadside folios and books. Dorothy, who was living in Winnipeg, teaching at St. John's College, and I were having a rather voluminous correspondence on a number of issues. Dorothy was burning up with the idea of starting up a new magazine. In previous years I had travelled over to Vancouver Island and visited her several times when she was teaching at the University of Victoria. She had introduced me to PK Page and then took me to meet the ancient blind editor, Alan Crawley, who was living with his son Michael in a little house near Cordova Bay Road. Crawley, who was close to 100 years old, had been the editor of a seminal Canadian literary magazine in the '50s called *Contemporary Verse*. The magazine, co-founded by Crawley, Dorothy, Anne Marriott, and Floris Clark, became an important place to be published for aspiring poets. Dorothy already had plans for me. She thought introducing me to Crawley might allow some of his ancient genius to rub off on me. As it was, I found it difficult to ascertain if Crawley knew how many people were in the room. To speak with him we sat close, clutched his arm or hand to get his attention and shouted into his ear.

Now Dorothy had the brilliant idea of starting a new literary magazine to be called *Contemporary Verse II*, and she claimed she needed my help. I had told her that I would be travelling across the country promoting Blackfish books in the winter of '74. She made me promise that I would stop in Winnipeg, where she was teaching at the time, and help her put her magazine staff together. She had saved approximately $1000 and she had done the preliminary work in brainstorming the publication and now she needed my help to pull it off.

In November I booked myself a flight to Toronto with a stop-over in Winnipeg on my return to Vancouver so that I could be of assistance to Dorothy in her ambition to float this new magazine. I arrived in Winnipeg on the last flight before the airport was closed. A humongous snowstorm had struck the city and nearly everything had ground to a halt. I managed to get a cab and gave the driver Dorothy's address, which was at the University Women's Club residence. At the time, Dorothy maintained a small apartment there as well as a small cottage out of town on the bank of the Red River. When I got to the address I unloaded my heavy suitcases, which were full of book samples, and I yanked them across the snowy sidewalk onto the porch of the stately building that appeared to contain apartments. I rang the bell for several minutes without any result. After 15 or 20 minutes of trying to get in I walked along the length of the veranda and peered into a window. There I spied Dorothy lying on a couch fast asleep. I tapped on the glass but to no avail. By this time I was getting nervous, since it was cold out and I was burdened by two unwieldy suitcases and I was almost broke. The thought of getting it together to find another place to stay was bothersome. I looked at the list of tenants on the wall and decided to pick one and buzz. Before long a woman with her hair in curlers wearing a rather tatty flannel robe came to the door. I explained my predicament and she allowed me to stand in the hall while she banged on Dorothy's door but to no avail.

"Wait here," she said in a gruff voice. I was wondering where she expected me to go when she returned holding a pass key. She opened the door and I followed her into the apartment. Dorothy was snoring like a band saw and I noticed an empty apricot brandy bottle on the rug beside the couch. The woman shook Dorothy but she merely adjusted her position and began to snore even louder than before. No matter how often or how hard she poked Dorothy there was no waking her from her deep loud slumber. I suggested to the woman that it was fine, that I would merely sleep in the armchair or on the carpet. Anything would be better than being forced to make tracks in the deep snow that was piling up outside.

"But this is the University Women's Club," she answered, "and men are not allowed here."

"Oh don't worry about it," I said. "Dorothy is my grandmother and I've come to visit. We were planning to meet here and travel out to stay at the cottage on the river but with this awful freak storm I'll just bunk in here with her tonight."

In the morning when she awoke, Dorothy was astounded to see me sitting across from her in the wingtip chair. We decided to go out for breakfast. Against my better judgement I decided to let her drive. In our previous dealings I had been so terrified by her driving that I always insisted that I drive her around in her own car. But since I was still exhausted and she seemed bright and bushy tailed I got into the passenger side. A few minutes later we pulled onto the main drag and Dorothy put her foot on the gas pedal. I sat looking straight ahead into the snowy curtain that had just begun coming down again.

"Perhaps you're going a bit fast for the conditions," I cautioned.

"Don't worry about it, dear," she said, proceeding at a faster clip.

I noticed a bus ahead pulling out from the curb. Dorothy for some reason failed to recognize the back of the city transit vehicle that was soon looming in front of us in the snowy air like the side of a mountain. Smash! Dorothy drove straight into the back of the bus in her Ford Escort. I sat in shock. We stayed in the car for a few seconds before the bus driver appeared and helped us get out of the vehicle.

"It was the conditions," she said.

I had no choice but to agree, indeed it was those awful conditions of swirling snow and limited visibility as she accelerated right into the back of the slow moving bus. Dorothy was amazed at how composed and kindly the bus driver was toward us.

"Well, I suppose he's taking it well because it's not his vehicle," I answered.

The attending police officer was not as forgiving as the bus driver, especially when he noted that Dorothy's driver's licence had expired some months previously. She got the beguiling look on her face that afflicted her when she got in trouble from her drinking and attempted to charm the officer. He said little as he surveyed the damage and put in a call for the tow truck.

By the time the policeman was through with us it was too late for breakfast. We were late for our appointments at the university where we were going to interview prospective candidates to fill the positions in Dorothy's new magazine.

"Dear, you take over," she said. "You know what to ask and I'll stay in the background and assess each person."

For the balance of the day we interviewed a number of students and others who were applying to fill the two main editorial positions that Dorothy had advertised in the newspaper. In the evening Dorothy's old friend, a Manitoba Judge named Roy St. George Stubbs, came and picked us up and drove us out to the cottage on the river and we continued our deliberations long into the night. Finally we decided on hiring S. G. Buri, who worked as a librarian at the university medical library, to become the editor of *CVII*, and a student named Robert Enright to fill the position of book review editor. The rest is history.

That night it started to snow with a vengeance and it continued on for three more days and nights before it ceased. I had missed my flight, which had probably not been able to take off, anyway. On the fourth day, another friend of Dorothy's, a grad student, came out and picked me up and delivered me to the airport and I was able to catch a flight to Vancouver.

In December, Dorothy phoned and informed me she was coming to Vancouver in January. She wanted me to go to the library and visit the political bookstores around town to familiarize myself with the work of the left-wing poet Joe Wallace. She told me Joe was an old friend of hers from her days in the movement. He was a politico as well as a poet who had achieved notoriety in the

Soviet Union and China and in other socialist countries since the 1950s up to the present time. She said that his work, while relatively unknown in Canada, except in left-wing circles, was distributed in thousands, even millions, of copies behind the Iron Curtain. Dorothy told me that Joe, who was 84, had just returned from a trip to the Soviet Union. She wanted to interview him for the first issue of *CVII*. It was scheduled to come out in the spring. She figured this might be the last time we'd have a chance to interview Joe because of his advanced age and she thought putting him in the first issue of the new magazine would be a real coup.

On a miserable wet January morning in 1975 I picked Dorothy up at the airport. I had already taken a trip to the SFU library and checked out a reel to reel tape recorder from the AV department. We travelled across the city into South Burnaby and finally found the high-rise where Joe lived. Joe Wallace, a tallish thin man with sparse white hair, greeted us at his apartment door, which was on the fifth floor. Padding around his sparsely furnished apartment, he made us a cup of tea while I set up the machine. Dorothy was full of chit-chat about the old days. She and Joe prattled on about organizations and people I had no idea about. Finally, we got down to it. Dorothy asked most of the questions. I chimed in from time to time. We spent most of the day talking with Joe until we had two reels of tape. He was a fine gentleman who took particular attention to ask me questions about the student movement and to ask me which poets influenced me. When I told him I was a fan of Milton Acorn's work he answered that he, too, had once liked Milton's work but in recent years had lost interest in keeping up with the poetry scene. I thought that to be a rather simplistic point of view, but as the day wore on I got a fairly good idea about Joe's poetics. While I mused to myself on the probability that Joe, a hardcore traditional Communist Party soldier and Milton a Canadian nationalist, had political differences, it did not occur to me that Joe's indifference to Milton's work would be largely caused by poetic differences. Joe couldn't be classified as being overtly political in his writing. He was a purely lyrical poet. He was a traditionalist whose writing had more in common with the Georgian poets than it had with modern poetry. I liked him a great deal and I found a handful of poems in his work that I enjoyed reading. The best of them, the love poems, reminded me of some of Leonard Cohen's work. His unfortunate lapses into writing political poems created a form of doggerel that was similar to the rhymes of Robert Service. Joe was quick to point out that his reputation in Russia was based on his lyrical tradition. He claimed the revolution had succeeded and the Russian public was already the converted, therefore it was unnecessary for him to write political poetry. Joe thought Acorn and contemporary poets such as Earle Birney and Al Purdy had gone way over the line by abandoning traditional forms. He was more critical of their use of language and their literary structures than he was about the content of their poetry.

Joe Wallace was a humble man who certainly believed in his political point of view with passion. I was astounded a communist could possess such deep Christian roots and still thrive in left-wing circles. I sensed an inner hurt in Joe that came perhaps from the fact that he was largely ignored in Canada. He made some issue of the fact he had done some recent readings, including one in the recreation room of the building he lived in. These events sounded like small potatoes to me. I wasn't convinced he was completely content with his lack of a wider audience and reputation in Canada. However, I was astounded by the light shining in his eyes as he proudly talked about his literary fame in the Soviet Union and told us stories about how well he was treated whenever he travelled there. Joe was particularly enthusiastic about telling us about the excellent treatment he received from Soviet doctors when he visited spas on the Black Sea. I had it on the tip of my tongue to ask him why he bothered with Canada at all but I was too polite a soldier to insult him with such a loaded question.

Eventually we got around to asking him respectfully on tape about such matters and he pooh-poohed any feelings of hostility or resentment at being largely ignored in the nation of his birth. He was humorous in discussing the harsh home life he endured as a child and the assorted trials and tribulations in his personal life and in his political life that saw him imprisoned for a time. In 1933 Joe was selected as a spokesman by his fellow unemployed who were marching on Ottawa to protest the prevailing social conditions and he had an encounter with the prime minister of the day. His description of the event appeared in the inaugural issue of *CVII*:

I was part of a delegation that went to see him [R.B. Bennett, Prime Minister of Canada] about the eight [labour leaders] who were jailed in Kingston Pen. Tim Buck and the rest. And this time I was the spokesman for the delegation, but Bennett wasn't going to allow any spokesmen. He had his press there, he had a couple of mounted police there and he just blasted me from the beginning. I said, "You granted us an interview. This is not an interview. This is a monologue. I have something to say. . . ." He interrupted, "You have nothing to say." I made several attempts and then I said, "You shot Tim Buck." That started it you see. Actually Tim Buck had been fired on in the penitentiary and Bennett was responsible to the extent that the kind of men that he upheld and the fact that he upheld them after and nobody was ever arrested, nobody was ever tried for this. So then his face turned purple, neck turned purple. "Get out." "All of us Mr. Bennett?" And he choked and he said, "Well the women can stay." The curious thing about Bennett was that, after I was out, he turned to Alice Buck as if she was a willing colleague of his, which was ridiculous and said, "You know, Joe Wallace would be quite a man if he didn't have these wild ideas."

In 1941, Joe was picked up and thrown into Camp Petawawa for being a Communist organizer and a danger to the security of Canada. He bore the country no ill will for his imprisonment. He grew in stature from his martyrdom.

Meeting Joe was an interesting experience for me on a couple of levels. I had been to Czechoslovakia in 1968, before the Soviet invasion, and in visiting my various relatives in the country I had had my eyes opened to some of the realities of Soviet-dominated culture: long line ups for food, long line ups at train station wickets, and in government offices. When I rode the ancient sputtering black wrought iron-encased elevator in my relatives' shabby apartment building in Prague, I smelled the cooking from the various floors wafting into the open shaft. All I could think of was poor Winston Smith in *Nineteen Eighty-Four*. Those thoughts went through my mind as Joe told us how the kindly doctors at the honoured writers spa on the Black Sea stooped to clip his toe nails and massage his feet.

When we left, Dorothy said she'd take charge of the tapes and find a grad student who needed a credit to take over the job of transcribing them. I balked at first, knowing that Dorothy was a disaster when it came to looking after things. She was always forgetting her handbag or leaving her briefcase behind. I had plenty of experience backtracking to find whatever objects she misplaced or lost. However, she assured me that she needed the tapes transcribed almost immediately for the coming issue. It was only sensible she take them with her back to Winnipeg. She had a selection from the tapes transcribed (but not even half of the interview) for the first issue of *Contemporary Verse II* which came out in the spring of 1975.

Joe Wallace lived until the following December and then he passed away without much notice.

After the issue came out, I asked Dorothy to package up the tapes and send them to me by registered mail so I could make copies of them and get the whole interview transcribed. She agreed but she wanted to publish the second half of the interview in a future edition of *CVII*. She told me I would have to wait because she had a deal pending with the CBC in Winnipeg to review the tapes toward producing a radio documentary. Dorothy was positively giddy about having the Wallace material edited for a radio broadcast. She was good at starting things but was weak on the follow-up. I fretted because of my past experience dealing with her. Hiding things in drawers and then forgetting and drowning in the resulting depression of her own folly was a constant problem with Dorothy. If she could leave it on the bus, forget it on an airplane, or lend it to someone and then promptly forget who, she would do it in a minute. She had a tendency to want to include everybody extant in her various schemes and projects. If she could get the CBC to transcribe the tapes to promote a potential broadcast she would be accomplishing two things at the same time and have the bonus of the transcribed tape for a future issue of *CVII*.

I cautioned her not to give the tapes to anybody before we made copies. She promised me she would get the AV department at the university to make copies. Later, she confessed she had given the tapes to the CBC man without taking the precaution of making copies. When I professed my concern that we might never see the tapes again she told me not to be silly, that she had a perfectly reliable connection at the CBC who would guard the tapes with his life. A few months passed and I wrote Dorothy a letter asking her about the proposed CBC radio program. She wrote back saying she would visit her producer friend and get the tapes back if he didn't hurry up and show some interest. Six months later, when her connection had gone cold and she finally got around to going to the CBC building in Winnipeg, Dorothy discovered, much to her horror, that the tapes had vanished. Eventually it was assumed by the CBC that somebody had taken the tapes and recycled them thinking they were old worthless material that nobody was interested in. I wasn't at all surprised.

The next time I saw Dorothy on the coast, she admitted she was a little chagrined about the loss of our Joe Wallace tapes. She was already showing signs of boredom with her new magazine. Dorothy was a doer, she had no intention of settling down and saddling herself with the day to day drudgery of running a magazine for long. She was already talking out loud about giving the magazine her attention for at tops, another year or two. Dorothy had too many projects on the go, too many places to visit in Canada and elsewhere, too many people to look up along the road, and too many books to write. She had taken the ideal and name of her former '50s small poetry magazine and with limited funds and the strength of her will had jump started a new literary review. *CVII* was nothing like its predecessor in shape or format. The only thing the two publications had in common was the name. Dorothy had planted another literary seed, this time in the name of Alan Crawley and now she was watching it grow into a plant and flower before her eyes. Not in Victoria this time but halfway across the country in Winnipeg, her home town. Dorothy was not interested in saving money, accumulating wealth or worrying about her old age and at the end of her life she survived on meagre resources. She lived her life to the fullest and she donated to a variety of cultural enterprises over the years. She had used her own savings from her modest teaching salary to finance the first issues of the magazine.

Dorothy's extensive network across the country gave *CVII* a constituency and she empowered its editorial staff to gradually take over the magazine and lessen her role. She was in full knowledge of the fact that new projects were already percolating in her consciousness. By some fluke of fate the magazine *CVII* still exists some 30 years later, albeit in a different form, but still treasuring its association with its long absent and long-departed founder. I was the wild card she plucked from the deck to help her establish the bottom line. The greenhorn she thought might, if I was lucky, evolve into becoming a minor Alan Crawley. I hung around for about 10 years, a soldier-recruit in her army of cultural adventurers from 1971-1982 (110 pages in her literary font at the University of Manitoba library), until we had a falling out and drifted apart. I figured at the time it was probably for the best, since we all need to move on every now and then to follow our own paths. I'm sure she felt the same way.

Dorothy wrote poems by hand early in the morning on a pad of paper, and letters and essays and other prose during the rest of the day. She listened to classical music and attended many concerts and musical events. She was always rushing off to an event at a gallery or a political meeting. She was extremely well-connected with artists, musicians and performers in other disciplines. Dorothy received an inordinate number of literary awards and numerous honorary degrees. The annual British Columbia Book Award for poetry is called the Dorothy Livesay Poetry Prize. Dorothy never stopped travelling the poetry trail until she was too frail to walk. I don't imagine she ever stopped her daily habit of writing.

The times I remember best about Dorothy were the many visits I spent with her at Rock Cottage perched on the rocks above the ocean in a small coastal alcove near Victoria. She asked me to come there in the summer of 1975 and handed me a huge stack of poems she had been working on. I spent two days putting the poems into a semblance of order and helping her decide which ones to weed out. Later in the year the manuscript, called *Ice Age*, was published by Press Porcepic. The collection was Dorothy's poetic take on growing old.

Although her body had the appearance of being old during her last years, Dorothy never got old in her mind. Her life was a series of collaborations. Her endless energy had matched up well with the advent of the alienated '60s generation that were challenging the establishment. She had become a symbol for her own '30s generation and she was still alive artistically when the cultural revolution came around again. Late in her life, she was caught up in the nationalist movement that catapulted writers into notoriety and fame. The universities had become "Canadianized," and Dorothy received an enormous amount of attention, especially in academic circles. She became a figure to be celebrated by the women's movement and at the universities. While she was encyclopaedic on the past, she stayed firmly in the present. She remained interested in what the emerging artists and new voices on the scene were all about. She sought out the young artists and writers in every generation that she encountered in her long, productive life.

Until her death in 1996 at the age of 87, we had a cordial relationship as we passed in our travels or found ourselves for a brief time at the same location or on the same program, such as in 1986 when an anthology I edited, *Vancouver Poetry*, was launched at Canada Place. It was one of the largest readings that was ever held in Vancouver. Dorothy beamed at me and told me that I had done a good job because she taught me well. She was already a bit unsteady on her feet when she walked across the stage, but it seemed she would go on forever. Whenever we met, we gossiped about what was going on in our own lives. Each time she told me about a new writer or a great new book she was reading and at least a dozen things that I did not previously know. Dorothy was a passionate exponent of living life in the fast lane. She was a confident personality who had strong opinions about everything. At meetings and conferences, whenever the boring cry came up to change the word "chairman" to "chairperson," Dorothy was on her feet lambasting the debasement of the language. The feminist constituents that adored her would quickly abandon their quest to alter the nomenclature when their elder spoke. They would rather argue with a hungry alligator than trifle with Dorothy when her hackles were up. She was an academic without the usual pretenses, a political organizer, a feminist literary crusader and a writer of great distinction. She covered the century of her birth, 1909-1996, with a career that will never be matched.

MEMOIR OF MINAGO, 1983

FLYING OVER THE GULF OF SAINT LAWRENCE in a Boeing 727 that is having problems finding Prince Edward Island. Suddenly, it's there below, beneath the swirling fields of fog; a green eye ringed with red like a planet. The prim Japanese school girl sitting next to me is reading a Japanese translation of Lucy Maud Montgomery's *Anne of Green Gables*. I fidget, holding a copy of Milton Acorn's *The Island Means Minago*. The Summerside air terminal is early 20th-century turkey shed. Transport planes practice takeoffs and landings, drifting out bumblebee awkward over Malpeque Bay. Climbing down the stairs from the plane I am assaulted by the smell of salt water and the stink of lowland fields. There is nothing hard or tall to look at against the height of sky. My eyes are bathed in a pastoral glow.

The taxis here have big yellow stars wired to the roof tops. I am greeted by the notorious novelist, Ved Devajee, author of the *Nemesis Casket*. He is an extrovert behind the wheel, watching the road from the corner of his eye, gesturing with hands and eyebrows. "Cars seldom attempt to pass, the natives are too polite," he remarks. "However, they might pull up beside you in the wrong lane and drive along having a chat." There are few cars in winter in PEI and no freeway systems. I tell him it reminds me of Czechoslovakia, an island in the middle of a continent with hardly any cars and taxis with similar stars.

Ved's alias is Reshard Gool, he's originally from Brixton and is married to the artist Hilda Woolnough. Reshard and Hilda, who I have not previously met, lend me a car and hand me the key to their house in Charlottetown. They give me a map with detailed instructions on how to find my way back to their country place. A wonderful packing-crate house, with two airtight wood stoves, and an enormous pile of slab wood. The house is an organic museum; full of strange books, Haitian wood carvings, ferns, ice plants, prints, paintings, pottery and a bathtub with claw feet.

There are two dogs, cats, and a frost-damaged garden overflowing the fences. A trout stream with darting shadows playing under its banks is a sanctuary flowing below the wood lot. No fishing allowed. A grouse whirs up into the dead limbs of a convoluted spruce tree. The forest floor is carpeted with mosses. Reshard argues about everything; so do I. We are the bookends of conversation. Hilda, an artist of considerable merit, consumes 10 cigarettes per hour. Making art from life, they serve squash soup, salad, a cauldron of mussels, a platter of paella and cod tongues garnished with lobsters. Hilda and Reshard have followed each other from island to island across three oceans. Reshard wears a deep pile red satin bathrobe with braided cord lapels that might have been tailored for Robert Garrick. After dinner they dance to 1920s music. We drink five bottles of Hilda's homemade wine. I fall asleep in her attic studio amid the curiosities and unfinished works. In the morning, before they are awake, I find my breath in the wood lot and in the garden's green wreckage.

In Charlottetown pay phones cost 20 cents and you dial four numbers. It's a tiny city you can walk in an hour. I did, stopping at St. Dunstan's Cathedral to sit in a second-row pew, craning my neck at the immaculate rose window. Hypnotic streaks of light pass through the openings carved in imported stone. There is no granite or any form of rock other than soft red sandstone on this island. An old woman stared at me from a side door until I left with a handful of pamphlets about the history of the cavernous church in Lilliput. Spent five minutes in the only second-hand bookstore I could find, then sauntered past the bottling plant down to the harbour. There were big guns at Victoria Park. From across the water sailboats out on their tethers seemed like a bunch of toys.

Milton Acorn lives in Parkdale, a suburb of Charlottetown, on Donwood Street, adjacent to his future permanent residence, the Peoples' Cemetery. Where else for the "Poet of the People"? Gravestones in PEI are so old and wind-abused that dates can be impossible to read. The Island is porous rock eroding into red sand, an hourglass sifting into salt water. Acorn sports a goat tail on his chin and walks with a shiny cane. He has heart trouble. In his hands he clutches an ornately bound red and blue notebook that contains the draft of a poem he is writing about his mother.

In PEI, Acorn is not an unusual name, though I have not heard it often other places. Kimbell C. Acorn sells cars. Milton Acorn is a poet. Another Acorn, Milton's brother, also writes poetry. And so it goes, thumbing through the phone book. According to Milton, it all springs from the union of a Germanic Acorn and his prodigious Scottish wife — 20-some children. If you examine the flag of Prince Edward Island closely, you will discover that it is covered with acorns. Milton is 60 this year with a face containing both sorrow and joy in the same expression. It is earth-red; the Island, the beaches, the roadways, the potatoes, the furrowed fields, the stones in the People's Cemetery. A shade of red-erosion touching everything, living or inanimate.

After three decades of living in urban Canada, the poet has returned to the Island. The Waverley Hotel, corner of Spadina and College in Toronto, loses its most famous resident. I remember picking him up in the early '70s at the train station on Main Street in Vancouver. He got off the Transcontinental with the typewriter strapped to his rucksack, bobbing along behind his neck like some kind of mechanical head-dress. He was enthralled from watching a UFO that flew along beside the train across the prairies. The stench from his stained clothes smothered the blustery cigar in the middle of his scraped red face. He reluctantly took a bath and stayed a month on the living room couch. Every morning he got up early, made coffee and put cups beside our bed. The kids rode around on him like he was a pet mule. During the night the machine clacked and the cigar flared until by morning light the hallway was filled with clouds.

Milton was a voracious reader who kept his library in his head, the books he picked up mostly in second-hand stores were left scattered behind him in the trail of debris that followed his life. In the '60s he had come west to pursue his dream of being a full-time poet. Milton had a theory on how he could increase his profile and become a national figure. A favoured son in the Maritimes, it amounted to him getting himself known, some might say getting notorious, in the Toronto and Montreal scenes before moving to Vancouver and becoming a player in that community. Once he had achieved coverage in these main centres he was content to make his headquarters in Toronto and just visit the other regions of the country from time to time. I was always curious as to why he had skipped establishing much of a presence on the prairies or in the north. Maybe it was the cold weather or perhaps the vast distances were too much for one who never bothered to learn to drive. His preferred mode of travel was the train. However, he most often took the bus, waxing on about the Sudbury bus station being the last place in Canada that served coffee with small glass milk bottle creamers. The Islander in him was a social fellow who liked cities because of the endless nature of the action.

In the mid-'60s, Milton lived in Roy and Pat Lowther's basement in their spooky rented house in Vancouver on East 46th. The house in which the depraved Roy Lowther, in the mid-'70s, took his wife's life with a ball-peen hammer. Milton, a man of action, was a perfect fit for the times. His bohemian nature allowed him to fit right in with the street scene and hippie culture. He thrived in the heady atmosphere of left-wing groups and activism during the years of massive opposition to the War in Vietnam that spread through the western world, making villains of governments and corporations. Milton's reputation as a communist poet and a Canadian nationalist had been forged from a lifetime of labour organizing and navigating the political waters that were so well defined by the Cold War. Milton, a committed activist and organizer, was one of the founders of *The Georgia Straight.* The height of the counterculture saw a huge change in writing and publishing in Canada. The mimeograph revolution and the subsequent availability of relatively cheap offset printing came at the same time the rebellious baby boomer generation, now at university, discovered Canadian writing. Milton's astonishing collection, *I've Tasted My Blood*, a selected poems, chosen by Al Purdy, came out in 1967 to great success that came tainted with controversy that helped keep Milton in the public eye for many years. He made more hay from losing the Governor General's Award for poetry to George Bowering than he ever could have gained from winning it.

Milton, the ultimate in dishevelment, wore crumpled worker pants, running shoes, and plaid flannel shirts, usually bright red to match his complexion. He memorized most of his poems and he was a dynamic reader with a remarkably varied repertoire of poetry that included many dynamic virtuoso reading pieces. He was a poet of delicate lyricism with astonishing insights about the human condition. Unlike most of the poets who wrote political poetry, Milton was a craftsman and an innovator who was fascinated by the possibilities in language in merging content and emotion into form. Late in his career, he fiddled around with the sonnet form and developed the Jack Pine sonnet, which he jingoistically labelled a Canadian sonnet. Milton was successful because he understood that he was a professional poet rather than a professional politician. He never let propaganda get in the way of a good poem, although at times it wasn't always obvious or such a clear cut choice. I have heard him described as a "militant improbable humanist worker who traded his carpenter tools for a pen."

I think he was. He wrote poetry with the same kind of skill and exactitude as that young carpenter in his deep past. He thought of himself as a worker all his life, rather than as the artist he was. Al Purdy, who witnessed Acorn's carpentry skills at Ameliasburgh, always claimed Acorn was a much better poet than he ever was a carpenter.

Milton became a favourite reader in the underground at union halls, coffee houses, left-wing book stores, art galleries, and demonstrations. He also became a popular figure in the vast network of events and readings on colleges and university campuses across the country. Poems such as "I've Tasted My Blood," "I Shout Love," and "The Natural History of Elephants" became his signature pieces from coast to coast. Once witnessing Milton reading at Sparticus Books on their second floor location on Hastings Street in Vancouver, I was amazed when the whole audience of committed lefties, almost all dressed in khaki, came to their feet and joined Milton in reciting his famous elephant poem. It was a magical moment for me because it showed the absolute beauty and power that language could create and how it could transcend the writer.

In the early '70s Milton came to stay with us for a few weeks nearly every year. We lived in Louis Riel House on the Simon Fraser University campus on the top of Burnaby Mountain. Brian Brett and I had already founded a little magazine called *Blackfish* and we published Milton's poems and his diatribes against George Bowering and the literary "ism" that was known as Black Mountain. Since we were located at the heartbeat of the movement our magazine issues caused a great deal of posturing and gnashing of teeth. When Milton showed up, the Bad Mountain (as Milton called it) devotees behaved badly, as expected, but it made no difference. Milton was far too primitive and clever for them. In a public place he was a virtual loudspeaker of opinions, he mowed them down with a torrent of sound that was neither logical or even always coherent. They ran for cover. Milton did not recognize any rules or niceties in the face of the enemy. The only people I knew who could match him in that regard were the young poet/politico Jamie Reid and my fellow student William Hoffer who was already well on his way to becoming a controversial book seller/literary figure, having opened a second floor book store (by invitation only) in Gastown. Milton relished a rhubarb; it kept his name in the headlines. The "language poets," as they were known, were a patrician lot who displayed little talent in the field of street fighting. They gave Milton a wide berth, as if he were some type of dangerous beast from another planet. His persona — indeed his table manners — troubled them.

Milton worked hard at his craft, no matter the situation, be he at home or on the road. He slept on a temporary bed in our living room. He pounded on his portable Smith Corona long into the nights, suffering monumental nosebleeds that sometimes put him in the hospital. Each time, after Milton came to visit, we found wads of draft pages and half-written letters in every nook and cranny of the apartment. Paper fluttered out from him like a normal by-product of life. He travelled light, and when he finished his endless drafts, he plunked out one pristine copy of each new poem and added them to the manuscript in his binder before he moved on down the road. Sometimes, in frustration, he abandoned whole manuscripts. He had a way of compensating for his chaotic working habits. Wherever he travelled, he usually stayed with friends and he relied on them to take care of his overflow. Theoretically, it was possible for him to recover his lost works and, when things went wrong, it was usually possible for him to get back his abandoned manuscript pages. One got a pretty good idea about who Milton's friends were over the years by the boxes that had been left in people's houses.

Milton, the midnight workaholic, padded around the campus in the daytime on the balls of his feet, in the curious way he had of moving, or he took the bus to the city where he followed a routine of visiting his favourite book sellers and shooting the breeze with his political cronies and the fellow travellers who he met for coffee in working-class cafés. Sometimes after dark, I would drive him in my old truck into the west end of the city. On Friday and Saturday nights, Milton liked to drop by Cool Aid, a place of sanctuary where people brought the unfortunate victims of the street scene who were having acid flashes or suffering from psychedelic drug reactions were looked after. Milton was good at dealing with schizophrenia and other psychological disorders. He was particularly adept at calming down freak-out artists. He gave them his baleful eye, staring into their faces with his own broken visage and somehow they usually managed to land back on earth. I saw it a few times with my own eyes — a person in a catatonic state suddenly snapping back into place under the influence of Milton's crazy eyes and the mewing/gravelly sound of his voice.

Once a friend called to tell me that a young woman artist had taken so much chemical mescaline that she had basically left for another dimension. He wondered if I could bring Milton around to see her. We drove down to an old rooming house that survived across the street from the main Vancouver Post Office. The woman in question, a young Chinese girl in her mid-to-late teens who had left her ultra-conservative traditional family, was carving jade for a living in Gastown while she produced a steady stream of drawings and paintings in her fourth-floor perch in the top of an ancient rotting wooden structure that had no heat and a leaky roof. Her friend met us at the front of the building. He told us his girlfriend had been sitting in the dark upstairs staring at the wall for the past 48 hours. He guided us up the rickety wooden staircase that hung precariously to the outside of the building. It seemed so flimsy that a fly would have had trouble landing on it.

Milton made a joke about danger pay as we climbed the slippery stairs, holding on to the railing for dear life. Her friend ushered us into the tiny dingy, cluttered living room that was virtually a picture gallery. Drawings and paintings were hanging by clothes pegs on a wire that stretched across the room. He lit a fat white candle in a cup and put it on a small coffee table in front of us and began boiling a pot of water for tea on a Bunsen burner. Milton and I sat on the floor across from the young woman who sat cross-legged with a bemused expression on her face but remained silent the whole time we were there. We sat for about an hour in the same spot. Milton stared straight at her for the whole time while I peered around in the gloom at the interesting works, mostly pencil drawings, that littered the floor. Finally, he tapped me on the arm and made a gesture with his head toward the small kitchen light at the other end of the hallway. We stood up and stretched our cramped legs and followed the light into the far room. The boyfriend was rolling a handful of joints, preparing to go out and listen to music up on 4th Avenue.

"Sorry," Milton said, "I can't locate her."

"Maybe you should try professional help," I offered.

"Yeah, sure," he said. "One of these days when I get the chance."

A few days later, I ran into the boyfriend at Don Stewart's bookstore on Pender Street.

"How's she doing," I asked.

"Look," he answered, "it was really only about sex and we were only together for a short time. I moved out yesterday."

Later I learned that he had not only moved out but departed with her supply of jade and her finished carvings and most of her pots and pans, books, jewellery and clothing which he sold to a secondhand shop in Kitsilano. I told Milton about the situation.

"Let's go back and see her," he said. "She probably needs our help."

We arrived at the side of the building and stared up at the light in the window at the top of the rickety spiderweb of rotting wood.

"This'll be my last trip up there," he said. I agreed.

When we got to the top landing we noticed the railing was coming unnailed. We stood there for a while and then Milton tapped loudly on the glass.

"Maybe we should just go in," he offered.

"I dunno, why don't you knock a little louder," I suggested.

Milton made a fist and banged on the door. The sudden shock of his pounding gave me a start. It reminded me of the police I observed banging on a hippy house on Boundary Road. Suddenly the door opened about a foot and half and the tall shaggy bearded face of a man in his mid-20s appeared in the space.

"She's my girlfriend," he said. "I just moved in with her."

"We thought maybe we'd drop in for tea," Milton added.

"Where is she?" I asked, peering into the side window.

"She's hanging out in the living room," he answered. "But I'm awfully sorry, we're pretty busy with me moving my stuff in."

He shut the door in our faces and we could hear the sound of the deadbolt slamming into place.

"Good view of the city up here," I mused, turning up my collar.

We stood paralyzed in the mood while the wind rudely bumped the staircase against the peeling shingles. Seagulls screamed at the cold blue sky.

"Well," Milton said, holding on to the railing with his white knuckles, "let's get the hell out of here."

I have witnessed Milton throw the most awful tantrum in the Crest Grill and seen him so depressed he couldn't face getting out of his bed at the Waverley Hotel. Every time he moved, the three inch, yellow corkscrewing toenails on his feet tore the sheets into shreds. His corpulent, rubberized body was covered in large yellow-headed boils. The toilet in the dank bathroom in his hotel room was roaring like a major cataract in the Nile. Every towel, sheet, and piece of clothing in his room was blood stained from the chronic nosebleeds that plagued him. Crumpled sheets of typing paper that had been discarded on the floor splattered from the blood storm that exploded from his face and was so hard to stem. I have walked with him in alleys just off Spadina in the middle of a blizzard while he looked in the rubbish piles for passed-out winos who might need to be helped out lest they should perish.

For years he made this practice of prowling the alleys in winter a routine. When he found a candidate who needed his help he staked his charge to endless cups of scalding java in an all-night café while he entertained with stories about the "winged dingus." The whole experience for some must have seemed like an encounter with a rather seedy down-and-out uncle. I have visited Milton three times in Sunnybrook Hospital, each time thinking he was on his deathbed.

Now, by some fluke of fate, I am driving around Prince Edward Island in a borrowed car with Milton staring balefully out rain-splattered-windows. The main Island highway is the Great Blue Heron Way. We see the birds, everywhere in ditches and fields, like so many David Nivens unruffled before the apparition of poet's eyeball and tongue. Milton is writing poems about birds. We stop at Rustico beach to watch black ducks in the drizzle. Milton thinks perhaps ravens start out being what's commonly known as blackbirds, then turn into crows before they succeed in becoming ravens. I argue that hamsters turn into pigs before they metamorphose and become hippopotami. We walk through a bitter wind at Cavendish, a furious mottled tide hammering the beach. Milton utters a hundred historical facts in two minutes. I am saved by the black-backed Atlantic gulls that attract him and cause him to burst out into a kind of pseudo bird language.

Milton is as close as Canada has come to producing Vincent van Gogh. He is a bachelor who has spent the major part of his life in fleabag hotels. He has literally consumed tons of bad restaurant food and neglected his health with a passion. He has obsessively danced with the visions that have haunted his life. He has the gift of speaking in tongues, the wild eyeball, the palette of brilliantly scrambled brain cells, the great love, and limitless anger. He is a gentle, considerate friend with a smouldering personality prone to misunderstandings and conflicts. Acorn is an extremist in all things, with an appetite for controversy. In his old age he is a raging anti-abortionist and homophobic.

Although he has won the Governor General's Award for Poetry and was given the singular honour of receiving the "Poet of the People" award in 1970 from his peers, he has remained the rat in the woodpile of Canadian letters. His Marxist politics, his personality, and his lifestyle have precluded him from the spoils of the establishment. Academics generally avoid him like the plague. The Lieutenant Governor does not invite him over for tea and schnapps. It is safe to say that Milton Acorn does not get invited to chi-chi parties; neither did van Gogh.

Acorn's best poems are cannon shots fired at the universe, or delicately crafted passages that invoke great reverence and hope for the human condition. He is an omnivorous generalist who has spent 40 years writing because it wouldn't stop coming. In the semi-gloom, he squints his eyes and watches a flock of killdeers circling the bay, the wind biting at his chapped face.

Milton's mother is seriously ill in hospital. He knows she'll never get out. He mutters, "I was a different kind of kid," rubbing his red eyes.

"I'll bet, Milton, you're a different kind of adult."

He chuckles like an exotic bird.

"Do you want to hear the black duck?"

He starts a tempest of quacking. I look down to the point, several groups of black ducks lift off the bay and head for unknown territory. He stops and exclaims with glee, "That was the warning call!" Rain sweeps down from grey banks over the brownish sea.

We climb back into the car and drive off, looking for a hockey game. Milton finishes telling me about places in the world where one square foot of earth contains five thousand different species of worms. I'm impressed.

"You know, I could have been a bird just as easily as a man," he says. "Blue Herons write poetry without trying." I agree. Who can argue with that?

GOOD NIGHT LOUIS

I have arrived in Winnipeg by air in the early evening. Either of two things is possible: there is a snowstorm and a wind making drifts against the houses or the roads and tree branches are coated with ice. The world is in the deep freeze. I adjust my collar and remove the brittle pair of glasses sticking to the bridge of my nose. I am trying to take a picture of Patrick Friesen at Louis Riel's grave near the Grey Nuns in St. Boniface. It is a ritual of many years of winter nights. It is either blizzard weather or colder than living memory when we pay our respects to Louis. He's buried under ground that is harder than a bowling alley lane. I snap a few shots with my automatic camera. Pat, dignified and composed, is standing beside Riel's monument. He might be a visiting European professor of linguistics or a Jesuit out for a night on the town.

While the rose window hole in the burned out cathedral wall makes a huge voice of the wind, we wander the snowy graveyard and climb treacherous cathedral stairs. After a while we drive past Gabrielle Roy's house and come to a dead end on a shanty-house-street in St. Boniface. Pat jumps out of the car and scales the brick wall of the St. Boniface Glass Company and sits on the roof. Snow begins to fall again, just a whisper of it caught by the wind. We drive through downtown Winnipeg at 3:00 am among odd-lit windows and dark and shadowy shops. The square granite buildings in the industrial district stand in the fields of the city like enormous tombstones. In the railway yards we climb on boxcars and skid down the gleaming rails. In the park beside the Red River we find huge ice sculptures bathed in artificial light. History and humour portrayed with the medium of frozen water and air. My feet fly out from under me and I land in the middle of my back.

I FIRST MET PATRICK FRIESEN in Toronto in the early 1980s at the rat race known as the League of Canadian Poets. He was the executive member from Manitoba; I represented British Columbia. When I first saw him I thought he might be recently arrived from some Siberian work camp. It was in the look. His butchered hair, piercing eyes, and the earnest measure of his face combined to make a serious statement. I expected a thick foreign accent to go with the sombre fashion of his clothes. He didn't speak much but sat and observed the game of literary ping pong. I recollect that BC and Ontario were arguing about appallingly sordid matters. Probably something to do with missing funds since money is what poets require more desperately than any other single commodity. When we finished our bickering Friesen leaned forward and dissected our problems with the dexterity of a surgeon. His judgement seemed to me to have been delivered by the voice of a benign executioner. I watched Ontario shrivel up like a slug under the salt shaker. My god, by some fluke of nature we found ourselves to be natural allies.

We left the meeting and walked the streets looking at humanity. I soon realized I was in the company of a man who was in the best sense possessed by his vision. With the passing of the years it has become apparent to me that artists who achieve this condition have arrived there by a curious method. They have worked like fiends trying to convert the energy of the imagination and the vision into creation. They have worked through thousands of pages of false starts and variations until they have finally begun to understand the underlying structure. Pat Friesen is a poet because he can't help it. He has reached the place where poetry has become a life sentence. The long journey of the process explains everything to the writer and nothing to the reader. In the end, only the writing matters. When it's good it has its own life. Pat Friesen's books are like that. They have powerful lives. No matter what the *genre* — poetry, dance, film or plays — the voice of the poet is the music.

IN THE MORNING WE DRIVE TO STEINBACH. I have wondered about the place after reading Pat's books. It is all I thought it might be, a bustling town surrounded by big fields and bush lands. I want him to give me a tour of the car dealerships. Instead he takes me to meet his mother, Margaret Friesen. She is recovering from a skiing accident. She has her own woods and cabin where she skis the trails and finds her own meditations. A gracious, charming woman, she has theories and interesting ideas about civilization and society. Patrick takes me by car into the country to visit the house and the farm where his father was born. I pull out the camera and take a picture. Pat is standing in front of this tiny white weathered house. There is a kind of dignity in its structure. The camera is attracted to the figure in the foreground. It makes me think about the solitudes and the memories generations interpret in their own lives. Maybe the austerity and the struggle for the land have left their mark. The man in the picture is saying nothing but feeling everything. It's as if he's taken on the job of trying to explain good reasons for being alive. The rules for life are not easily explained. The large painted sign in the Steinbach cemetery boldly proclaims the rules for the dead:

- A cemetery is a sacred place. Quiet and reverence must be observed by everyone at all times. The town reserves the right to refuse admission to anyone at any time.
- Dogs or other pets are not allowed in the cemetery unless controlled by leash or other means.
- Automobile speed is limited to 20 kilometres per hour.

- Artificial and real flowers are allowed. Artificial flowers and wreaths will be permitted on new graves for approximately three weeks, at which time they will be removed by the town.
- Fences of any kind (wood, iron, plastic or brick) are not allowed on any plots.
- The Town has the right to access any lot or plot, as necessary, to carry out required duties.
- Plots are generally levelled 3 weeks after and seeded one to two years after burial. All grave sites are to be ground level, raised or mounded graves will be levelled for the winter.
- Flowers are permitted, providing that they are planted within two feet of the head stone, planting of the entire plot is not allowed. Trees may be allowed, subject to receiving the caretaker's permission. Large trees interfering with neighbouring plots will be pruned.

Pat Friesen's haunted, mesmerizing language portrays the people of his place in time. He is the boy in the small town sitting out beside the gate watching the real world pass by. He is the one who wonders for his generation. The mythical west begins at the Ontario/Manitoba border and moves across the plains and mountains to end on the fissured rocks on the distant coast of Vancouver Island. Patrick Friesen and I live at opposite edges of the west. I have coastal dreams and a big ocean vista. He has the great prairie and the stars calling down to earth. We have many things in common. We are about the same age. Our grandmothers came from a great distance away.

I am of Czech ancestry, he is a Mennonite. We've had wild roller coaster rides in our respective personal lives. We are Montreal Canadiens fans and have a serious attitude about playing baseball. We are fond of city nights and small towns. We are fellow travellers, who have been skating on the small pond of Canadian writing all of our adult lives.

IN 1985 I RECEIVED A POSTER IN THE MAIL. It was advertising a National Book Festival event in Manitoba. It was called "The Missing Mennonite Cabaret." I was a little confused trying to imagine how "cabaret" went with "Mennonite" even if it was "missing." A few months later I was talking with Elin Logan and Randy Ware who worked for the Canada Council. They were sitting on bar stools with tears rolling down their cheeks while they retold tales from "The Missing Mennonite Cabaret" that was organized and MC'd by Patrick Friesen. They were laughing so hard they couldn't stop long enough to tell me what was so funny. I was aware of the great tradition of Mennonite writing in Canada but I never thought of it as being very humorous.

Last winter I persuaded Pat to show me the video of "The Missing Mennonite Cabaret." Friesen was the bizarre MC in a loud checked jacket. He was behaving like a sleazy nightclub comedian. The jokes were flying, drinks were being served and the audience was in a state of euphoria. Friesen had a steady stream of patter going. I realized suddenly that he was living out the fantasy role of the Mennonite version of Don Rickles. The audience was having a hell of a time. There were a few sour faces in the crowd, some of whom were writers waiting to go on. As I watched the video it dawned on me that some of these distressed faces were nervous because they had never been required to be funny in print in their lives. Now they were expected to get up and play for laughs. The waiting writers were getting gloomier while the MC was getting nuttier. I understood what my friends had been laughing hysterically about. Friesen's comic routines were extending his tradition. He was balancing on an edge, changing the rules, poking fun at his culture's rigid image. The writers soon got into the spirit of the evening and the audience was in heaven.

WINTER HAS NOT YET MADE AN APPEARANCE in White Rock so far in 1992. The months have passed through a blur of heavy grey skies and torrential rains. On February 6 flowers are peeping out from the ground. Trees are beginning to bud and the flowering shrubs are putting out false displays. I'm off to Winnipeg to spend another winter weekend with Patrick.

The lights in Winnipeg in the middle of winter's night shine on a frozen cityscape. I wonder how Louis is doing in his hard bed. There is no lack of winter in Manitoba, no signs of false spring. The wind is always blowing in from the vast prairie. I hear Pat Friesen's voice resonating in a theatre or laughing under the open sky of bitter weather. Now, in the middle of his career, the books and plays have established him as one of the best writers of his generation. I have no doubt that the best is yet to come. Pat Friesen is a writer of integrity and a man of distinction. I value him immensely as a writer and as a friend.

MEMOIRS OF A SMALL PRESS JUNKIE

THE GREAT LEAP FORWARD in small press publishing in Canada took place in the middle of the 60s and hurtled on into the '70s. I arrived at the end of the beginning in 1971 and started-up Black-fish Press with Brian Brett.

Brett was a boy wonder who could learn any difficult job. He had an attraction to old printing presses and became a jack-of-all-trades at fixing and running them. He could make anything run. We eventually acquired a rebuilt Multilith Press from Western Offset and installed it in the basement bathroom of his brother Leonard's house in White Rock. We produced a magazine and a series of publications that included broad sheets, pamphlets, and books in trade and limited editions. Our plate maker, complete with egg timer, was built into a cupboard. The press chugged away in the bathroom, pumping out pages of poetry books which were collated by hand and then bound in the homemade binding system that Brett devised in his spare time. We tried harder than most and the result was a variety of editions in one- or two-colour printing on text papers in boards or hand-sewn deluxe editions.

We lived in fear of the city bylaws which stipulated no home businesses. We covered the basement windows with rice paper and played loud music to hide the familiar ka-chink ka-chink that rattled on day and night. We were sure the dogcatcher was going to turn us in or the woman next door who came over on the lawn and asked politely about the noise in the basement. Brian answered quickly, "Oh it's just that darn washing machine." After that incident he was careful to cultivate Peg by tolerating her miserable dog and helping her each time she forgot to set the handbrake on her car in the alley. It was always running away down the hill.

One of the prime customers for our limited editions was the bookseller William Hoffer. Hoffer had been a student radical in the '60s at Simon Fraser University acting as security for the SDU during the student strike and in various confrontations with authority. Hoffer wore a full-length black leather overcoat to intimidate campus security who were always putting ringers in student meetings and taking what they thought were surreptitious photos of student radicals.

In his spare time, Bill was accumulating a huge collection of Canadian books and periodicals which he stored in his second floor walk-up store in Gastown. By the time he fled for the west end of Vancouver and set up a store on Dunbar Street he had cornered the market on esoteric print materials and was putting out an irreverent catalogue that raised prices significantly and captured a large market share of the eccentric antiquarian book trade in Canada, supplying dealers, collectors, university special collections, and a walk-in clientele.

Whenever our newest publication, passing through our basement mini-production plant, was ready, I would make the foray to Hoffer's store and attempt to make a sale. It was usually at a time fraught with peril because we were haunted by phone calls from bill collectors, usually about paper bills and printing supplies. To make matters worse, Hoffer was abrasive, prone to vicious attacks, and highly critical. He abhorred most aspects of the writing scene and poured equal amounts of vitriol on authors and publishers. There was no browsing in his store, unwary customers often fled unable to cope with his sarcastic verbal onslaughts which were designed to find out if the customer was up to the level of debate he required. He wrote nasty entries in his catalogues and offered big prices on books he ripped up. It worked, business boomed.

I learned to enjoy the taste of crow whenever I entered Hoffer's book palace. It was never easy withstanding the immense wall of energy that was thrust into one's face with the force of a howitzer. Years later it evolved into a tank metaphor; the colophon on his publications. I was always choking on my words waiting for the cash so that I could escape and make a substantial payment to the nagging bill collectors. There was always the possibility he could be in a mellow mood. Time passed effortlessly as we looked through books he had bought recently. Perhaps a mint copy of Raymond Knister's *White Narcissus* that had somehow survived untarnished in fragile dust jacket or a presentation copy of Dorothy Livesay's first book, *The Green Pitcher*, a nice $300 entry into the new catalogue.

On one of my forays to ring in some cash I was astounded to find Bill almost dancing with pleasure when I walked through his door. He stood up and patted his hands on the tops of two boxes and began to open them.

"There is a time when the bookseller must step forward and deal with the exegesis of time," he remarked, while he revealed the contents of the cartons. Seventy-five copies of a white book entitled *Woman Reading in Bath*, poems by Anne Szumigalski. "This is an amazing debut book. I couldn't resist. It's the bookseller's job to decide what is great literature and what is not, and I have decided." He handed me a copy, "Now sit down and do yourself a favour, read these poems." The rest of the afternoon he read them to me, waving customers out of the store with wide, sweeping gestures of his free arm. "If only some of you around here could write this well," he snorted.

"It has an unusual imprint for poetry," I remarked, noting the Doubleday Canada/USA, 1974, shared imprint. Printed in the United States of America, First Edition.

"Well, you're right for once," he said. "It's obvious what's happened." He looked at me with his paralyzing stare. "The cosmic blunder, occurs rarely in the publishing business. An accident that happened. Big publisher releases an astounding poetry book that will disappear in the system and never appear again until it is remaindered in New Jersey in a shopping mall parking lot in July."

"But it's a new book," I blurted.

"Precisely why I bought mine now. It has a white cover, returns will be dog-eared and the rest scattered like seeds in a wild garden. Put these babies away in the back wrapped up. Wait a year or two and it'll be fifty bucks per pristine copy."

"Who is she?" I wondered out loud.

"Doesn't matter," he said, "all great Canadian authors are unknown or dead. We mustn't stray from the strength and beauty of these brilliant poems to find an author. Poets are always trouble. When you get them it's like having roaches. I poison them in the catalogue to keep down the numbers."

I began speculating about the pronunciation and ancestry of the name when I remembered that Hoffer was studying Hebrew, Russian, and several eastern European languages.

"Polish," he rose from his chair and pronounced SZUMIGALSKI with flare and read me the poem "Nettles." One of the best poems I have ever heard. A memory in images that haunts the reader for life; an eternal story about an old woman and a cricket.

ABOUT ONE YEAR LATER I was sitting at our display table at a small press publishers' conference at Robson Square in Vancouver. A thin woman with dark curly hair and black horn rimmed glasses stood at the edge of the table looking at our various publications.

"How do you finance these?" she asked.

"Well, we don't really finance them," I answered. "They just happen from time to time as we can afford the cost of materials and then we try and sell as many as we can in order to generate some income."

Just then Loyd, the weirdest of the weird booksellers on Pender Street, came back for the third time and attempted to low-ball me on all of the copies of the limited edition of Al Purdy's *On the Bearpaw Sea* that were on the table.

"I'll give you nine bucks apiece for them," he said holding out his cheque book.

I was hoping to make a sale and each trip Loyd had offered an additional two bucks per copy for the 20 numbered copies bound in the Japanese manner with rice paper hand-sewn covers.

"Loyd, they're $15 apiece and I can only give you a 20 percent discount." Loyd's neck turned red and he started stamping his feet and waving his cheque book around his head.

"Look," he said, "I use to drink with Purdy in the Alcazar when you were in diapers. This is his junk, at this price I'm doing you a favour."

The thin, dark-haired woman stepped in front of Loyd until she was looking straight into his eyes. "Junk", she said, "you call this book junk!"

Loyd turned redder, his eyes popped a little and his neck twitched in its ill fitting wool jacket collar. I figured it was just a matter of time before Loyd paid the price. I knew he was planning on stashing the books away until they were out of print.

The young woman with dark piercing eyes was livid. "You're a cheapskate, why don't you shove off."

Loyd was trying to smile but his face was caught like a red fox in a trap. He stammered out the side of his mouth, "I know what you're up to, you're one of Purdy's sluts." Turning to me he said, "I'll come back when this dame's gone."

"My name's Caroline Heath," she said, handing me a light green coloured magazine with a grain elevator on the cover. "I'm from Saskatoon. I came out here with a friend to see what we could learn about publishing. This is *Grain*, our magazine. Pretty soon we're getting into book publishing."

She had a wiry build and small determined face that seemed more austere than necessary because of her severe glasses.

"How could you stand it when that guy called your books junk?"

I explained that Loyd was an amateur dealer who knew little about the book trade but had compulsions to buy certain books at different times. Nobody took his cheques but occasionally when he was serious he would turn up with a handful of cash.

"But he was such a gauche uncouth jerk."

I agreed with her, but explained that couth seldom came with cash.

"If you think he's a challenge wait until you take your magazines over to William Hoffer."

For the next hour she asked me questions about publishing. Mostly about things I hadn't even considered yet. We were new and old at the same time. New in that we were caught up in the offset revolution and old because we still clung to our ancient 7,000 pound Chandler and Price letter press. I told her that like her Brett and I started out with a magazine, graduated to books and had become small press junkies and by now there was no hope, we were confirmed life long writing addicts. She mentioned that she and her friend were in the same state and that *Grain* was just the beginning because there were so many writers on the prairies who needed a publisher. I told Caroline about my periodic forays across the country, suitcases bulging with books, crashing here and there each place, travelling by bus or borrowed car from bookstore to bookstore. I suggested she take some magazines to Binky Marks in the basement of Duthie's across the street.

The next day I ran into Caroline again when I went to hear the conference proceedings. She was with her friend Anne, a poet and her fellow editor from Saskatoon. They might have been the most opposite people on earth. Caroline, slim, intense, aesthetic in her black boots, black jeans, black jacket, black hair, and black horn rimmed glasses. Anne, a plump woman with an angelical face behind enormous slabs of glass in wire frames wore a colourful flowing dress with a huge scarf. Caroline was telling me that Anne was a fine poet. We were having a few laughs. I casually asked Caroline Anne's last name since I missed it the first time around. "Szumigalski," she said. Suddenly I thought of Hoffer's eyebrows going up and down in ecstasy, his voice hitting the rafters while reading me those astonishing poems from *Woman Reading in Bath*.

Now, July 28th, 1996, 20-plus years later I realize that *Woman Reading in Bath* is a selected poems from the first half of a writing life. The poems before the books of poems started arriving. Forty poems, 88 pages, poetry of inordinate quality, *Woman Reading in Bath*, title poem about a woman swimming in the sea with God, is a book of revelations about the lives of ordinary people. The fat woman who waits for the stooping thin man, addicted by her sexuality, to come back to her in the night. The couple joined by an operation who become a roosting place for birds. The young wife who goes to visit her cousin and returns to her husband decades later, an old woman resuming her place. The aunt taking a gruesome home movie through a glass bottom boat while on her vacation so as not to waste the occasion. Grandma's chalky knuckles growing up out of the grave like the twigs of a tree. These are powerful poems that examine the human condition with humour, pathos, and understanding. They reveal the poet, observer, and participant; skilled in her craft, moving the reader through the pages with a narrative of startling metaphors.

From this auspicious beginning, Anne Szumigalski has fashioned a remarkable writing career that spans three decades. Her collections of poetry which include *Doctrine of Signatures*, *Dogstones*, *Instar*, *Rapture of the Deep*, and *Voice* are the legacy of a major poet. She has written prose, plays, and translates other writers. Her play, *Z: A Meditation on Oppression, Desire and Freedom* (1995), is a powerful work about survivors from the holocaust. Szumigalski has documented her career in an unusual way in *The Word, The Voice, The Text: The Life Of a Writer* (1990). She starts at the beginning of her life and writes eloquently about childhood and the simple but profound experiences and emotional keys that unlocked the vaults of poetry and endowed her with the voice of the poet and a life of creativity from childhood that never stopped growing through the years. If you want hardcore biographical details, it is easier to find them in the poems. This prose memoir, illustrated by poems from various volumes (notably from *A Game of Angels*, 1980) is a kind of classic treatment of the art form that has blessed the writer. The child who played a "game of poetry" with her family and became absorbed with word play and the mysterious process of finding voice became inspired by angels. "As soon as they entered my work — for by that time I had begun to think of poetry as my life's work — angels became themselves, fiery messengers, glowing transcendent beings, and in this guise they have remained with me ever since."

Anne died in 1999 at age 77. For many years before that, she lived in a small brown house on Connaught Crescent in an industrial section of Saskatoon. The house remains sequestered in trees, on a lot that the poet and her late husband transformed into a series of small gardens. The result is a completely private enclave hidden away from traffic and industrial clatter. The poet's garden in detail like the pages from a book; a spiritual place, a small oasis of poetry in the middle of the great plains, perhaps the most notable literary address in Saskatchewan. The perfect place to interview the poet on July 25, 1996.

When I look at your work I think that Woman Reading in Bath *must have been a "selected poems" from all your early writing?*
That's right, quite true. I'm one of those people who are a really enthusiastic mother. When I had small children, I really had two families of small children with a space in between. In the space in between I began publishing a lot of poetry in Canadian magazines. But then I had two more children. If you're an enthusiastic mother the same energy that you use to write goes into your children. It's creative energy. So I didn't stop writing but I stopped trying to publish anything when I had small children. My time belonged to them when they were tiny. They soon grow up. When they grow up you can do what you want. You can select your po-

ems. Look at children, the mother or father call them out of the void. You called them, you wanted them, then your time belongs to them. That doesn't stop you writing poems. It does stop you from doing anything but write. You put them away, you take them out and look at them. As for publishing them, no, it's not the right time to publish them. Nothing could ever stop me from writing poems. I can't help that, it's part of my life, always has been.

Your children appear in your poems about halfway through A Game of Angels. *That book starts out in childhood, only a few poems. It moves to the Daisy Filman poem, which is about an awakening during adolescence, a period of hard scrabbling in the times, then a handful of incredible poems about the war years before you continue through other phases of your life; childrearing, home life, and midwifery. Did you write other poems about the war?*

Yes, I wrote a lot of poems about the war. I remembered things. You have all these things that collect in your mind and then you write poems about them. The problem is writing poems too soon after events happen. If you do that it usually doesn't work out. In fact my poem which I called "Halinka," about the baby, probably in *Rapture of the Deep*, is about the child I lost. It was quite a few years after. It just didn't work out. Then after about fifteen years had elapsed I could suddenly write the poem. I like to be at a distance from the things I write about. I do go over things in my head a lot. I talk to people. I talk to my parents. I argue with them because it occurs to me that I haven't argued something out with them. So I'll get really angry and yell at them. I'm not one of those people who thinks I'm going to get an answer in voice, the thing answers itself. You're better able to understand what happens. I do this often with my husband. I get really annoyed at some of the things he did and I sort of yell at him. Then I'm able to see exactly what happened. It's rather useful sometimes to be alone. If you want to talk out loud to somebody who isn't actually present there's nobody to laugh at you.

My husband used to annoy me a lot because he didn't like my writing poetry. He didn't like this, he didn't like that. Then I realized this poor guy had to put up with this woman. I was young when we got married. He was quite a lot older than me. He obviously thought that I'd grow up in time. Of course I didn't. He was probably disappointed about that. Then I'd laugh out loud thinking this guy had to put up with me. Why am I fussing? It's probably annoying to have a wife like that. Certainly annoying if you're not interested in poetry and you have a wife who wakes you up in the night and makes you listen to something. Must have been infuriating. I think he liked it. But I think he wanted to keep me for himself as a sort of private person. These things work out in the end. Of course now that I have lost him for more than ten years I miss him a great deal.

You've spent all those hours learning how to be as good a writer as you are. A continuous meditative experience that places you in a receptive space for the work you do. It almost seems like a way of controlling an emotional and intellectual life. Keeping the process you started as a child going. Building an infrastructure to deal with things other people don't have the luxury to think much about.

Yes. They want to do something else. This is what I chose to do. I keep on making new ones. Sometimes you remember. There is a photo of my sister and me. I'm four and she's six. We're having our photo taken. For years I hadn't thought about that but when I saw the photo I immediately remembered the feel of her hand. I didn't want my photo taken. She was very comforting. When she took my hand hers was warm and sticky. She probably had jam on her hands. I was comforted. I felt great, I knew she wouldn't let anything bad happen to me. I look back in my life and think about what everyone was wearing and what they said. It's really important for writing poetry. I can go back so easily and remember. It's only when these things are at a distance they become poems. When they are right under your nose it never happens. When you can go back to this particular day when you were 15, or 12, or 25. Not only are you there but you are illuminated. You don't remember every single day of your life but just these particular ones. Even then we must begin thinking this is a poem. *A Game of Angels* was written when my husband and I were courting. We were in Germany and we played this game. We pretended to be angels. I think that was what he liked because he found it really difficult to be a child, but I didn't.

The major body of your work is the poetry. Did you always think you were going to tackle Z?
Of course. I always knew I would write about my experiences from the war. The question was if I kept putting it off would I be there to write it.

Did you have a dilemma whether it would be poetry or some other form?
I thought it might be a novel or a long poem. I didn't think of it as a play, although I always was attracted to theatre. I didn't think of it as a play but as time moved along that's how it turned out. If you were a young woman would you not be horrified if a probably formerly dignified old gentleman who had been most likely a professor at a university in Europe was to fling himself at your feet and thank you with tears in his eyes that you had given him a piece of bread? Wouldn't you be horrified? You'd think to yourself, why is he doing this to me? I'm nobody. I'm not even a person yet really. That's a terrible experience. I haven't got that in Z. That's one of the worst experiences in my life.

You have that experience in Z over and over again. You have people making choices about surviving.
Praise be to those who manage to survive. Praise to those people who ate the dead bodies of other victims of air crashes in order to live on. They deserve to survive. They don't want to do that but

survival depends on it. So they did it. It would be an entirely different thing if they killed the people to eat them. But when they're dead already of course they should eat. I have no qualms about that at all.

The story about the piece of bread is the central question that occurs between Itzak and Horst in Z. You have a scenario where you have this prisoner who is an organizer, administrator and clever survivor who runs a kind of pawnshop of souls. He tells stories to his jailer who reacts like a critic demanding more from him each time until it becomes a deadly game and the survivor is given the power of God because he is forced to select the victims for the gas chambers.

Yes he does, and the man throws it all away by suddenly breaking down and yelling out the names of all these people who are not supposed to have names. Because he really knows that's the end of the ship when that happens. He can't help doing it. At last his passion takes hold. We're all very close to being one of these people. If you were to meet these two people, and they weren't in this situation — Horst, a schoolteacher, and Itzak, a storyteller — you might have liked Horst much better than Itzak. He was a kind, steady guy before he got his wartime position. And it has totally corrupted him. Now he doesn't know what he's doing. He takes one step toward being a Nazi and another step in the opposite direction. It's obvious to the audience or reader that he's giving in to the worst side. He'll kill people quite happily. If the war hadn't happened to him he would have gone through his whole life being a village schoolteacher. Retired in his sixties, being liked by everyone. Gone in for village council, good citizen, fine neighbour, but it didn't work out like that. He was put in this corrupting situation. While Itzak might never have ever come to his great moment when he suddenly rebels and realizes he has to take risks. All the time before he has been licking boots. Suddenly he says no, puts himself in total danger and the whole thing turns around on him.

Itzak isn't a very likable character.

No, he's not. He's in the position of being a hero although he isn't a very likable person. While Horst is really a nice man but he gets corrupted. But just because somebody is a victim doesn't make them a nice person. Lots of victims are horrible people. You have to realize that. I think we are often bamboozled by the idea for example that all native people are wonderful because they have been victimized. That's just not true, some of them are wonderful, some of them are not. Just like everybody else. The people in concentration camps were victimized and treated in a completely inhuman way. Presumably the victims somewhere sometime are going to gain something from that because they suffered so terribly. Those people who used to be thieves will suffer as greatly as those who used to be theologians. It doesn't make any difference. They're just people. If you took a thousand people at random from any community you would find good and bad people. Some of them will have no strength of character, some of them will be mean, some of them will be cruel, some of them will give up, and some of them will be noble characters. If you took one hundred Germans before the Nazi era and a hundred Jews wouldn't you find the same proportion of good and bad people? Every community does. Is there such a thing as a good or bad person? They're always mixed. In Z, Itzak and Horst are really one person, in a way different sides of one person, the good and bad and indifferent parts of their own people.

These are difficult things to talk about.

That's what happens to people in their lives. Whatever situation you're in you don't really know how you'll react. It's all very well for me to say if I was tortured I'd never give anybody's name out. Balderdash! You don't know that about yourself, you don't know how far you'd let things go. Nobody knows that until they are tested by it. Of course everybody would rather not do the wrong thing. If you were Itzak put into this position, if you were more intelligent than most people and knew how to get around things, wouldn't you? Everybody can speculate on this. None of us know how brave or noble we are. We just don't know that. There's no way of knowing but being tested. Think of the nuns who took little Jewish boys, dressed them as girls and took them into their schools. They had classes full of little girls, some of who were little boys in disguise, to rescue them from the Nazis. If they had been found out not only would the nuns have been shot but all the children as well. They took that enormous risk. I don't know if I would have taken that risk. I just don't know. But the people who did you have to say were noble and brave. The test of life is experience really, and that is the only test. It's amazing what really brave things people will do. It's also amazing what despicable things people will do to save themselves. It's just human nature, up and down, high and low. You don't know which one you are.

Nobody knows that. That's what I wanted to say, nobody knows which one they are.

CITIZEN JOE

WHEN I THINK OF ROSENBLATT THE POET I think of the most complicated human being that I have ever had the pleasure to know. This man, while serving a life sentence enslaved by the muse, is also a fine prose writer who excels at drawing, etching, and painting. He has produced a huge catalogue of books and visuals. He remains a unique artist who has endured for over forty years, without sign of slowing down. Now in his late 60s he continues to produce books and fill galleries at a prolific rate.

I was in my early 20s in 1974 when I first met Joe at the Bagel restaurant at College and Spadina in Toronto and had lunch with him, Patrick Lane, and Milton Acorn. It was the beginning of a lifelong friendship with Joe that has endured until this day. On my various journeys to Toronto from the West Coast to peddle the literary books that my friend Brian Brett and I produced at Blackfish Press, I invariably ended up hanging out with Joe. Rosenblatt was then and still is a connoisseur of café life. He introduced me to bagels at the Harbord bakery, cappuccino at the Diplomatico at Clinton and College, hot veal sandwiches at Bittondos down the street as well as the divine pasta, freshly made by two extra large Italian mamas, upstairs at the Monarch Tavern. We ate split quail at the Brazilia in Kensington Market, gorged on blintzes at the United Bakery, watched road warrior movies at the Tropical Island

and ate plate after plate of marinated shrimps at the Lisbon Plate (now the Amadeu's Bar and Grill). Sometimes we went to the all-night Portuguese bakery on College or the Sangria, a second story dive further down the street.

On Saturday mornings we usually met for breakfast at Barney's in the book district on Queen Street before we hit the book stores. Usually we stopped by the Village Bookstore and engaged Marty Avhenus in conversation while we looked over his large collection of esoteric publications. We often visited the Gadatsy Gallery located in Yorkville. There, for the first time I had my first glimpse at Joe's more than remarkable cat drawings. They were huge drawings of stupendous cats that captured the public imagination. Joe donated the proceeds from his cat drawing shows to the Toronto SPCA for the benefit of homeless cats. This was a brilliant strategy that attracted an audience and got Rosenblatt the artist ink in the popular media including *Maclean's* magazine. Not to mention the good it did for Toronto's itinerant cat population. Homeless cats have remained a cause that Joe and his wife Faye still support today. During most of the '70s, Joe and Faye lived on Greensides Avenue in a brick house with Guiness, a slight Siamese, Esther, a plush grey beauty and Maurice a massive orange male — all of them more eccentric than their housemates. When the Rosenblatts eventually moved to Qualicum Beach in British Columbia, all three felines made the transition to living on the west coast. Guiness walked around like a stiff old man in long johns. He lived to be about 14. The shimmering sexpot, Esther, and the athletic Maurice, who if human would have been a heavyweight boxer, lived to be over 20. I'm sure their great age had something to do with the quality of their diet. Joe the avid fisherman rowed miles in the saltchuck trolling for salmon or jigging for bottom fish to provide gourmet seafood for his ancient friends.

On lazy weekday afternoons we often opted for a visit to Allan Gardens so that we could refresh our minds by staring at the intricate orchids that had just opened or at the beauty of the myriads of tropical plants that languished beneath the glass of a Victorian greenhouse. There was something addictive about looking at exotic tropical plants while the strange influenza inducing Toronto winter sleeted outside the curvaceous panes. I learned that Allan Gardens was the location for one of Joe's purest triumphs. Here in 1963, he and Milton Acorn made a stand against the Major Hooples who formulated decades of city policy. In those days, walking on the grass in a Toronto park was almost a capital offence. The lawns of city parks had little signs on the green matter warning against walking on it and the sidewalks were rolled up on Sundays. By the time I started taking yearly trips to the mysterious east in the early '70s things had loosened up a trifle but Sundays were still pretty lame. A visitor in the know could always find entertainment by strolling around Christie Pits, going out to the Beaches district or visiting Ward's Island just offshore in Lake Ontario.

Acorn and Rosenblatt started a Free Speech movement and decided to challenge the authorities by reading poetry and making speeches in the park. The result was a large crowd of supporters and a full-scale punch-up and riot when the police showed up. The two poets were forced to go into hiding while Toronto's finest attempted to hunt them down. The incident became known as the "Allan Gardens Free Speech Fight." In the end the two fugitives gave themselves up and after a brief legal hassle the whole issue was dropped. In the years to come Rosenblatt and Acorn were to become legendary characters in the annals of Toronto cultural and political movements. That subject I'm afraid would be another article in itself. While thinking about this piece I have determined I could easily write a book on Rosenblatt without much trouble and certainly without consulting sources. There are so many sides to the man and his work. It is difficult to even imagine how to tackle writing about the immense scope of his unusual career and the depth of his amazing phobic personality. The latter subject is probably at least a three-volume undertaking. Needless to say Rosenblatt the writer/artist is a meaty subject who will make any critical study a veritable banquet of exotic dishes.

There was no disputing Joe's talent for getting people together. During my visits to Toronto we literally walked hundreds of miles around the city, going from attraction to attraction. Invariably, Joe led the way and I followed. Usually Joe had already planned our adventures. At each stop we would be joined by one or more people, usually writers, artists, broadcasters, critics, librarians, PR flacks, publishers, book sellers, academics or journalists as well as his secular friends, who ran the gamut from restaurant workers to blacksmiths. His circle seemed endless and changeable as we picked up companions and moved on to the next location. This might include a stop at Longhouse the Canadian bookstore on Yonge Street or a visit with the Dreadnought Press hippies on Huron Street or on to the Royal Ontario Museum or the Art Gallery of Ontario or Hart House at the University of Toronto (where Joe swam and used the weight room) or to the Thomas Fisher rare book room at the Robarts Library, or to view the priceless volumes tended by Desmond Neil behind the portcullis in the basement at Massey College or a visit to the ancient CBC buildings in Cabbagetown (where Joe went to have lunch with Barbara Frum or one of his legion of cronies who worked in front of or behind the microphone).

Joe introduced me to the painter Florence Vale and we spent many delightful hours talking with her about art or listening to her play the piano in her old house on Hazelton Avenue, in what, by then, had become an exclusive neighbourhood. The walls were crammed with paintings, both her own and those of her deceased husband Albert Frank. Sometimes we visited Gwen MacEwen on Roberts Street sitting at close proximity in her small cramped living room that was so full of furniture there was barely room to breath. Often we tripped around town with the poet Diane Keating who has more class in her little finger than most of us could ever hope to possess. We must have appeared a pair of unruly bumpkins in her patrician companionship. Speaking of patrician personalities, I once heard PK Page another writer/artist who defines dignity by her very being, call Joe "my little Minotaur." It was an affectionate summary that always seemed appropriate to me considering the content of his artworks. Joe helped establish the Victoria Hotel on King Street (its bar filled up at lunchtime and late in the afternoon with stockbrokers from the financial district), as a refuge for out-of-town poets who eagerly rented the cheap rooms, which were mostly taken by railway workers and actors.

Whenever he was in Toronto, Robin Skelton, a man of many literary *genres* and a practitioner of Wicca to boot, took the joint over. We often sat in the large wingtip chairs in the once opulent but by then faded bar and drank whiskey with Robin, resplendent in his Swedish cavalry officer's hat, while he regaled us with side-splitting-tales of his adventures in the British military service. A field he claimed he was supremely unfit to serve. The staff at the hotel regarded him with awe as if he was a celebrity who had just arrived from accomplishing some sacred duty for the pope. He could do no wrong as the front desk, barmen and waiters tripped over themselves in their efforts to please. Robin hated walking and his presence in the bar insured a steady stream of patrons coming in to pay homage and who imbibed at the same rate as himself and tipped lavishly.

Usually, by the end of the day of one of our sojourns around Toronto, we ended up on College Street, in Chinatown, or Kensington Market (not far from the location of the flat on Kensington Lane where Joe spent his first few years) dining on cheap ethnic food — easily the best thing about a cosmopolitan city in a multicultural society. Late in the evening, just after midnight, we often walked several blocks along College Street so Joe could pick up the new day's first edition of the *Globe and Mail*. Rosenblatt had long before sussed out the delivery trucks first stop. He was a newspaper freak eager to get at the news before it got too old.

Rosenblatt has never possessed a driver's licence or a wallet full of plastic cards. He has also never been burdened by what most people would call a regular job. He is a full-time writer and visual artist who has from time to time indulged in various periods of editing, teaching, and residencies. His longest manifestation in the former guise was the 13 years he edited *Jewish Dialogue*. This memorable publication that began in 1970 and ended in 1983 served a constituency of about 1200 subscribers; in addition, thousands of magazines were given away free. It was a seminal publishing place for many new authors and visual artists. Matt Cohen's first published story appeared in *Jewish Dialogue*. The issues throughout the years remained a virtual who's who of literary writers. In many cases, not only a first publication but a first paid publication. *Dialogue* was one of the best paying literary mags of the times. While the magazine celebrated Jewish writing and writers and focused on that tradition, it remained open to good writing from any quarter. Rosenblatt was not into maintaining a literary ghetto. The most amazing thing about *Jewish Dialogue*, apart from its long years of publication, was that it survived by selling numerous business-card sized ads to Jewish businesses and professionals in various locations in North America. While Joe handled the literary affairs of *Jewish Dialogue*, the business side of the publication was run by Murray Barrett, a white-haired, pear-shaped man in white shoes and belt. He sat in a small office in his oversized chair and made hundreds of calls each week to various cities in search of advertisers: usually Jewish businesses or professionals, including a good number of doctors, dentists, and lawyers.

On a few of my trips to Toronto, I accompanied Joe out to Downsview to have dinner at his parents' house. This invariably meant that we refrained from eating anything for several hours in advance. Joe's mother, a tiny energetic woman, rushed about in a whirlwind, serving up a veritable feast of Jewish fare, including knishes and blintzes. By the time we finished eating we resembled bloated lobsters as Mrs. Rosenblatt urged us to eat and in the end invariably professed disappointment at how little we managed to consume. I can remember both of us stretching out on a bus stop bench, groaning at the leaden weight of the food that protruded from our distended bellies. It was an exercise in familial duty for Joe who in his life had gone through some periods of alienation from his parents. I think he liked to take a friend along with him on these visits in order to lessen the pressure he often felt, especially from his mother. I'm not sure that Joe's parents had much knowledge about the extent of his artistic life.

One of the most vivid memories that stays in the forefront of my thoughts about Joe concerns his parents. Being a rather high-strung person who hates the sounds of silence, I engaged his parents in a lively conversation that I will never forget. They had emigrated to Canada from Poland in the early '30s (Joe was born in Toronto in 1933) at the urging of Joe's Uncle Nathan, who needed help in his fish store on Baldwin Street. The result was they escaped the fate that tragically obliterated their parents, siblings, relatives, and friends. His aged parents, a petite couple, sat across from us on the couch holding hands and showed us pictures of their respective entire families that had perished in the Holocaust. It was a powerful experience.

Being a poet and not an academic, I'm afraid I am not competent to articulate intelligently on the effect biography might play in the creative process. In Rosenblatt's case, let me refer you to one of the most delightful books that has ever been published in Canada. *Escape from The Glue Factory* (Exile Editions, 1985) is a classic in the creative non-fiction *genre* that has never been equalled. The book is written in a beautiful lyrical style that focuses on the poignant details of nostalgia. It reveals an immense depth of understanding about the issues that are encountered in the journey of life. Only a true poet, under the bright truthful light of self-discovery, could have written this book. It is an incredible work. I read it on a yearly basis just to help motivate my own bumbling attempts at writing prose.

In this volume of astonishing memoirs, Rosenblatt has recorded his early school life attending Lansdowne Public School on into early adulthood. Here the young child from a Yiddish-speaking household that follows Orthodox Jewish practices is thrown into the strict Anglo cauldron of public school. The description of the horse chestnut trees in the streets, the memory of Rebbe Noble and the elders at the author's bar mitzvah, the action at Uncle Nathan's fish store, the sad life of Harvey "the friendly giant" who lived on Major Street, and the story about Moose the boy who tormented the lads in young Joe's cabin at summer camp, are evocative pieces that instantly remind one that childhood is the glue that holds the adult together.

Rosenblatt the boy, who impulsively put a pea in his own ear and lusts after his luscious elementary schoolteacher, Miss Orchard, is victimized by a sadistic platoon of teachers. One of them, Mr. Chick, takes it upon himself to correct a curvature of his spine by forcing the young Joe to stand erect with his chest thrust out while holding a pointer in the small of the back. He learns to recite Kipling and to memorize the King James version of Isaiah under the tutelage of his demanding ex-military male teachers. The dreamer is born again. The result is a charming book with so many incredible cultural insights that the reader feels joy and pathos at the same time. The innocent school boy finds out about the Holocaust at the movie theatre when he foils the clearing out of children by hiding in the washroom. He journeys back into the dark balcony to what he imagines will be a rumoured "Minnie Mouse with tits cartoon" only to view the startling news reels that first revealed the horror of the Holocaust to the general public. Rosenblatt's kid is a misunderstood fall guy who learns the major lessons of life at an early age and quickly becomes a survivor who makes money by selling condoms door to door. Early in life the poet is already in training for a lifetime of exploiting his experience and imagination, although he doesn't know it yet.

In real life, Rosenblatt attended Central Technical high school — ironically, one of the most progressive schools of the times in presenting innovative artistic programs — where he frittered away his time trying to look busy until he dropped out. Most likely he was a partially dysfunctional student in a system that processed under-achieving candidates like himself toward the industrial workforce without imagining any of them might possess special qualities of artistic genius. After his high school experience, Rosenblatt studied welding at the Provincial Institute of Trades in Toronto. After knocking around the workforce, Rosenblatt obtained employment as a Canadian Pacific Railway bull worker, loading boxcars. It was in this rough industrial frontier of a largely multi-ethnic workforce where Rosenblatt first emerged as a social activist and poet who was encouraged to write by Milton Acorn the communist poet. Acorn, a gifted poet who left behind a marvellous legacy, saw Joe in the light of his own life. Before he became a full-time poet Acorn was a carpenter who shared Rosenblatt's labouring background. In conversation Milton came across like a propagandist who advocated social revolution and Canadian nationalism. Despite his political views, the bulk of Milton's literary production remained untainted by his biases. He wrote uniquely constructed poems of great power and beauty that astounded his contemporaries. Most of whom were terrified of him. For good reason, since he disliked many of them for a variety of reasons. For example, he attacked George Bowering at every opportunity because his work was influenced by American writing of a certain ilk that Acorn despised and Tom Wayman who he regarded as a no-talent poser of tepid left-wing persuasion — bereft of craft. When Milton discovered that Wayman had dedicated a poem to him he went off like a Roman candle.

Milton viewed Joe as the son he never had and championed his work for many years. He grew upset that Joe had abandoned a certain political sensibility that Acorn demanded from his fellow poets. As Rosenblatt grew in stature, winning the Governor General's Award for Poetry in 1975, Milton became increasingly more critical, until the two had very little in common. This was a pattern with Milton that also saw him turn his back on bill bissett and Patrick Lane, two poets that he openly admired for decades, along with Joe. They were all repudiated suddenly in an unfortunate magazine interview in *Cross-Canada Writers Quarterly* in 1986 (vol. 8 nos. 3 & 4), near the end of his life as if he was trying to terminate poets that he had begun to view as rivals. I believe this unfortunate interview destroyed Joe's feelings for Milton as a friend, although he continued to admire his work. In his old age, Milton became an outrageous opponent of abortion, a raving advocate for the Ayatollah in Iran, and a shocking homophobe.

In the early '80s, when Rosenblatt was running for the presidency of the League of Canadian Poets, I encountered Milton on a street corner and went with him to the Crest Grill on Spadina Street for breakfast. Milton and I had a long history. I was one of the few poets who was not avoiding him for fear of inciting one of his outrageous attacks. We each shared a lifelong passion for the Montreal Canadians. Whenever I was in Toronto during the hockey season I watched Hockey Night in Canada with him on the TV in the lobby of the Waverley Hotel, where he lived for many years. I employed a strategy with Acorn that allowed me to avoid issues that I could not tolerate discussing with him by sidetracking him in wonderful discussions about the technical and mental aspects necessary for writing poetry. Whenever the Ayatollah came up, I whipped out something from my bag and showed him a poem or a clipping. Since Milton was a prolific reader I patiently waited for the diatribe to lessen and then presented him with a book on some subject I knew he couldn't resist, thus instantly gaining a change of subject, which mercifully spared us the ignominy of a huge blow-up. Others perished under his onslaughts and avoided him like the plague. On this day I committed one of the worst blunders imaginable. I suggested that, since he was a League of Poets' member, Milton should come to the business meeting the next day at the Bond Hotel and support Joe's run for president. This was a mistake of huge proportions that resulted in one of the most astonishing encounters I have ever witnessed. The League was fraught with peril because of the militancy of the feminist caucus and the aspirations of several different factions who were rightly demanding recognition for certain social and sexual biases.

Within seconds of entering the fray, Acorn was on his feet attacking an Indo/Canadian poet (who was trying to pass a gay rights resolution calling for support for gays who were being harassed by the police at Toronto's steam baths) with a screaming narrative that raved on about sodomites and perverts. Knowing that he was probably the only person in the room capable of interrupting the stream of bigotry, Rosenblatt jumped to his feet and began to attack Acorn's points of view. This led to an amazing slagging match that left the members largely speechless in their chairs, viewing one of the most vicious exchanges anyone had ever witnessed. Rosenblatt finally managed to accomplish the near impossible by silencing Acorn's attack. This exchange caused the rather woolly-headed Aussie psychiatrist/poet Craig Powell to leap to his feet and proclaim Rosenblatt unfit for office since he obviously could not control his emotions. The result of all this turmoil was a surprising series of events and occurrences. Joe lost the election for president but he became a champion for the feminist caucus and the disenfranchised writers who felt alienated for their sexual preferences. This would hold him in good stead in the future when he was elected president of the League in subsequent years and served two successful terms in that office.

At the end of the day, Milton wandered around, squinting out from his baleful eye, docile as a lamb, wondering why everybody was upset. He wasn't mad at Joe, whom he avidly supported for president. It was merely a father/son spat at the workplace. I felt terribly guilty that I cost Joe the presidency by opening my big mouth at the wrong time, reminding Milton about the meeting he would not have attended, but I confess I knew the vote for president was going to be close. I saw Milton as a potential vote in the Rosenblatt column. Later, at subsequent League meetings, whenever Milton showed up I often sat with him isolated at a table while others cleared out. By that stage in his life he had that kind of effect on people. Rosenblatt has documented some of the events I have outlined in a humorous article that appeared in 2002 in *Books in Canada*.

What is great about Rosenblatt the artist is present in all of the various disciplines that he works at. There is everything you might want to know about love and sex and debauchery in the fantastic carnivorous world. The great horny lumpy bull frog leaning over a bath tub, the free standing love lamp, domestic chaos, the playful sexual buzz in his line drawings remain vivid in my mind when I close my eyes and remember his black and white images. The remarkable metaphysical environments with a wide range of odd mythological-like creatures with cat heads and female human bodies, odd demented horses, satyrs, fat birds hanging around like helpless idiots, frogs copulating with disembodied women, fluttering butterflies, ominous spiders, flaccid snakes, and fish that swim in every direction out from the recesses in the streams of the imagination. The domestic conditions of human habitation are celebrated in a cluttered recreation of the interior landscape complete with mini airplanes flying among the detritus. Always those ubiquitous cats — in magic belts, smoking from hookahs, drinking from martini glasses, wearing human breasts. My favourite, the mausoleum picture entitled, "Monument To Dr. Anaconda's Favourite Tom Cat, Maurice C Bagels. Maurice C Bagels, Favourite pet/who loved his master & served him well thru/this wretched terrestrial/life. Honour/to thee o feline." Lying on top of the monument, a naked woman with tiny breasts is about to make it with a frog above the sign of "9 lives." God, how can it get any better than that!

Over his career, hundreds of exotic drawings have documented Rosenblatt's metaphysical existence. I run into them time and time again in people's hallways or in bathrooms or positioned strategically in a den or on the walls of a library, often in the possession of an artist or a writer. Quite properly, he has always been avidly collected by his fellow travellers. In the past 10 years or so Rosenblatt has transformed his art by changing his medium as an artist. For several years he abandoned drawing altogether. I think his absence from that field began a long gradual evolution toward a slightly more refined vision that is progressively growing in magnitude. In recent times he has been painting wildly great pictures that explode in blossoms of vivid colour. I am astonished to notice that the man who created art from the margins in a kind of efficient utilitarian process on the kitchen table is now painting boldly in oils. The result is his fat birds are slyer and seem even more vulnerable to being raped and pillaged by the peril lurking in the innocent world.

Finally, it is the prodigious output of books of poetry that will be totalled up at the end to put a cap on the Rosenblattian reputation. Perhaps only a handful of Canadian poets have even approached the massive publication record that has garnered him national and international recognition. A career that began in 1962 with *Voyage of the Mood*, a little 10-page pamphlet from Peter Dorn's small private press, Heinrich Heine Press, has reached 40 years across the bridge of time bringing us to *Parrot Fever* in 2002 from Exile Editions. By my count, Joe's been a player in the game for 40 years with approximately 30 individual titles. That is the kind of output that is necessary for a writer to be regarded as a major poet, and Joe Rosenblatt is easily all of that. He has had a multifaceted poetry career that never stopped taking chances, be it concrete sound poetry, beautiful delicately balanced lyrics, or bizarre surreal prose poems that expand the edges of the *genre*. His work has been published by the gamut of publishers in Canada, from virtually all of the important small presses across the country to McClelland & Stewart. The variety of editions of his work have included almost every publishing form imaginable, from limited edition folios to trade paper and hardcover editions. His books usually will be illustrated by his own hand, although it is not an ironclad rule. Along the way, he has achieved many milestones that include being the first Coach House Press author, winning the Governor General's Award and the British Columbia Book Award, seeing volumes of his work published in Italy. He is easily one of the most anthologized poets in Canadian history. It doesn't matter where you travel in this country, whenever Rosenblatt reads the audience hopes he will perform the "Extraterrestrial Bumblebee." It is possibly the best known sound poem in all of our literature.

The thing that sets Rosenblatt apart is that he has always exploited his own inner resources for his material. He is a deeply spiritual man who practices the deception of black humour to illustrate the most basic organic aspects of the human condition. He delves into the metaphysical world in a modern context creating brilliant poems from the palette of the language. His visions are unique and startling while he uses humour and satire to disguise how serious he is in his views about the relevance of humanity. The creatures in the world are his *métier*, through them he defines his own place and our place in the great clear eye of the universe. They live and thrive in both the external and internal worlds the poet chooses to visit. Rosenblatt is an original poet who works in a realm of his own making. There is no other poet in our literary culture who is comparable.

What is great about Rosenblatt the man is that throughout his life he has been a social activist. He has remained an independent thinker who cares about people and all the other creatures that live on this earth, be they downtrodden humans, homeless cats, or threatened species of fish in depleted oceans and streams. Joe is a self-effacing man. He has eschewed publicity and kept a modest profile in the face of his important artistic achievement. He is personally responsible for helping a huge number of Canadian writers get published because of his unique ability at bringing together writers and publishers. Joe is truly a national figure who has friends and contacts in nearly every corner of Canada. His generosity has never really been acknowledged. I, for one, owe him a great deal for his unstinting support and faith. I don't know how I will ever be able to pay him back except by telling him in print that I am forever grateful for his friendship. I am sure many of his fellow writers and artists feel the same way I do. Without much trouble I can sit down and think immediately of about 40 writers whose careers have been greatly accelerated by his efforts. Thanks, Joe, for all your help and your inspiration. Without you and your absolutely fantastic visions, the world would have been a far less rewarding place to be.

WATERMARKS

IT ALWAYS STARTS UP AGAIN with a mysterious phone call. On the other end a stranger wants to ask me questions about Pat Lowther, the poet who was brutally murdered in 1975 and discarded in a creek in North Vancouver by her demented husband Roy. What is my connection to Patricia Lowther that keeps me dealing with mysterious phone calls 30 years after her death?

I knew Pat Lowther for five years, from 1970 until her death in 1975. During that time, Brian Brett and I published a number of her poems in our little magazine, *Blackfish*, as well as an edition of her poetry entitled, *The Age of the Bird* (Blackfish Press, 1972). From the beginning, Pat and I became close friends. I talked with her on the phone once a week and saw her two or three times a month. Eventually, we began to move in the same circles and because she had no car I often stopped to pick her up or drop her off after a reading or literary event. In addition, both Brett and I were extremely fond of her work and we saw Pat as an important contributor to our publishing ventures.

After her murder and the sensational publicity that occurred before and during the trial, I received a number of phone calls from journalists and media people from across the country, including Paul Gresco, who wrote about Pat in *Weekend* magazine and Peter Gzowski, who broadcast a couple of programs about the whole debacle on his CBC radio program. After the media interest died down the calls most often came from bibliophiles or poetry fans who wanted to purchase *The Age of the Bird* or from poets, usually young women, who were writing suites of poetry about Pat's life and wanted to ask questions about Pat as a personality. At least one of these poets received a literary award from The League of Canadian Poets for a book of poems she produced on the Lowther murder. Later, the calls came from organizers of literary events who were putting on a Pat Lowther memorial reading or symposium, or from academics who were writing articles or books and wished to interview me in person or on the telephone or have me answer detailed questionnaires about Lowther's life and work. For about the first 10 years I dutifully answered questions and attended events where I usually spoke briefly about Pat or read a few of her poems or took part in a panel discussion. In 1980, I attended the launching of Pat's posthumous poetry collection, *Final Instructions: Early and Uncollected Poems* (Intermedia) at the Literary Storefront and did a reading in Pat's honour along with Lorraine Vernon and Dorothy Livesay. In 1985, I was MC and spoke at an event at Robson Square, also in Vancouver, that was a fundraiser to help establish The Pat Lowther Poetry Prize that has been awarded annually ever since by the League of Canadian Poets. The same year I gave a talk about Pat at Harbourfront in Toronto at an event that also included Dorothy Livesay. As the years passed, it became more difficult for me to dredge through my memories and find the courage to relive the whole sordid business over again by turning up to speak about my friend. I continued to enjoy reading Pat's poems, a large selection of which I was happy to include in my 1986 centennial anthology, *Vancouver Poetry*, published by Polestar Press. In 1987 and again in 1989 I was interviewed by Toby Brooks who produced a book entitled, *Pat Lowther's Continent: Her Life And Work* (Gynergy Books, 2000). However, not long after that I made a decision to no longer make myself available as a source of information about Pat Lowther or attend any events that were associated with remembering her and her literary legacy. I was burnt out on the subject and tweaking my memory gave me nightmares. The body of rumours and misinformation that had taken over left me appalled and depressed by the way history was being constructed like bad plumbing that leaked all over the place.

For me, Pat Lowther's murder and the way things were resolved never allowed closure, even though Roy had been convicted and spent the rest of his life in prison. The sensational trial that was reported on daily in the media escalated everything to another level. Just as Pat's murder elevated her literary reputation, the coverage of the murder trial elevated her into becoming a kind of celebrity victim. The coverage of the trial put the whole issue into another perspective that was far wider than her friends or family could imagine. The murder and trial was public knowledge and the public had an interest in trying to understand what was going on. Insiders and those following the proceedings knew Roy was a diabolical man who had committed a heinous crime. However, the average Joe in the street figured he might be innocent. Where ever I went people were having conversations about whether Roy was guilty or not or whether Pat was a slut who deserved what she got. Once in a convenience store I heard an elderly woman tell the clerk that "the poetry woman who was murdered was probably peddling it on the street." When Roy cracked halfway through the trial and changed his story I knew he would be found guilty and he would go to prison for a long time. When he was found guilty, sentenced, and imprisoned things died down but there was still no real sense of closure. Pat's body, evidence for two years, was finally released to her family and cremated. The whole sad story came to a conclusion without any of us having had the time to stop and properly say goodbye to our friend. Pat's absence was greatly felt. For Pat's friends the world immediately around us was intensely wrapped up in the events surrounding her demise. In a sense, we never had a chance to miss her properly because we were always talking about her. When the limelight was over we came to realize just what we had lost in our lives. Pat Lowther was a calm person with a great deal of dignity. She often had interesting insights and observations about the natural world. She was a committed socialist who worked tirelessly to help other people during her lifetime. She did not have a mean bone in her body. Her murder was the work of a madman.

When I read her poetry today, I realize the work she had already accomplished was only a hint of things to come. Pat Lowther was 40 when she was murdered, a young age for a writer who was just entering the productive stage of her career that would have seen her produce perhaps 20 or more books of poetry in her lifetime. However, now we will have to be content with just four volumes.

As the years passed, it became more difficult for me to control my emotions. I often thought about what happened to Pat and pondered the difficulties in life that her young daughters must have faced growing up without parents. Especially after their champion and loving grandmother, Mrs. Virginia Tinmuth, who died at the age of 90, was no longer able to take care of them because of infirm health. I felt a terrible sadness. Mrs. Tinmuth, who was already 67 when her daughter was murdered, had stepped in and faced off with provincial officials in recovering her granddaughters from foster homes after their mother was murdered and they were taken by the authorities. I remembered Beth and Chris as preschoolers, during the years I knew their mother and made frequent visits to the Lowther family home. In the few years after Pat's death I made occasional visits to North Vancouver and saw the daughters again. However, as the years passed by I heard rumours that Virginia was in poor health and that she was no longer able to provide a home for her granddaughters. They had once again been shuffled into the foster home circuit. I felt guilty for losing track of the girls and for letting my relationship with the family grow distant. I also had become suspicious of the motives of some individuals who were attempting to use Pat Lowther's memory as a bandwagon for their own ambitions. I was tired of correcting misinformation and talking to people who saw Pat Lowther's legacy as a source for creative or academic fodder. There's no doubt that in the end the academics will turn up to sort out and sift the details no matter how obscure or disguised they have become during the passage of so much time. Sometimes when I started thinking about Pat, I would start to cry uncontrollably, so I chose to go into a state of denial rather than try to find the courage to deal with mystery callers. I stopped returning phone calls and I threw letters of inquiry away.

In my recurring dream I saw the prosecutor pointing with his pen at some feature in the ruined skull, as he did during the trial, to make a dramatic point to the jury. The skull was kept in a basket in the courtroom unless it was taken out to be used as evidence, then it was displayed on an evidence table. Before the authorities can charge someone with murder they need to have a body. Pat's body which had been defiled — teeth smashed in, hair cut off and unceremoniously dumped into a rugged mountain creek by a desperate murderer (cadaver number 929-75) — needed to be positively identified by experts before there could be a case. Since Pat had been beaten to death with a ball-peen hammer the broken skull was an essential piece of evidence that was discussed and examined *ad nauseam* to satisfy the legal beagles on both sides. Pat's poor damaged cranium seemed almost to preside over the courtroom.

During the discovery and murder trial, each time Roy walked into the courtroom, he peered around looking for familiar faces. Several times he tried to catch my eye and he nodded at me whenever he got the chance as if to welcome me to his fiasco. He was preening and performing as if he was enjoying every second of being the centre of attention. Roy, normally an uptight man with anti-social tendencies, was firmly in control of himself for the first time in my experience. I had previously only witnessed Roy as a troubled, disorganized man who had difficulty functioning in public and who was basically a social maladroit who was wearing himself out with rage and jealousy blaming everybody else for his misfortunes in life. Roy had been a public schoolteacher who could not seem to hold down a job and his modest literary career had almost dried up.

I first met Pat Lowther at a small literary gathering in 1970 at Seymour Mayne's apartment in the basement of a wealthy neurosurgeon's house in the residential area on the UBC campus. Seymour was finishing up his PhD in Canadian Literature and he had his hand in a number of small publishing concerns. He had been a partner with Patrick Lane in Very Stone House Press which had published Pat's first book, *This Difficult Flowring* in 1968. Brian Brett and I were students at Simon Fraser University and we were planning on starting a little magazine called *Blackfish*. We decided early on that, of all the local poets, Pat was the one we wanted to feature in the first issues of our magazine. In 1971 the fall issue of *Blackfish* contained a dozen of Pat's poems.

When I was working with Pat on her broadside folio, *The Age of the Bird*, which was published in 1972 by Blackfish Press, I became aware of the friction that existed between Pat and her husband Roy. By the time I knew Pat, she and Roy had been through nearly a decade of troubled times and their marriage was in wreckage. Roy was largely living in the basement while Pat occupied a bedroom upstairs in the tall A-shaped house on 46th Ave. East just off Fraser Street. They had shifted to opposite ends of the house but because of their two daughters they remained together and shared the main floor. Pat had become a huge fan of Pablo Neruda's work and *The Age of the Bird* was a homage to Neruda while being a beautiful lyrical sequence about revolution and the spiritual cost of the struggle. We had little money to spend on the project. I was sitting in Pat's kitchen at the table looking at some tattered pages from a rumpled, broken volume of South American pottery designs. It was a damaged book that Roy had found at a junk store in a collection of art books that he purchased. Pat had suggested perhaps I could cut out a few small images with an exacto knife from one of the pages and use them as a design feature in the text. While I was removing a half dozen small designs on one of the pages I heard a noise like rustling. Pat stood up and dropped a section of the newspaper on top of my working area and held her finger to her lips to warn me to stop what I was doing. It soon became obvious that we weren't alone. Roy, quiet as Tinker, the family cat, had snuck up the stairs and manoeuvred himself into a position behind a tall book shelf so he could listen and observe us before we could detect his presence. When finally he came out from his hiding spot he gave me the creeps. Soon he went back down into the basement again and Pat heaved a sigh of relief.

"Why are you so afraid?" I asked. "It's just a damaged old book with no binding and a hundred loose pages mostly spoiled by mould. Surely he won't begrudge us one page of it so we can grab a few designs."

"You don't know Roy," she answered. "He specializes in throwing fits at the slightest offence. Seeing you cutting up that tattered page would be enough to drive him into a state of frenzy."

By this time in their relationship most of Pat's friends had little use for Roy. It was well-known that Roy inflicted self-abuse on himself whenever Pat attempted to discuss leaving their loveless marriage. Subsequent information that came out years later, from members of both sides of the family, revealed that Roy was an explosive, abusive man who sometimes resorted to physical violence and committed domestic abuse on members of both families he had fathered with two different spouses.

During the years I knew Pat, Roy never really acknowledged me. I was in my early 20s while Pat was close to 40. Roy, a decade older, was a poet himself, albeit a bad one. He wrote doggerel and was completely convinced that he was a misunderstood genius. It burned his ass to think people saw more in Pat's work than they saw in his feeble output. Rather than rejoice in the quality of his wife's work and use their companionship as vehicle for elevating his own literary interests Roy chose to go another route.

At the beginning of their relationship, Roy was the more established writer with left-wing and literary connections and he and Pat both gradually began to meet other writers in the Vancouver scene. However, Roy sank further into the realm of being an amateur versifier while Pat was becoming a strong poetic voice in the rain forest region where she lived and she was gaining national recognition. Roy's relationship with the writing world was seriously slipping because of the limited vision he projected in his own work. He eschewed former literary friends and opted to hang out in the community arts scene where poetry was regarded as a hobby subject. Roy wrote rhyming lyrics that had limited appeal, although occasionally something of his would appear in a publication, usually sponsored by an amateur writing group or a political organization.

Whenever I was at their house and Roy was home he talked obliquely about writing or writers as if I were not present. He made outrageous statements about various poets, including Pat who he felt was being unfairly promoted by a certain element in the literary community who wanted to see their relationship fail. Pat told me he imagined that she had sex with almost every male she spoke with. Each time I left she had to deal with his sarcastic commentary about my relationship with her. I suppose he found it difficult to imagine our friendship was solely about writing and publishing. Roy had sunk into middle age believing that he alone possessed insider knowledge on what constituted good writing. When fellow left-wing writers like Dorothy Livesay and Milton Acorn (who stayed in the suite in the Lowther basement when he was living in Vancouver in 1968) heaped praise on Pat for the astonishing new work she was producing, Roy took it as a defeat for his own aspirations. Not only was Roy failing as a writer, he wasn't able to hold down a job as a teacher. Roy put his vocational failure down to being a by-product of his political beliefs. He felt he was being discriminated against and eliminated from being a teacher because he was a communist. There may have been a glimmer of truth in that premise but Roy was a difficult personality who was always involved in controversy. The result was the Lowthers, with two small daughters to raise, lived below the poverty line and had to resort to taking welfare to survive. At some point, Pat decided that she would have to become the bread winner and she began a series of political and cultural jobs that were supporting the family while Roy stayed home and looked after the children. At least he was half decent at child care although subsequent events have shown Roy used this opportunity to brainwash his children about their mother, during the day, while she was out of the home. Years later when they grew up, the Lowther children, Beth and Chris, who were 9 and 7 years of age when their mother died, remembered their father engineering the scenario of Pat's demise. He demanded their childhood loyalty and filled their lives with a litany of complaints about their mother, who he assured them might go away at any time without telling them.

The green eyed monster had Roy by the throat and he could not seem to ease up on his feelings of panic. In a plot and scenario worthy of Alfred Hitchcock, Roy Lowther decided to murder his wife in order to redress the anger and rage that had become daily preoccupations in his somewhat lacklustre existence. The single issue that pushed the Lowther domestic struggle over the edge was the poetry reading scheduled for September 27, 1975, at the Ironworkers Hall on Columbia Street in Vancouver. The reading was sponsored by a group affiliated with the NDP. The event was labelled, "Work and the Working Life." Patrick Lane, David Day, Peter Trower, and Pat Lowther were invited to read. Roy, who considered himself an important "work poet" and long-time labour supporter, was furious that he was not included. He went to great difficulty trying to gather support among his political cronies to get himself added to the list of readers. He even enlisted the aid of an NDP Member of the Legislature to try and bring pressure to bear on the organizers but they were not willing to add a lesser quality poet like Roy to the bill. The fact Pat had been chosen and Roy was rejected became a huge issue for Roy. He struggled to hold his emotions in place but in the end he blew up at the organizers and acted like a child having a tantrum. For several years in his own demented mind he had been in a head to head struggle with his wife for poetic supremacy in their relationship. It is doubtful that Pat ever understood the full implications inherent in Roy's increasing bonfires of rage. What she probably regarded as a minor issue escalated in Roy's mind to becoming tantamount to WW III. Pat was a gentle person who readily supported a wide range of writers and activities in the scene. She would have been just as happy to be a member of the audience as she was being a reader. I never recognized a competitive spirit in Pat as far as writing went. She had no desire to compete with Roy. She wrote because she was addicted to the process of writing poetry and she pursued it like a job. She banged away on her Remington at the kitchen table every chance she got, while she filled up an ashtray half as large as a hubcap with Matinee filter tips. Roy on the other hand walked around with a shopping bag full of his poems. He was like a sleazy salesman promoting his tenuous relationship with the muse, always looking for someone to proselytize to about his own poems. The reading at the Ironworkers Hall was the final judgement for Roy Lowther, who decided it was time to play God. Anybody who would kill for poetry could not have seen it any other way. Roy made plans to insure that if he wasn't going to be on the bill at the Ironworkers Hall, neither was his wife. On or about the 23rd day of September, a few days before the reading, Roy terminated Pat Lowther's life with a succession of hammer blows. Roy was successful in killing the poet but he had no control in deciding about the life of the poems. On the 27th, when the reading at the Ironworkers Hall went ahead, fellow poet Jeni Couzyn stepped forward and read Pat's poems.

One night in September 1975, probably the 23rd, Roy Lowther climbed the two flights of stairs into the upstairs hallway and quietly entered Pat's bedroom carrying a ball-peen hammer, which he proceeded to use with a vengeance as he beat his sleeping wife to death, smashing her skull in a wild frenzy of murder. The completion of this grisly act left a blood pattern on the wallpaper on the wall at the head of the bed (later discovered by the police when they lit the wall up with bright lights). After he murdered his wife, Roy put her body in the bathtub so her blood would run down the drain. After wrapping the body in a plastic sheet and storing it in a bedroom closet, he poured strong disinfectant into the drain, cleaned up the bathroom and scrubbed the bedroom walls. Two nights later, on a full moon, after putting his children to bed, Roy loaded Pat's body into the trunk of his car, strapped the blood-defiled matrimonial mattress onto the car roof, and drove through Vancouver on his way to the North Shore where he dumped his wife's body into Furry Creek. He discarded some of her clothes and possessions in the bush and he abandoned the mattress beside the Squamish Highway.

I had been informed about Pat's disappearance before her absence was reported in the newspapers. Lorraine Vernon, a poet and one of Pat's closest friends, a person I respected greatly, phoned me at the end of September to tell me Pat had suddenly gone missing. Lorraine reported that Roy Lowther was telling the family Pat had walked out on him and the daughters and that she had probably gone off to be with a lover. This was not the possible behaviour of the Pat Lowther we knew. Pat was a dreamer, constantly at work on her writing to the detriment of house work and she was a bit absent minded but she was extremely close to her mother, sister, and her children. She was the last person one would expect to hear had run off. Lorraine and I took it upon ourselves to make lists of every writing and literary connection that Pat might have across the country and began phoning people in nearly every province in search of Pat. The negative results our phone campaign garnered only reinforced the feeling of dread that began to dominate our conversations. Already Lorraine, Kathy (Pat's older daughter by a different marriage), her sister Brenda, her mother

Virginia Tinmuth and the rest of the family feared the worst — that Roy had possibly snapped and murdered Pat and buried her body at some undisclosed place.

I began to talk with Virginia Tinmuth on the phone and I took a trip across the Second Narrows bridge to North Vancouver to discuss the situation with her and other family members. Mrs. Tinmuth, a woman of conviction and strong personality, possessed a backbone of tempered steel. She had a close relationship with her daughter and she suspected right from the beginning that foul play had occurred. Virginia knew the circumstances surrounding Pat's failing marriage and she had had plenty of experience dealing with Roy Lowther.

When the Vancouver Police Department were first contacted about a missing person by Pat's daughter, Kathy, they made a superficial investigation and determined that Pat probably had run off on her husband. The fact she was a poet and the spin Roy put on her, that she was a beatnik woman with loose morals, only reinforced the police decision to take the matter lightly. Most of Pat's close friends knew she was having a long distance relationship with a writer by the name of Eugene McNamara who lived in Windsor, Ontario. This relationship had consisted of them spending a couple of weekends together over the years, notably at Dorothy Livesay's Rock Cottage near Victoria. Pat was not promiscuous, nor was she a plausible candidate for running away from her life. However, Roy was able to use his knowledge of the affair with McNamara as the basis of his story to the police that Pat had run off with a lover. Kathy had filed a missing persons report with the police department. The police told her that they had no authority to search the house but suggested the family enter the house surreptitiously and look for clues. The police reaction to the situation upset the Lowther family. They became terribly frustrated at the lack of action. At the beginning of October, 1975, after consulting with Virginia, I contacted one of my friends who was an intern reporter at *The Vancouver Sun*. I informed her that Pat Lowther's children were planning on digging up the backyard at the Lowther home in search of their mother's body. This information intrigued the newspaper's editors, who instructed a reporter to investigate. On a wet, blustery afternoon the family dug up the garden at the 46th Street property looking for traces of Pat while reporters from *The Vancouver Sun* gathered in the alley to observe the exercise.

On October 13, 1975, the nude body of a woman was discovered by a fisherman, jammed under a log in Furry Creek, one of Pat Lowther's favourite haunts. By this time Roy Lowther had already gathered up his two young children and some of his possessions as well as his dead wife's manuscripts and had retreated to a relative's cabin on Mayne Island. After Pat's body was discovered, the police focused their attention on Roy. The bizarre story he told about his missing wife did not jibe with what others had to say about her and his behaviour became erratic. It is possible the police were applying just enough pressure to panic Roy into making mistakes in his attempt to cover up his awful crime. Roy was eventually arrested in a police operation in the middle of the night on Mayne Island. The authorities decided to move in because they feared Roy might harm the children. Buried under the cabin on Mayne they found a hammer and some other evidence from the Lowther bedroom.

During the next couple of years, a remarkable series of events and revelations transpired. In fact, the trend was established even before Pat's corpse was discovered when reports of sightings of her began to come forth. At the League of Canadian Poets annual general meeting in Victoria in early October (Pat was co-chairman of this national organization) the assembled membership was told a woman who matched Pat's description had been found wandering in Portland. The members' jubilation was short-lived when information proved that this amnesiac was somebody else. There were also reports Pat was spotted on the University of British Columbia campus, where she was scheduled to teach a creative writing course for George McWhirter who was going on sabbatical. After being charged with murder on October 18th, 1975, Roy Lowther was eventually let out on bail until the preliminary hearing in April 1976. The case didn't come to trial until a year later, nearly to the day.

During the time he was out on bail, Roy haunted Virginia Tinmuth, driving past her house and making weird phone calls at all hours from pay phones, and he tried to intimidate other members of the Lowther family. He was also involved in a bizarre incident in which his malfunctioning car careened around in a parking lot, inflicting considerable damage on a police car. There was a rumour that Roy, a few years earlier, had been called to the morgue to identify a relative who had committed suicide by jumping off the Port Mann Bridge into the Fraser River. Some people speculated that the gruesome sight of a decomposing corpse that had been in water for several days gave Roy the idea of dumping Pat's body into water, because he knew it would make her remains more difficult to identify.

By the time the case came to trial in April 1977, the murder of Pat Lowther had become a case with national significance because of her rising literary reputation and the horrendous nature of the crime. The general public was hard-pressed to believe that poetry could be a reason for murder. The media began to troll for prurient details that might titillate their audiences. Sadly, Pat's brief affair with McNamara and the letters between them were just enough evidence of infidelity to convince some casual onlookers that Pat was a wanton woman. Roy was also quick to point a finger at McNamara accusing him of the murder. Was Roy Lowther a madman who brutally murdered his wife or was he a poor cuckolded child-rearing husband who was being framed for murder because of his social deficiencies and his political beliefs? Once the court case began, insiders who knew the Lowthers, or who, for one reason or another, were closely involved in the court case, knew that Roy Lowther was enjoying his finest hour. Suddenly he was getting the public attention that he had always craved and failed to receive for his body of work, the unpublished reams of bad poetry that piled up in the corners of his life.

For me, the trial is a foggy memory. At a point in the proceedings, when Pat's broken skull was taken out for display one more time, I lost it and decided not to go back into the courtroom. I had heard enough, and in my heart I felt strongly that Roy Lowther was going to be found guilty of the murder of my friend. I could no longer endure seeing her remains laid out like pieces from some archaeological dig in the foreground of my life. As I lost track of the day-to-day proceedings in the courtroom I grew more reliant on the media to provide information. The picture that I was receiving from the media was much distorted from the proceedings I had been following in the courtroom. In the middle of the trial, suddenly Roy Lowther took the stand against his lawyers' advice and changed his story. Now he claimed he had returned home and found his battered wife dead and, knowing he would be a suspect, he handled, hauled, and disposed of his wife's body in Furry Creek. His bizarre admission sealed his fate as his defence gradually was reduced to a pathetic story that could not hold even a semblance of truth.

Roy never admitted or repented his crime. On entering prison he became a model prisoner. He affected an Earle Birney white beard, and his postures were reminiscent of Earle's, as Roy further developed his persona as a poet while becoming the librarian at William Head Prison in Victoria. In May of 1985, a dim light in a dark passage of time went out for good when Roy Lowther died in prison of natural causes.

It seemed a good time to move on in my life. Pat had been dead for 10 years and now Roy was also deceased. I would never be able to forget her or forgive him. By the end of the '80s, I stopped answering the mystery callers and I threw their mail into my piles. Their missives sank into the miscellaneous dead letter file in the fruit cellar in our basement. In later years, I deleted unwanted emails with a vengeance. I had exchanged my life in a metropolitan city of nearly 2,000,000 people to live in a town of just over 500 people. My life had slowed down as I dropped out of the urban rat race more than a thousand miles east of Vancouver on the northern plains in rural Saskatchewan. I needed to go somewhere else for a while to better appreciate the place I was born and raised and spent the majority of my life. I was not surprised when I came home one day in 2002 to the news that a stranger had left a message on the answering machine. She was a filmmaker from Montreal who was on the coast interviewing people on film for a movie she was making about Pat Lowther. She wanted to speak with me. I decided to ignore her and I succeeded for several months. However, she continued to leave messages. Eventually I suggested to Dolores, my partner, that she could do me a favour and tell the filmmaker to get lost. Dolores spoke with her on the phone and annoyed me by saying she thought I was being hasty. She said that Anne Henderson was an interesting woman and she urged me to have a conversation with her myself. I was sceptical because I knew the Pat Lowther story was a morass that came with a thousand different opinions. I could not see how telling this story on film would ever be possible without continuing the distortions that have grown stronger in time. I told my friends on the coast to tell the filmmaker I wasn't available or interested in her project. I had nothing against her, I just assumed she would be digging in the archaeological fields of my past. I was sure her movie would be nothing short of a complete fiasco. She continued to call and finally, more out of frustration than anything, I decided to set her straight with the facts as I knew them. In a short time I realized how wrong I had been in my assumptions about Anne Henderson.

Anne told me she wasn't making a movie about Pat Lowther. She was making a movie about Pat Lowther's daughters, Beth and Chris, and their search to find their authentic mother. A quest they had set out upon years before when they helped bring out the collected poems of their mother's under the title *Time Capsule*

(Polestar Press, 1996). The frontispiece in that book carried the following message:

> The children of Pat Lowther are looking for written or recorded documents or photographs that will shed light on the life and work of their mother. Correspondence or other material may be sent to them care of Polestar Book Publishers in Victoria.

My offer to answer a few questions and help to clear up a few issues suddenly turned into long conversations. I discovered that Anne Henderson was a considerable person. It soon became apparent she was a professional who really knew what she was doing. Her knowledge of the case, the fact she had connected so profoundly with Pat Lowther's children, and her willingness to persevere in the face of my reluctance finally convinced me to take a chance. I decided to be as honest as I could be in retelling my version of the events that surrounded Pat Lowther's life during the period I knew her. I told Anne she was free to check the record by looking at my correspondence from the mid-'70s in the Blackfish Press archives in the National Library of Canada in Ottawa. I discovered from Anne that her brother was Ace Henderson, a British Columbia Supreme Court Justice, who in 1977 as a young lawyer had defended Roy Lowther in his murder trial. Anne was a good listener and she asked thought-provoking questions. One day she phoned and we got into a long conversation that delved into regions I had not entered for a long time. I realized that our conversation was becoming a narrative and I was doing the talking. Suddenly Anne stopped me and asked if I would reconsider and travel to Vancouver to be interviewed on film. I was taken aback. I had convinced myself there was no way I was going to Vancouver to talk on film about Pat. Anne told me that Beth and Chris, who I had known when they were young children, had remembered me from the past. I had last seen them at the Pat Lowther event at

Robson Square in 1985. My heart began to race and I started feeling queasy but for some unknown reason I changed my mind and agreed to go to Vancouver.

Anne sent me an airplane ticket and somewhat reluctantly I flew out to the coast. I went directly to the Blue House on the hill in White Rock where my son, Jevon, lives. I started ransacking the filing cabinet and cupboards, looking for Pat Lowther material. After a lengthy search I found two copies of the limited broad side folio, *The Age of the Bird*, and some copies of *Blackfish* magazines that contained Pat's poems. I also located two copies of the "Canadian issue" of *Inscape*, a small literary magazine from Arizona that I edited in the early '70s. That issue also includes a selection of Pat's work.

The next morning, a young man in a van came to pick me up and drive me from White Rock to Vancouver — actually to a rendezvous in a parking lot in Little Mountain Park in Vancouver, where I finally met Anne Henderson. I decided I would put myself in her hands because I had really grown to like and trust her from our phone conversations. Anne dropped a bomb on me. She wanted me to meet Beth and Chris and talk with them on camera about their mother. I was absolutely terrified at the thought of meeting them spontaneously while being filmed. For years, whenever my mind wandered back to thinking about Pat I became emotional and sometimes I just broke out into tears. I accepted the fact that I no longer felt comfortable talking about Pat in public. I was afraid of openly showing my grief. I had wrapped myself into a cloak of denial about attending any more Pat Lowther events. I knew in my heart that I would crack up when I saw Beth and Chris who had long ago become mature adults. I felt that I might not be able to withstand the shock of speaking with them about their mother while being filmed. I tried to dissuade Anne but she reassured me that somehow it would all work out and that it would be a necessary scene in her movie. Unknown to me, Anne had already chosen a place for this meeting. She would seat Beth and Chris at a picnic table in the middle of Jericho Beach Park and she wanted me to walk across the grass to them where they would greet me and we would have a reunion followed by a conversation about Pat. By the time we arrived at the park, I began to realize how well-organized an operation a film shoot in the hands of a professional like Anne has to be. Later, when I saw the film, I realized why Anne had chosen Jericho Beach. She and her crew of filmmakers from Quebec were in love with the blueness of the coast and the special light that exists there and they were intent on capturing its qualities in their film.

I sat in the back of the van, choking on my emotions. I was already losing control. I was trying to stem the flood of tears that were close to drowning my composure. I stalled for as long as I could by hemming and hawing and trying to talk Anne out of the idea. In the end, I took the walk across the grassy field on a beautiful sunny fall morning, wind whipping seagulls in the air with a film crew shooting from behind. I was soon in a daze, moving ahead realizing that I could not guarantee what would happen when I reached them. When I approached close enough, two figures came out from behind the table to greet me.

I burst into tears, I was overcome by a huge wave of emotion that nearly knocked me off my feet. Standing before me were the two Lowther girls, who I best remembered in my mind as preschool and primary students, and here they were now in their mid-30s. On that walk in Jericho Park my mind had played its own movie. I had fixated on the most vivid memory I had of Beth and Chris eating cookies in their mother's kitchen when they were 8 and 6 years old. I thought of the stories I had heard of how hard their lives had been in various foster homes, how they had become involved in drugs and delinquency and became alienated toward one another in their teenage years. They had suffered the ignominy of their father killing their mother and in essence lost both their parents forever. Only a few people are ever marked in this tragic way. Growing up in the shadow of that experience must have been monumentally difficult. Now they were united in their effort to find out as much as they could about their mother and they were succeeding. My encounter with Beth and Chris in Jericho Beach Park, thanks to Anne Henderson, set me free of denial. I burst into tears but I was able to talk freely with Beth and Chris on camera and give them copies of their mother's publications they had never seen. After the shooting we had a lengthy lunch and we were able to talk for a couple of hours about many important things. I guess it's fair to say we caught up with each other and though several decades had passed, we were able to benefit from the experience of being able to talk about my friend and their mother who was so brutally and unnecessarily taken away from us in a sudden and unbelievable manner.

Late in the afternoon, I was once again whisked away in a van and driven to a mysterious locale in Vancouver's Chinatown that turned out to be Peter and Meredith Quartermaine's astonishing house and fenced-in yard in Chinatown. In the back, under a canopy of leaves nestled into a corner of the remarkable Oriental garden, is a studio that contains a printing press and shop. Anne's camera and sound people were already in place and the room was illustrated with Blackfish Press publications from the early '70s. It reminded me of the print shop that Brett and I had set up in White Rock so many years in the past. Anne had decided to ask me a number of questions to get me talking and she wanted me to just kind of ad lib and recollect the years I knew Pat Lowther, including during the awful period of her disappearance and the subsequent events that transpired thereafter. I had already discarded my denial in the morning when I was freed by the open and generous way I was greeted and treated during the encounter I had with Beth and Chris. I knew when I saw them that they were okay, that they had made it despite all the horror and hardship they had endured. They wanted to learn about their mother and wanted to tell their own stories. Who could argue with that? I felt liberated and I was able to talk articulately about my opinions and feeling concerning the many issues and events that surrounded the whole Pat Lowther affair. Watching Anne Henderson, the filmmaker and her crew in action, was a minor revelation. Anne knew exactly where she was going and what kind of a film she was making. There was nothing left to chance except chance itself. Later I was driven back to White Rock and I stayed in the lower mainland for a week before I flew back to the prairies.

About a year later I received an excited phone call from Chris who told me that Anne's movie was complete and that it was going to be shown in a few weeks on a CBC program called *The Passionate Eye*. I was happy to hear the news. Chris went on to tell me I should be prepared for the reality that I had become involved in the way the movie was constructed. Thinking back to my on-camera experience, I wondered how that could possibly be true. A few days later, a Purolator truck showed up in Dundurn and I signed for a package. When I opened it I discovered I was holding a video of Anne Henderson's *Watermarks*. All I had to do was put the cassette in the VCR and I could finally watch Anne's movie. It took several hours before I was able to summon the courage. When I finally did, I was amazed at the blueness of the coast through Anne Henderson's camera lens as she told a story about two sisters who overcame so much adversity and grew up to become strong women with a common goal, a quest to discover the mother they had little opportunity to know and to honour her memory by remembering her life's work and getting to know her as best as they could. Beth, the intense intellectual city girl with a precocious little boy named Rowan who reminded his great grandmother, Virginia Tinmuth, of his grandma, her daughter Pat. Chris, the environmentalist who lives part of the year on a float house with her partner Warren in an inlet not far from Tofino on the West Coast of Vancouver Island, more laid-back than her sister, but just as persistent in her drive to find out truth and to fill in the details of her mother's life. Two very different sisters and a powerful story told without pretensions. When I viewed the film I was in shock because I suddenly saw the method in Anne Henderson's genius. Rather than have endless points of view about Pat Lowther, Henderson decided to minimize non-family members. She concentrated on telling the story by following the lives of Beth and Chris while relying on the memories of Pat's oldest daughter, Kathy, who was 19 when her mother was killed, to recall important details about Pat's home life and her disappearance and subsequent events and the trial. Anne took the interview she did with me and alternated it with an interview she did with the writer and journalist Sean Rossiter. I told the story from the position of a literary friend while Rossiter told the story from the point of view of being a reporter covering the events and the trial for *The Vancouver Sun*. These were the positions we occupied in life at that time in the mid-'70s. Surprisingly, both Rossiter and I were telling the same story, but from different perspectives. It was as if we were corroborating each other as witnesses called in a court case might have done. We witnessed the Pat Lowther story from different angles, but we reached much the same conclusions. Henderson had chosen to discard many of the interviews she had done with various people on the coast and opted to keep her film on track by narrowing its focus. Anne Henderson is a brilliant film maker. She made a film about a family. A film about daughters in search of their lost mother. She made a film full of poetry that was told on a backdrop of coastline. The writer of those poems, Pat Lowther, treasured this landscape. She was a poet of the rain forest and she lives again in the lives of the little girls, Beth and Chris (now grown-up daughters), she loved so much and who have accomplished a miracle with Anne Henderson in keeping their mother's work and memory alive. Now when mysterious strangers call and ask me questions about Pat Lowther I will advise them to watch *Watermarks*.

ACKNOWLEDGEMENTS

Earlier versions of these essays have appeared in the following publications:

"Dog Gone, "Terror Time," and "Bridge to the Past" in *The Saturday Review* (*The Vancouver Sun*);

"In Darkest Alberta" and "Dear Mr. Greyhound" in *The Vancouver Review*;

"Music in the Dark" in *NewWest Review*;

"Memoir of Minago" in *Poetry Canada Review*;

"Good Night Louis" and "Memoirs of a Small Press Junkie" in *Prairie Fire*;

"The Chance to Sing" in *Western Windows*;

"Have Poem Will Travel" comprised part of the introduction to *How I Know The Sky Is A River: Selected Shorter Poems 1978-1998* (Hagios Press); and

"Citizen Joe" in *Literary Criticism Writers Series 15* (Guernica Editions).

Thanks to Suzy Miller and Fred Eaglesmith for *Ditched*. With thanks to Scott, Jeff, Jake, Emily, and Hank for making my days more interesting than they might have been, to Dolores Reimer for outrageous comedy, Donald Ward for typography, Yves Noblet for his design, and Paul Wilson and Donald Ward for their editing skills.

Born into a commercial fishing family in Vancouver, British Columbia, Allan Safarik was raised on Vancouver Heights in North Burnaby and later lived for 15 years in the Blue House on the hill above the pier in White Rock. Safarik has published a prodigious amount of poetry in magazines and anthologies as well as a number of poetry collections, and he edited the anthology *Vancouver Poetry* (1986). In addition, his reviews, essays, and stories have appeared widely in Canadian publications and he is the author or editor of several non-fiction books. The essay "Notes from the Outside" received a Saskatchewan Writers Guild Non-Fiction Writing Award in 1994. In addition, Safarik was a winner of the 2003 John V. Hicks Manuscript Award for Literary Non-Fiction for *Notes from the Outside*, and the Saskatchewan Book Award for Poetry (The Anne Szumigalski Award) in 2005 for *When Light Falls from the Sun*. He currently lives in the 100-year-old Jacoby house in Dundurn, Saskatchewan.